D1601205

UNBRIDLED PASSION
SHOW JUMPING'S GREATEST HORSES AND RIDERS
NORTH AMERICA

UNBRIDLED PASSION
SHOW JUMPING'S GREATEST HORSES AND RIDERS
NORTH AMERICA

JEFF PAPOWS, PhD

PHOTOGRAPHY BY
Gretchen Almy and Tony De Costa

FOREWORD BY
George Morris

ACANTHUS
PUBLISHING

Printed in the United States of America
ISBN: 978-0-9842173-7-3

Published by

Acanthus Publishing
343 Commercial St., Unit 214
Boston, MA 02109

The following photographers have graciously contributed their work which has been incorporated into this book with permission:

© Gretchen Almy: pg. 7, pg. 19, pg. 23, pg. 26, pg. 33, pg. 34, pg. 41, pg. 44, pg. 49, pg. 52, pg. 57, pg. 63, pg. 70, pg. 83, pg. 87, pg. 114, pg. 129, pg. 133, pg. 134, pg. 149, pg. 150, pg. 194, pg. 197, pg. 203, pg. 204, pg. 208, pg. 242, pg. 251, pg. 261, pg. 293, pg. 300, pg. 309, pg. 312, pg. 318, pg. 330, pg. 336, pg. 345, pg. 348, pg. 353, pg. 356, pg. 369, pg. 376, back cover

© Tony De Costa: front cover, author, pg. 13, pg. 60, pg. 73, pg. 104, pg. 119, pg. 120, pg. 124, pg. 186, pg. 232, pg. 322, pg. 326, pg. 366, pg. 367, pg. 368, pg. 370, pg. 378, pg. 379

© EquiFit: pg. 159

© ESI Photography: pg. 10, pg. 110, pg. 136, pg. 372

© Flashpoint Photography: pg. 140

© iStockphoto.com/kurga: pg. 224

© Janet Hitchen Photography: pg. 78

© Jayne Huddleston: pg. 14, pg. 16

© Jacqueline Knutson: pg. 218

© Bob Langrish MBE: pg. 20, pg. 24, pg. 30, pg. 36, pg. 38, pg. 66, pg. 96, pg. 130, pg. 180, pg. 191, pg. 200, pg. 212, pg. 226, pg. 230, pg. 235, pg. 238, pg. 247, pg. 248, pg. 256, pg. 264, pg. 269, pg. 272, pg. 278, pg. 283, pg. 288, pg. 296, pg. 304, pg. 340

© Randi Muster Photography: pg. 375

© James Leslie Parker: pg. 2, pg. 144, pg. 154, pg. 161, pg. 164, pg. 168, pg. 173, pg. 174, pg. 177, pg. 252

© Tish Quirk: pg. 321

© Stephens Family: pg. 92, pg. 101

©Ashley Yanke: pg. 183

Course Design Illustration © Steve Stephens: pg. 364

DEDICATION

I dedicate this volume to the athletes, human and equine, who are profiled here. Their performance records speak for themselves. The introspective, up-close and personal struggles, sacrifices, triumphs, and heartbreak tell a much richer story than I imagined at the outset of this journey. Honor, nobility, sacrifice, and commitment are the texture and fabric of the unique and beautiful relationship between horses and riders, and the staff who support them. The horses do the seemingly impossible because it comes naturally, out of love and generosity, and because we ask it of them. There is no more noble partnership on earth. So, I dedicate this book to the athletes who are my friends and my heroes, and to the horses who are theirs.

ACKNOWLEDGMENTS

Where do I begin? As you might imagine, no author completes a major book that merits actual publication without a lot of people contributing directly or indirectly in a way that merits a thank you. Even though I've published several business books previous to this, *Unbridled Passion* was a matter of the heart for me, born of a need to illustrate how truly special the sport of show jumping is. That context causes me to really reflect and think about all the help I've received in the sport as well as in the writing of this book itself.

First of all, I have to thank my wife, Pat, and my children, Doug, Tom, and Molly, who have put up with over a decade of my boots clomping across the large expanse of hardwood floors in our house at 5:00 AM *every* morning, of *every* year, except on Christmas days, in pursuit of some measure of modest success in a sport where every day represents an obligation to one's horses and homework for oneself.

Second, I have to thank my longtime coach Greg Prince of Woodridge Farm for putting up with my never-ending inadequacies and concurrent manic drive to fix what my muscle memory often seems incapable of acting on. Greg is an enormous talent and has the patience of a saint. Also, Jerry Kenney of Ascot Riding Center, who got me started, is always on my mind when it comes to gratitude. Lastly, my barn manager Katelyn McGrail, who provides my horses loving and meticulous attention, has to be mentioned.

As for the work at hand, *Unbridled Passion* would not have been possible without my publisher, and a world-class publisher they are. From the beginning, Acanthus Publishing, and its president, Paige Stover, believed in this project, and that's a lot to ask a business to aspire to when you know nothing about such a mysterious sport. Also, Acanthus's creative director, Tazuko Sugajima, has added incredible value to the finished work with her sense of design, astonishing creativity, and artistic talent. Other members of the Acanthus team contributed very significantly to the excellence of the final product: Gabrielle Corrado, Lois Hager, George Kasparian, Klaus Givskov, Nancy Weng, Eliza Rosenberry, Genevieve Kim, Stephanie Mann, James Molinaro, Luke Messecar, Ericson doRosario, Ted Rogers, and Ryan Baker.

In this same field, Gretchen Almy, a longtime friend and the official artist for the Jumper Classic, added much with her hard work, images, art, and photographs—both candid and intimate—of many of the horses and riders in question.

For that matter, let me also thank Melissa Lovasco, President of the Jumper Classic, for her help. Similarly, Tony De Costa—who has been photographing horses for longer than I can recount—added dozens of important images of horses and riders in action and beautifully captured the power and grace of the sport, including the cover photograph of McLain Ward and Sapphire. James Leslie Parker Photography, located right here in the good old USA, was very generous and lent beautiful and important images to this finished work. Also, Bob Langrish Photography, from the United Kingdom in merry old England, contributed many important images captured at the Olympic Games and responded in real-time whenever asked for assistance.

Finally, in the category of staff support, my assistant of more than 25 years, Sharon Ricci, has always managed a million details for me and also made serious contributions to the book itself. This project would not have been viable without her talents and dedication. Further, Pamela Mansfield did a number of interviews and conducted countless hours of research to ensure the accuracy of each story line represented here. Pam is a talented communicator in her own right, a good friend, and a valued and important resource to me.

Finally, the athletes who, without exception or hesitation, put so much of themselves on the line, detailing their trials and triumphs, jubilations and heartbreaks— they are both the inspiration and the substance of the book you hold in your hands. In many cases, the caregivers, managers, and support staffs of these world class figures also made critical contributions. It's the friendships I'm proud to say I have in the sport that made *Unbridled Passion* both necessary and possible.

Additional copies of this book can be ordered at
www.UnbridledPassion.net

TABLE OF CONTENTS

FOREWORD
BY GEORGE MORRIS

Having spent a lifetime in the sport of show jumping I am thrilled to see a substantial book come to print that amplifies the incredible efforts of North American riders, owners, and support staff and conveys the real texture of our sport. We need books such as this one that go beyond the technical considerations of show jumping and tell the real stories that inspire and motivate people to get involved. We have to be aware of the level of support required to make international and Olympic-level competition possible. I have personally sponsored horses for U.S. riders over the years and have been directly involved with leading our gold medal teams for decades now. I understand clearly that we need grass roots involvement in order to attract the spectators, sponsors, owners, and patrons that support our country's best equestrian athletes. Books like *Unbridled Passion* help raise awareness for the sport and provide a basis for the required understanding that often translates into full participation.

Unbridled Passion is a well-written, up-close, deeply personal, and truly inspirational book that chronicles the incredible achievements, frustrations, and postponed gratifications that are unique to show jumping. Jeff describes show jumping as "the world's most beautiful sport" and I, of course, agree. But it is the beauty of the human and the equine spirit rather than the visual aspects of the sport that really makes that statement resonate with me. Remember horses do not care what you know, but know when you care.

The world *Unbridled Passion* brings you into is a special culture filled with incredible people who represent America's finest and perhaps best role models for our young people today. These men and women, as Jeff aptly explains, are of tremendous character and have dedicated their lives to representing the USET on the world stage. Equestrian pursuits teach our young people dedication, commitment, and the true meaning of responsibility. I have traveled the world and accompanied the athletes Jeff acquaints you with on the sport's biggest stages and have seen them tested under extraordinary circumstances.

If you are a horse lover, even if from a distance, and have in the past admired or been affected by a young person involved in the sport, this book is for you. These are indeed the role models for our youth and great ambassadors for our sport and our country. I encourage you to make an intellectual investment in this book so you will come closer to understanding the real stories behind these superb athletes. I invite you to take the time to read this worthy effort. I further invite you to get involved in our sport in whatever manner best suited to your individual aspirations. Not all of us need to be in the saddle to make a valued contribution.

George Morris

AUTHOR'S PREFACE

As my technology career reached its apex, I was thirsty for a new challenge. I first put my toe in the water of show jumping in 1999. I had harbored a distant desire to participate for a long time. From the first moment I watched Ian Millar, Norman Dello Joio, Margie Engle, and Leslie Burr Howard—my early heroes in the sport—gallop toward what looked like seemingly impossible obstacles, I could not put the vision out of my mind. It was like daring me to do the impossible, as had often been done in my professional life regarding technology breakthroughs and corporate turnarounds—only worse. Being an animal lover at my core, I was smitten. I had an undereducated notion of how trusting the rider's connection with the horse had to be to attempt a jump, and I began to watch the superstars of show jumping as often as I could. The more I learned and understood about how difficult it was, the more committed I became to developing some proficiency in the sport. I became obsessed.

Having lived it now, I can tell you this sport is more difficult than anything I have ever attempted. I am reconciled with the fact that I have yet to truly succeed. My horses have touched my soul, given so generously and courageously, and have supplied a whole new meaning to my life. In an exciting twist of fate, my early heroes are now, in many cases, my friends. This is a bonus that helps make up for the fact that I have been forced to accept that I lack natural talent.

Before I take you into the up-close and personal world of show jumping's great partnerships, I want to offer a brief explanation as to why I have chosen the people and horses in this first volume of *Unbridled Passion*.

Many of the choices are obvious; several of the greatest combinations in the sport are examined here. In addition to the obvious selection of such notables as McLain Ward and Sapphire, Ian Millar and Big Ben, or Margie Engle and Perin, I have included three amateur athletes with extraordinary skills. *Unbridled Passion,* is not, a quantitative or data-driven chronology of the resumes involved. The point is that there is more to the sport, and more to the story, than top performance. It is as much a journey to the heart, equine or human, as it is a pilgrimage to the brain.

I found, as I talked with the individuals showcased in this book (and I don't mean just the riders, but also the caregivers and support staff who are intimately involved with these great teams) that there is much about the stories of success, failure, jubilation, and heartbreak that has not previously been made public.

The challenges faced by participants in this sport are so much more complex than the skills examined under the harsh lights of competition. Bringing together the ownership syndicates, finding and retaining the right staff, and identifying the proper routines and programs for each individual equine athlete are daunting issues in and of themselves and perhaps not often considered or understood. Contrary to some of the folklore that circulates, this is not a sport of "blue bloods" or the ultra-affluent. As often as not, with obvious exceptions, the people involved are working professionals who have made extreme sacrifices to earn the monumental financial support needed to compete at the top level of the sport. These struggles and triumphant outcomes are a key part of the stories, regardless of the rider's prior economic status.

Unbridled Passion is a contemporary look at North American riders currently active in the sport. I chose not to turn back the hands of time, but to focus on today's human halves of the partnerships. The stories chronicled here in Volume One represent partnerships that are in the present or immediate past tense and, in all cases, involve athletes very much at center stage in the sport's largest venues today. In future volumes, I anticipate looking at historic horse and rider combinations and the superstars of the sport who are from outside North America. In the meantime...

Enjoy the ride!

Jeff Papows
Cambridge, Massachusetts
June 2011

Ch. 1

Jeff Papows & Roxett

Too many years ago, in search of a midlife challenge beyond the business world where I had enjoyed success, I became involved in the sport of show jumping. Others would later remark that I was in quick fashion, someplace north of passionate and just notionally south of demented. Upon some honest reflection, I have to agree with that rather self-deprecating assessment. The question is: why? I'm not a stupid or irrationally compulsive person. I hold several advanced degrees, including a doctorate. Conventionally, that should serve as proof to the contrary—so much for that theory. The real answer is simple admiration, actually outright love, for the other half of this team sport, the horse.

JAMES LESLIE PARKER
The author and his best friend, Roxett, in the heat of a jump-off.

The sport of show jumping is the only Olympic sport where men and women compete as equals. It is perhaps the only team sport without a spoken word. While the scoring of faults that define success or failure is very quantitative and unforgiving, it is at least easy to understand.

Show jumping is perhaps one of the **hardest Olympic disciplines** for folks outside the sport to comprehend.

For those readers who are not fully familiar with the sport, I will digress for a moment to give you some context. In the sport of show jumping, the rider gallops around a course of jumps, or obstacles of different designs and degrees of difficulty, and jumps over them in succession. It can seem like a simple enough endeavor to the casual observer. Wrong! I only *wish* it were that simple. In the Fundamentals chapter of this book (Ch.22), I have provided photographs of the types of fences or obstacles encountered on the course, and a world famous course designer's sample diagram of the course for a recent Grand Prix. If you are unfamiliar with show jumping, this section of the book will help you get oriented so that what follows will make more sense to you. If you are already deeply into the sport, you can skip the Fundamentals chapter.

The horse never enters the ring before the competition. The human member of the team walks the course, pacing off the distances between jumps and committing them to memory beforehand. A horse's gallop stride is 12 feet long, on average, so courses are designed in multiples of varying numbers of strides. Course designers set strides at technical distances, like half strides, to test the teamwork between horse and rider and the team's ability to compress and extend the natural stride length of the horse. As you move along in the sport, and advance to larger challenges (meaning bigger classes), the jumps grow in size to heroic heights and widths. Leaving the ground at a non-optimal take-off point can be disastrous because gravity will win every time. Horses have eyes on the side of their heads so that when they are in their natural element they can see threats coming with their peripheral vision. As a consequence, horses have no depth perception and leave the ground in response to a signal from the rider. The horse must blindly trust that his human partner will not allow him to get hurt.

How many of us would leap a 5-foot obstacle, perhaps 9-feet wide, carrying a 200-pound companion on such blind faith? As for the human athlete, he or she is executing this jump with a 1,400-pound partner sporting steel shoes, often affixed with sharp studs for traction. Ending up on the downside of an error in judgment can be life-threatening. I can tell you from personal experience that, at the very least, bones are going to be broken.

One of the many things I love about the sport of show jumping is that there are no counterfeits. You either do the hard work, make the day-to-day sacrifices to develop the partnership and skills needed, or you don't. No amount of money, performance-enhancing concoctions, or proximity of supporting team members changes the lonely reality

In the sport of show jumping, you can witness **BEAUTY** without vanity, **COURAGE** without condition, **SERVITUDE** without expectation. Not your average situation.

of riding through the in-gate and receiving the single beep tone that tells you to begin. The tone signals the start of the 45 seconds you have to pick up your gallop and cross the laser beam in front of your first fence on the course. At that moment, it is you and your equine partner; the two of you are very much alone. It can be a frightening place. Success, failure, and gratification, or an ambulance ride are separated only by your mutual trust and accumulated experience together. Your coach and supporters can only look on from a distance and hope.

It is this mutual trust, courage, and servitude that is the foundation for this book. When compared to many of the professional athletes we see in the media today who offer less stellar traits for young people to idolize, these stories offer something extraordinary. Having developed close relationships with many of this sport's elite riders, I can assure you that show jumping is populated with athletes of the highest ethical standards and impeccable character. This sport attracts individuals who rise to the upper levels of the "right stuff" and are deserving of the admiration of their young fans.

There are many books for your consideration on how to ride and the care of the equine partner. The technical and specific considerations of the sport are well documented. The emotional (I hesitate, but am tempted to call it the spiritual) aspects of the unique bond that develops between the famous horse-and-rider combinations are what I have tried to memorialize in this volume. Both the human and equine members of these teams, who have stood victoriously on the world's biggest stages, are deserving of no less. Not everyone discussed here is an Olympian or even a professional. I have also included three notable amateur equestrians who have risen to the higher levels of the sport. There are amateurs in the Grand Prix ranks whose accomplishments are worthy of examination.

GRETCHEN ALMY

Jeff and his spirited mare, Glorydays, train at home.

I made the choice to include these non-professional riders to encourage young readers to aspire to excellence and to make it clear that goals are attainable.

What got these athletes there? Hard work, most certainly. Sacrifice, undoubtedly. But also a more subjective component—the devotion of human to horse and horse to human that is at the root of their success. It is this element that makes their stories both heartwarming and heartbreaking.

How did I come to the point where I chose to undertake the kind of effort involved in authoring a book of this type? I have authored several business books dealing with the computer and software industry where I spent my professional career. I have been through the rigors of the publishing process before. That is, however, where any similarity to this project ends. You might think I would know better than to go down this path one more time.

I am no one of particular note in the sport. I am a dedicated amateur athlete who has had some measure of success, but I am not even in the same food group as the heroes of the sport discussed in this book. I am the Chairman of a not-for-profit horse show, the Fidelity Investments Jumper Classic, which the North American Riders Group has rated one of the top shows in North America. My role in this organization, in conjunction with my amateur pursuits, has given me the exposure, access, and, in some select cases, the lasting friendships that have made the writing of this book possible. This proximity to the superstars of the sport has resulted in an intimate inside look at the extraordinary relationships between the partners of the best show jumping duos that readers typically would not have the opportunity to experience firsthand.

A horse by the name of Roxett 7, previously owned by Linda Irvine Smith and ridden by Hap Hansen, came into my life and taught me firsthand about faith, love, courage, and service. I have been blessed to own this magnificent horse and ridden him as my partner for the past 12 years. I acquired Roxett just after he qualified for the World Cup Championships in Las Vegas in 1999. Roxett has a dozen Grand Prix wins to his credit, most of them with Hap, and a resume that includes an Olympic appearance; I will never have that in the sport. His tolerance of my meager talents and frequent mistakes, his total selflessness, courage, and devoted friendship warms my heart and soul in a manner I cannot adequately articulate.

> The truth is I can hardly talk about the **depth of my relationship with Roxett** without being overcome with emotion. It is part of what makes this sport so special.

Roxett made it possible for me to enter rings in competitive venues that I had no business being in. Roxett is now retired in my barn where he will remain for the rest of his days. He is ridden every day, comes running to the sound of my voice, and enjoys the best that can be offered to a horse. He has earned all that and more. I love him beyond reason. He loves me every bit as much in return (I am not all that lovable but he does not seem to notice). The Josh Groban song *You Lift Me Up* summarizes this horse's spirit, life, and gifts to me more articulately than I can manage on my own. I did indeed feel strongest when I was on his shoulders, and he never once let me down.

Several years back, I had a bad fall, caused entirely by operator error. I miscalculated a distance, forced it, and we flipped over a fence. Roxett and I ended up on the ground. A horse hates nothing more than being put off his feet; in nature, that makes him defenseless. In his natural

environment, the horse would flee because being on the ground is a frightening, unnatural condition. Roxett did not get up and run as years of evolution and instinct would mandate. All of us in the sport have seen that happen too many times—a horse and rider go down, and the horse gets up and runs out of fright. Roxett got up, walked over to where I was lying, got down on one knee, and prodded me with his nose. "Come on, Jeff. That was nasty! Are you okay? What are you doing on the ground? Get up!" he seemed to say.

I had broken my shoulder. It took several people to separate him from me so I could get to the emergency room.

> While they were taking the x-rays, and during the entire hospital drama, I had an **overwhelming paranormal sensation** that made me frantic to get back to the show grounds **to be with Roxett.**

I walked out of the hospital with a bone protruding from my shoulder and exposed under my coat, enraging the emergency room staff. I was a mess. Having escaped from the hospital, I returned to the show grounds. Roxett was screaming, his nose bleeding slightly, and he was completely frantic, which was totally out of character. I ran over to him and he calmed down instantly. "Rocket," his barn name, buried his face in my arms and seemed interested only in staying as close to my aching and bruised body as he could. I was equally relieved to see him. What waited for me at the hospital was a trivial concern at that point. I was at peace and happy to be reunited with my horse of a lifetime.

I've heard people unfamiliar with horses, and our sport in particular, denigrate their inherent intelligence. How then, do you explain this experience? For my part, nobody will ever convince me a horse's intelligence and heart are not extraordinary. I know better and experience living proof in my barn every day of my life.

It was the blessing of Rocket coming into my life that catalyzed my obsession with the sport of show jumping. My passion for the sport is what drives me to collect the stories behind show jumping's most spectacular partnerships. As the depths of the incredible bond that exists in and out of the show ring are explored on the pages that follow, it is important to remember these love affairs (if I can call them that) are somewhat more understandable when you consider, that for these athletes, the horse makes dreams come true. For professionals, their careers are made by the quality of their relationship with their equine partner.

Lifelong ambitions, aspirations, and goals, which are made not only by the rider but also by the grooms and support staff that make up the inner circle for these great athletes, are defined entirely based on the courage, service, and devotion of these partners. It is no small wonder when world travel, fame, fortune, and dreams are forged that an incredible range of emotions and endless mutual devotion result.

TONY DE COSTA

The author and his best friend share a quiet moment.

Ch. 2

Ian Millar & Big Ben

BECOMING BIG BEN

The accomplishments of the partnership of Ian Millar and Big Ben on show jumping's biggest stages are nothing short of astonishing. The obstacles Big Ben faced outside the competitive ring are no less heroic than his service inside the ring. But before we get to that story, let me put Ian's character and determination in perspective. Ian Millar has competed in nine consecutive Olympic Games spanning nearly 40 years (the only other athlete to have done this is Austrian sailor Hubert Raudaschl who competed in nine consecutive Olympic Games between 1964 and 1996). Ian has his sights set on London in 2012. If he is successful, he will be the only person ever to compete in ten consecutive Olympic Games.

JAYNE HUDDLESTON
Ian Millar and Big Ben in action at Spruce Meadows.

15

Captain Canada and Big Ben during a rare quiet moment at Spruce Meadows, Ben's second home.

It is impossible to discuss the accomplishments of Ian Millar without referencing Big Ben. This immense chestnut gelding was originally named Winston, a tribute to the political stature of Winston Churchill. Winston was born in 1976 on the van Hooydonk Farm in northern Belgium to a dam who was only 15 hands. In 1983, he was sold to another farm in the Netherlands and Dutchrider Bert Romps. Emile Hendricks became aware of the tall gelding who he soon purchased and renamed Big Ben.

By today's standards, the **price paid for Big Ben** is another piece of this **Cinderella story.** World class show jumpers today can sell for **seven figures** and prices in the very high six figure range are commonplace.

MAKING STRIDES

Big Ben began his career with Ian Millar in 1984. Ian's chance introduction to Big Ben came almost as an afterthought to a long trip across Europe. Ian had met Emile Hendricks at a Spruce Meadows tournament. On the last day of his European trip, tired, anxious to return home, and not without some extra effort, Ian decided to swing by the farm and have a look at the gelding that had grown to a tremendous 17.3 hands. Shortly thereafter, Big Ben was sold to Eve Mainwaring and Lynn and Ian Millar for $45,000 and permanently relocated to Millar Brooke Farm in Perth, Ontario, Canada.

Ian rode Big Ben to 40 Grand Prix wins. Equally as amazing, Ian and Big Ben were the first team to win two consecutive World Cup Championships—the first in Gothenburg, Sweden, in 1988, and then the following year in Tampa, Florida. Ian was ranked the number one rider in the world at that point, directly resulting from this legendary partnership. Ian and Ben won the du Maurier International, show jumping's then-richest purse, twice—in 1987 and again in 1991. This notable Grand Prix took place at Big Ben and Captain Canada's second home, the international ring at Spruce Meadows. The du Maurier was later renamed for other sponsors and became North America's first million dollar Grand Prix.

Aside from Ian, the person who enjoyed the closest relationship with Big Ben was his groom, Sandi Patterson. Sandi was his caregiver at Millar Brooke Farm and everywhere else he traveled for his entire career. Big Ben's enormous height and stature were exaggerated on the many occasions he appeared in public with Sandi, who is as petite as Big Ben was large. The love and adoration shared between Sandi and Ben transcended all the bounds of professional obligation.

Ian once told me that working with horses is like **drilling for oil;** if you don't try that extra exercise, or that different shoeing angle, or bit, you may never know you were **inches from a gusher.**

I think of that sage advice often when I'm tired and struggling at the barn with one of my own horses. I guess Ian's decision to make the effort to visit Ben on the last day of his European trip was his gusher. **And what a gusher it would prove to be.**

Shortly after Sandi went to work for the Millar Brooke Farm, she commenced a life of international travel, having never previously been outside of Canada. Sandi logged hundreds of thousands of miles with Big Ben. From Sandi's perspective, she got on the plane and went to the biggest international events in show jumping, representing the hopes and dreams of an entire nation. Her job was to do everything in her power to help Ian and Ben win. She did her job well.

GRETCHEN ALMY

Sandi Patterson, Ian's longtime barn manager, and crew prepare StarPower for competition at the 2011 Wellington Equestrian Festival.

OVERCOMING OBSTACLES

Big Ben survived two bouts of life-threatening colic surgery in 1992. Sandi said the hardest part of these ordeals was to see Ben, so huge, strong, and spirited, belittled by something so out of everyone's control. Many horses never recover from this kind of surgery; returning to competition is even more rare. Big Ben not only survived, but immediately returned to

BOB LANGRISH MBE
EQUESTRIAN PHOTOGRAPHER

Ian Millar and In-Style clear the massive water jump during the Beijing Olympics.

his winning ways. He loved the spotlight of the competitive ring as much as Ian did. A horse's digestive system is the weak link in an otherwise powerful and beautiful creation. Horses cannot burp, vomit, or relieve stomach distress the way people and dogs can, and they have miles of intestine that can become blocked or twisted.

Shortly thereafter, as if the surgery was not enough drama, Ben survived a horrific highway accident when the 18-wheeler in which he was being transported was hit and overturned. Two horses died in the accident and a third's career ended due to the severity of injuries. Horses have good memories, and a highway accident like the one Big Ben endured could change a horse's personality forever. Big Ben's publicist, Jayne Huddlestone, arranged for a press conference complete with TV cameras. (Yes, you read that right—Big Ben has his own publicist. He was, after all, a rock star). Jayne wanted Big Ben on camera just behind Ian during the interview. Ben was still shaken up, acting out of sorts, and a bit spooked and antisocial.

Ian described Big Ben to me as
1,600 POUNDS of DANCING DYNAMITE.

Ian agreed to try the interview with Big Ben looking over his shoulder, but insisted they would have to reshoot it without Ben if he wanted no part of it. The minute the cameras starting rolling, however, Big Ben, consistent with his lifelong showman's personality, pushed his way into the picture with Ian, nudging his rider playfully and hamming it up right on cue. This aspect of his amazing personality showed itself on a regular basis. As intimidating and over-spirited as this horse could be, he would sometimes reach down and lick the hand of a small child or shove his nose into a basket of muffins held by a young fan in a wheelchair, lighting up that child's face like a Christmas tree. Big Ben lived the life he was born to lead.

Sandi told me Big Ben had two personalities—his everyday barn personality, where he demanded constant attention from Sandi and his handlers, and his show-day personality, or his Sunday demeanor. When you came into Ben's barn you had to scratch his ears and deal with his every demand, or he would kick his door and insist his needs be met. By contrast, on show days, Ben was all business; he was extremely focused, not wanting you to fuss over that last tendril of his mane you wanted to tuck away. The bigger the class, course, or event, the more tuned in and focused Ben became. Sandi commented, "The more we challenged him, the more he would laugh at all of us, as if to say, 'I've got this figured out; you can't fool me.'"

In 1994, Ian made the decision to retire Big Ben from the competitive ring at the age of 18. After 11 years of competition, a national tour was arranged throughout Canada. People by the tens of thousands came to honor Big Ben and show their appreciation for this courageous athlete. In talking with Ian about this very emotional time, one very telling fact came to light. Big Ben's retirement tour came at a time when Polaroid cameras and instant photo development were very much in vogue. During the retirement tour, Polaroid film was sold out all across Canada. Such was the fame and fascination with this beloved gelding.

Big Ben was recognized as a Canadian icon when Canada Post honored him with his own postage stamp. Big Ben was also inducted into Canada's Sports Hall of Fame as only the second horse to be so honored, joining legendary Thoroughbred racehorse Northern Dancer. In 2005, the

GRETCHEN ALMY

Ian's daughter Amy Millar and her horse Costa Rica Z. put in a clear round during a big Sunday Grand Prix in the 2011 Wellington Equestrian Festival.

Perth and District Chamber of Commerce erected a life-size statue of Big Ben and Ian Millar jumping in a park on the banks of the Tay River in downtown Perth, Ontario.

On December 11, 1999, Big Ben was struck with a third case of colic. After consulting with two different veterinarians, Ian made the heartbreaking decision to euthanize Ben. He is buried on a knoll overlooking Millar Brooke Farm. A large stone and plaque mark his resting place. A fire in the shape of a horse show burned at his funeral service, and it is relit annually on the anniversary of his passing.

In recounting his life and times with Ben, tears and smiles came to Ian in equal measure. I have to admit it was challenging for both of us. During Big Ben's life several offers were made for millions of dollars. Ian remarked,

"The French wouldn't sell the Eiffel Tower. The United States would never sell the Lincoln Monument. Big Ben is a Canadian and belongs to an entire nation. To sell him would be unthinkable." Amazingly, the ownership syndicate behind Big Ben agreed without hesitation.

While listening to Ian recount the amazing story of his life with Ben, I got an intimate glimpse of these two larger-than-life athletes. It takes place on the occasion of Big Ben's final derby at Spruce Meadows. For those not familiar with the term derby, it represents show jumping's marathon event; instead of 10 to 13 numbered obstacles, the horse and rider are challenged with 20 or 22. The rider

The third member of the team Millar trio, Jonathon Millar, in action.

BOB LANGRISH MBE
EQUESTRIAN PHOTOGRAPHER

is faced with banks, table tops, the dreaded devil's dike, ditches, and all the natural obstacles (meaning banks and ditches from the terrain employed in the ring, rather than obstacles built from rails or planks) that strike fear through the hearts of both horse and rider in the sport. Big Ben loved these events. Ian did as well; he amassed a small fortune winning derbies with Ben.

MAKING DREAMS COME TRUE

On that last derby day, after they came down the bank at Spruce Meadows to the more demonstrable challenges on the remainder of the track, the crowd of 50,000 spectators went wild, and, to Ian's amazement, Ben jumped higher than usual. By the end of the track that day, he was a foot over every obstacle, levitated by the adulation of the crowd. The more wild and boisterous the crowd, the higher Ben jumped.

In a manner consistent with the Cinderella-like story of Ian and Big Ben's career, Big Ben won his final derby. The odds of that happening, given the depth of the international field of play on any given Sunday at Spruce Meadows, coupled with the risks involved in this sport, are truly staggering.

Big Ben, consistent with most winning show jumpers, was wired—pumped up, full of himself, and leaping all over the place. Why not? He had earned the right to act like that. He had proved his worth as a champion once again. As Ian and Big Ben made their way out of the international ring following the awards presentation, they were approached by Nancy Southern, daughter of Spruce Meadows founders Ron and Marge Southern. Nancy was accompanied by a young girl and her parents who were there sponsored by the Children's Wish Foundation. The girl was very frail and her mobility was aided by medical equipment because of her obvious physical challenges. Nancy and the child's

GRETCHEN ALMY

A personal moment with Captain Canada and his Olympic partner In-Style.

mother wanted her to get close enough to pat Big Ben. Ian was understandably nervous, given the exuberant mood Big Ben was in. Nonetheless, the foundation had granted this girl's wish to attend the derby, and Ian couldn't bear to deny her an up-close and personal experience with Ben.

When the girl approached with help from her parents, Ben was spooked. As the young girl came closer, she spoke to Ben and reached out with both her arms trying to touch the enormous gelding's nose. Instantly, he settled down, and lowered his head within her reach. In this simple way, he said, "It's all right Ian," and he let the girl stroke his face. Her mother was elated, and the child's face was literally glowing with adoration. Then Ian got a surprising request.

Nancy Southern asked, "Do you think we could lift her up on Big Ben and take her picture?" A small crowd had gathered, and putting the child on the horse was going to be dangerous. Experienced horsemen instinctively pause when they sense such a risky situation. Ian put those feelings aside, instead trusting his equine partner. Sandi and the other staff managed to get the young girl up in the saddle and astride Big Ben. Imagine what it was like from Ben's perspective, with a large number of people lifting a frail child onto your back. It was a moment Ian will never forget. Ben stood there like a stone; he became a school horse, totally determined to afford this young girl her wish. Time stood still and Ben clearly communicated that he understood the girl's special circumstances. Horses are like that. I have experienced it with my own horses and kids from the Windrush therapeutic riding programs that visit during the Fidelity Jumper Classic.

This moment is evidence of the special bond between that special horse, Ian, and his caretaker. Ben gave himself as much for the girl and her mother, as he had always given for Ian and Sandi. The unspoken understanding between the horse and partner cannot be quantified. It can barely be explained to the uninitiated. The absolute trust afforded each other is endless and special beyond all reason.

It was a magical finish to a star-studded career. When the crowd left with the little girl and her parents, Ben turned and playfully nipped Sandi as if to say, "You owe me one."

A few weeks later, Ian received a letter from the girl's mother which contained a copy of the picture of the girl sitting on Ben. The young girl had passed away. The mother shared with Ian that the girl had kept the picture next to her on her hospital wall up to the very end. It was her prize possession. The mother explained how much that day had meant to her and her husband, as well as to Ben's special fan.

With greatness comes great responsibility. Ian told me, "What makes a good athlete is not confined to what takes place on the field of competition, but the character displayed off the field as well." Ian Millar is greatness personified, much like his beloved Ben who was also a spectacular athlete by Ian's own expanded definition here.

Ian Millar is not only a great Olympian, but a father, grandfather, teacher, and partner. Ian's love of Big Ben is no doubt as large as Ben's stature and spirit. Despite all the accolades, gold medals, fame, and success, I know Ian would relinquish it all for a few more precious moments with his partner and friend. I asked Ian if there was a particular moment where he missed or thought of Big Ben. Ian responded, "There have been times when I am walking a course; I have this fleeting thought, 'This would be so easy for Ben.'"

It's my belief that if there is a superior being—call it what you will—that entity or force of energy looked down on Ian Millar and his horse from time to time and smiled with pride, knowing this was a very special thing.

Won over $1.5M in prize money

First pair to win two consecutive World Cup titles

Following the 2012 London games, Ian will be the only athlete to compete in ten consecutive Olympic Games

Ian Millar & Big Ben

Big Ben is one of only two horses inducted into Canada's Sports Hall of Fame

Until just recently, leading all-time money winner at Spruce Meadows, Calgary

2008: Team Silver medalist at the Beijing Olympics

1988, 1991, 1993: Canadian National Show Jumping Champion

1987: Team and Individual Gold medals at the Pan Am Games, Indianapolis

1986, 1987, 1989, 1991, 1992, 1993: King of the Spruce Meadows Derby

1984: Members of the 4th place team at the Los Angeles Olympics

CH. 3

McLain Ward & Sapphire

Like most people on the jumper circuit, McLain Ward is highly approachable. In every sense of the word, McLain is an ambassador for the sport of show jumping. The stars of this sport are emphatic about promoting the sport they love.

Years back, McLain and I were paired in a Pro-Am speed class. The professional's and amateur's combined times with faults being converted to added seconds determined the winning team. We were participating in the Syracuse Sport Horse Invitational, and like most big indoor shows, the place was hopping. Although we did not win, a serious friendship was born. In perfect honesty, I had a rail down. In classic McLain fashion, he told me, "It was a very light rub—you were just unlucky." In truth, I hit that rail so hard that the

BOB LANGRISH MBE, EQUESTRIAN PHOTOGRAPHER
McLain riding with a broken collarbone and Sapphire in Aachen, Germany.

lucky part was that it didn't end up in the front row of the VIP seats on top of some spectator's expensive dinner. McLain is just that kind of guy.

Most of my insights here are a mix of my own memory and interviews with McLain, Erica and Lee McKeever, the husband and wife team that manages the operations at the farm, and McLain's dad, Barney, who has always been a major force in McLain's success.

McLain Ward was born in October of 1975 in Brewster, New York, at their summer home known as Castle Hill. Like many people in the sport, their entire operation migrates to Wellington, Florida, during the winter circuit. Both of their properties are visually impressive and designed as world-class training centers. It is always fun to visit these farms and see the mix of dogs of every age and variety. Everyone on the property—Barney, Lee, Erica, and McLain—always seem to have time to welcome visitors.

McLain has been at the top of his class on the jumper circuit since his junior days as an equitation rider. When McLain was 14, he won the United States Equestrian Federation (USEF) Show Jumping Derby and the equitation medal finals. Internet records indicate that McLain was the youngest rider ever to win both in one year. Erica McKeever

McLain won the Grand Prix of Devon that **his father had won 20 years earlier** to the day.

McLain and Sapphire home at Castle Hill Farm in Brewster, New York.

GRETCHEN ALMY

Lee and Erica McKeever, Sapphire's best friends and critical members of the Castle Hill Team.

has confirmed this fact. Erica and Lee McKeever have been part of the Ward success formula since McLain was small, so she would know. McLain won these two events back-to-back from 1990 through 1992, a feat that has never been duplicated.

After leaping into the Grand Prix circuit, McLain wasted no time carving out the early milestones that comprise his resume. In 1999, when he was 24, McLain became the youngest show jumper in history to hit the million dollar mark in prize money.

Like all the inside stories of incredible equine and human partnerships, the most incredible aspect is not the exhaustive lists of wins, but rather the unique circumstances that characterize the heart of a champion.

SHATTERED COLLARBONE

McLain and Sapphire were in Aachen, Germany, in 2005 during the team finals at the Samsung Super League. In an early round, a rare mishap caused McLain to impact a jump standard, shattering his collarbone. For athletes in almost any sport, that would be it—end of story, competition over, weeks or months of recuperation and recovery. Not so for McLain. The reality was that Team USA and Coach George Morris needed another appearance from McLain and Sapphire to ensure the Super League Championship—the U.S. versus the European powerhouses. The pressure was on. Nobody had to ask McLain to ride, and nobody could have stopped him.

Picture the enormous field with all the immense jumps. Your collarbone is broken and you can feel the pieces moving about. McLain was able to block the pain and focus on the job at hand. Not only did he have the courage to enter the ring, but he also put in another keeper round for his country, enabling them to win the Super League. Most people could not walk up or down a flight of stairs, let alone mind pilot the mighty Sapphire and absorb the shock and stress a rider's upper body must endure. I have it on good authority that Sapphire pulls! Ouch! This is a demonstration of the heart of a champion: setting team before self, horse before rider, whatever it takes. That's McLain.

For those outside the sport thinking, "What's the big deal about show jumping? The horses do all the work. The riders aren't athletes!" Name a baseball player who has played with a broken collarbone.

McLain has won consistently on many different horses:

BOB LANGRISH MBE
EQUESTRIAN PHOTOGRAPHER

McLain and Sapphire in Beijing. Another clear round in the Olympics.

Goldika, Philipa, Antares, Potter, Rothchild, and Sapphire. The list goes on and on. Barney, McLain's father, recently disclosed that ensuring that the next generation of equine super stars is available to McLain is a lifelong responsibility. Like all the great stars of show jumping, the team support evident at Castle Hill is broad and deep.

OLYMPIC GOLD

McLain played a vital role in both U.S. team Olympic gold medals aboard the mighty Sapphire. For McLain, these Olympic moments were the culmination of a lifelong dream. McLain says, "I owe my Olympic dreams to Sapphire." He does indeed— two gold medals. It also has something to do with a lifetime of 4:00 AM mornings, sacrifice, pain, and unending work.

McLain is widely regarded as perhaps the **BEST RIDER in the history of our sport.** He is clearly the best pressure rider when the big moments come.

In 2008, McLain and Sapphire traveled to the Olympic Games in Beijing, China. The intense heat and humidity caused Sapphire's sides and skin to break out in a heat rash, making the already powerful and opinionated mare cranky and overly sensitive. These challenges aside, the mare responded to her rider's wishes and delivered an amazing six clear Olympic rounds, propelling the USA to Team Gold.

When I asked McLain what was his most unforgettable moment, I expected him to tell me about his moments on the Olympic podium. McLain, however, said something different: "The medal presentations and the playing of the national anthem were the country's moments, and they earned that for entrusting me to represent the team. The quiet moments in the barn before and after critical times where we had to perform and the quiet time spent with Sapphire, Lee, Erica, and the team—those were the special moments for me." I am all the more proud to call him a friend.

McLain and Sapphire clear 16 feet of Olympic water.

BOB LANGRISH MBE
EQUESTRIAN PHOTOGRAPHER

WORLD CUP FINALS IN SWEDEN IN 2010

Little could McLain have realized that, after riding into championship stadiums with broken bones and displaying poise and focus in two Olympic pressure cookers, his most difficult challenge lay before him. It was to play out at the World Cup Finals in Sweden in 2010. The character, class, composure, and integrity displayed are beyond description.

I am going to tell this part of the story in less detail than I am privy to. This episode makes me so angry that the longer the description, the higher my blood pressure will rise.

With multiple rounds into the complex World Cup scoring format where competitive placings were being converted to faults, McLain and Sapphire were in total command of the competition. Going into Sunday's final rounds, it was clear that Sapphire, piloted by the focused and determined McLain, was destined to add the one thing to her resume she had yet to capture: show jumping's World Cup title.

I am not going to mince words here—a shocking and unexplainable decision left everybody involved slack-jawed, angry, and outright disgusted. It was one of the sport's darkest episodes.

With no prior explanation, based on a totally subjective hypersensitivity test on her left front leg, performed at late hours of the night without McLain present, McLain and Sapphire were suddenly disqualified. You must understand how subjective this decision was. A representative of the Fédération Équestre Internationale (FEI), poked the mare in the leg multiple times and she reacted by moving her leg.

I have a chestnut mare named Glorydays, and if you poked her in the leg over and over again, she might just kick you in the head! Never mind pick up her foot. The decision was totally unsupported. Sapphire's reaction was natural. The disqualification was not substantiated by any real clinical evidence, and in the end was utter nonsense;

that is not good enough—it was total crap. Nothing but international politics—it was not sport!

Let us remember these animals can sense a tiny fly on their butt, so when you poke them over and over again, they will raise the limb in question. They are trained to pick up a foot to be cleaned every time a groom asks them—about six times per day.

There was no explanation as to why Sapphire was selected for this testing when others were not. Thermographic images, which detect the presence of heat that can indicate a problem, were negative, and the mare was then allowed to jump again. With all these concerns at the front of his mind, McLain put it on the line, galloped into the stadium, and placed second in that class, which clearly put Sapphire and McLain in the overall lead going into the final day. After the class, they were singled out and tested again. The scientific thermography was negative. Sapphire, after repeated poking by a so-called FEI official, picked up her leg.

The unspoken accusation was that deliberate procedures could make a horse over-sensitive, and, as a result, cause her to jump even more carefully to avoid impacting a rail. That said, the FEI was very careful to suggest in print and in press conferences that there was no evidence to suggest McLain, or anybody involved on his team, was suspected of any malpractice. In other words, they acted in one manner while attempting to be politically correct at the same time. "Walks like a duck, quacks like a duck; it's a duck." Tim Ober, the United States Equestrian Team (USET) vet, publicly stated the FEI decision was incorrect, and that his many years of direct experience with Sapphire convinced him there was no basis for the opinion rendered.

McLain asked to have the mare's legs swabbed and tested for foreign substances, and the FEI refused. McLain asked to have the horse jogged and tested for soundness, and again, the FEI refused. Clearly, a decision was made,

Erica McKeever gives Sapphire a pep talk.

and nobody was going to let facts or scientific evidence get in the way. Sapphire and McLain were not allowed to compete on the final day.

The World Cup went to Germany instead of the true champion. To add insult to injury, McLain was stripped of the prize money he had won up to that point. On what basis? Sapphire had been tested, allowed to compete, and won day after day before the corrupt decision prior to the final day.

McLain, the North American Riders Group, and the USET

combined forces in legal action. In the end, the FEI issued a statement declaring McLain's innocence and reinstated the prize money won. What does that tell you? The damage was done, however, and Sapphire and McLain were robbed of the title they would have earned and just about the only prize not on the 16-year-old mare's resume.

I am disgusted by the FEI. As Chairman of the Fidelity Investments Jumper Classic, I once considered applying for World Cup qualifying status for our Grand Prix. Not now—not ever!

Throughout this entire ordeal, McLain spoke out, not for himself, but on behalf of his country and his horse and showed enormous strength of character. Many of the other riders considered a boycott of the remainder of the World Cup that week. McLain spoke out against the boycott, showing incredible restraint despite the heartbreak that he clearly felt. I spoke by phone to McLain at the time, and his dismay for Sapphire's rights was all he talked about.

One might think this kind of stinging injustice would suppress an athlete's desire to compete. Not McLain—two weeks following this travesty, he not only returned to competition but returned to Europe and racked up victory after victory with Sapphire, Rothschild, Antares, and members of his younger string of horses. The true ending to this awful and shameful chapter in the history of the FEI is that McLain returned to competition in Europe with Sapphire two weeks later, was suddenly allowed to compete, and won in France and Rome. They were never challenged again. If you wanted a demonstration of character on the part of an athlete, or if you wanted somebody to rise above an injustice, it would be McLain and Sapphire enduring this nonsense.

SETTING NEW BARS IN 2010

SAPPHIRE has moved into the **top three money winners** of all time in the history of show jumping's Grand Prix horses.

Following this test of character, McLain and Sapphire's performance record set a new bar for the sport in 2010, while remembering the competitive anger that no doubt catalyzed a streak never before seen in our sport.

In the purely quantitative category of total prize money won, Sapphire was the 2010 super horse. Sapphire and McLain accumulated a staggering $873,716.64, according to Kenney Krauss, who catalogues statistics for Phelpssports.com. Kenney is one of the sport's best writers, and his Web site is one of the best real time news sources. In fact, Sapphire's three-year total ending in 2010 was an even more stunning $1,707,458.50.

Average money won per event by Sapphire and McLain topped the list in 2010. Sapphire's average pay day was just over $45,000. So in other words, McLain and Sapphire appeared less often than many, and always in the biggest money classes where course builders ask the hardest questions. More often than not, they won. According to Kenney, a win-analysis shows that Sapphire and McLain top the list again in 2010 with a staggering 31.57% win ration. That's an almost unimaginable winning percentage. Show jumpers compete with 40 to 60 rivals in almost every outing.

It is clear that while the unthinkable happened to our dynamic duo at the hands of the FEI in 2010, McLain and Sapphire's response was to win over and over again, making the folly they were subjected to all the more apparent.

McLain and his wife, Lauren, with Sapphire.

Sapphire's favorite treat is, of all things, donuts. **That's right, Sapphire runs on Dunkin!** If only the D.D. franchise understood, then there might be another big-time sponsorship in it for McLain.

SAPPHIRE UP CLOSE

For those who will never have the firsthand opportunity to get up-close and personal with McLain, Lee, Erica, or Sapphire, let me tell you a few other interesting facts about this amazing mare. Sapphire is by the stallion Darco, who was and remains one of the most successful Grand Prix jumpers of all time. It is also noteworthy that Darco has passed his talent and bloodlines to more than 3,000 foals.

In the barn, Sapphire is affectionately known by the barn name Sara. Seems a bit plain, given her stardom. "Queen something" would seem more appropriate, but Sara is what Lee, Erica, Lauren (McLain's wife), Barney, and McLain call her. Erica will tell you, by comparison to some of their other more demanding equine tenants, that Sara is easy to care for and very independent. Lee tells us that if Sapphire is not on the traveling squad, when the trucks leave for a show she gets moody and it truly seems to bother her that she has been left behind.

Sapphire is a chow hound. My chestnut mare has the same love affair with food—maybe that's part of the chestnut mare diva persona.

My favorite Sapphire quirk is her behavior at the in-gate, which is more pronounced the bigger the venue, crowd, or event. While the prior horse is in the ring and McLain is at the in-gate waiting, Sapphire always lets loose with a whinny. Before they go back in for the jump, she is even more animated; during the pre-gallop before her fans, the whinny is even louder and longer. She can't wait to get in there, and she's letting the prior horse know to get the hell out of her way, so she can show them how it's supposed to be done.

Years ago, I was in the office of another company with a Chief Executive Officer I respected. On his wall was an inscription, or rather a definition, for the word "commitment." The author of the message was anonymous, but I was so struck by it that I copied it, and it hangs, to this day, in my home, office, and barn. In my mind, it's as if it was written about McLain:

> Commitment is the word that speaks boldly of
> your intentions.
> It's the actions that speak far louder than mere words.
> It's making time when there is none, coming through
> time after time, year after year.
> Commitment is the stuff character is made of.
> It's the daily triumph of integrity over skepticism.

I can't think of a better way to codify McLain's character, contributions to his team at Castle Hill, the USET, and the sport. The story is far from the perfect fairy tale despite Olympic success. McLain's story comes with challenges, injury, and heartbreaks, as well as the cheers and accolades. Nonetheless, it comes because it has been earned. The road to Olympic Gold for McLain and Sapphire is well-stained with the sweat of a lifetime of perseverance that marks the path.

Winner of the CN International $1M at Spruce Meadows

Winner of the first $1M Grand Prix at HITS Saugerties, the Pfizer million, New York

Winner of the Fidelity Investments Grand Prix on Goldika

McLain Ward & Sapphire

2010: Won the $500,000 CN Worldwide Florida Open Grand Prix on Sapphire

2006: Team Silver medalist at the World Equestrian Games

2005: Team Gold medalist at the Samsung Super League, Aachen

2004, 2008: McLain is a two-time Olympic Gold medalist on Sapphire, Athens and Beijing

2004: Won the $100,000 Open Jumper Presidents Cup Grand Prix, Washington, D.C.

2002: Won the USET Show Jumping Championship on Victor

2001, 2002: American Grand Prix Association Rider of the Year

Cʜ. 4

Candice King
& Toronto &
Skara Glenn Davos

AN EARLY START

It is no secret that many show jumpers began riding at early ages—many of them as young as six years old. Candice King, however, began riding at the astonishing age of six months old. Candice was born and raised in California, where her parents, Al and Marlo Schlom, owned Quarter Horses. Candice credits her parents with piquing her interest in the sport that would later become her life's passion. As an infant, Candice rode with her mother by sitting in front of her while balanced in a Western saddle. At three years old, Candice competed in her first halter classes. She continued with Quarter Horses until the age of seven, when

GRETCHEN ALMY
Candice and Skara Glenn Davos warming up in Old Salem (Spring 2011).

she switched to the English saddle that was to be her life's office. Shortly thereafter, Candice began competing in the hunter, equitation, and finally the jumper classes.

Though Candice had a modest middle-class upbringing, Al and Marlo went to great lengths to provide the best trainers and mentors for their budding star. Candice's childhood best friend was Meredith Michaels-Beerbaum, who is also heavily involved in the show jumping world. Meredith eventually moved to Germany, married Marcus Beerbaum, and later went on to become the World Cup Champion with her famous mount, Shutterfly. During those early days, Meredith and Candice were inseparable and very competitive; they would often bet Cokes and Snickers bars on the outcome of a show. Each November, the girls would partner on a jumper team at a West Coast indoor affair. Their parents would decorate tables, and the girls would cheer one another on. The show was in Santa Barbara, California every year at the fairgrounds, and Candice tells me the ribbons were as long as she and her best buddy Meredith were tall. They remain very close friends to this day.

At age 15, Candice and her mother moved to the East Coast where they lived in a trailer, and Candice completed her high school education remotely. While some parents might have balked at such a sacrifice, Marlo and Al rose to the challenge, ensuring that Candice was able to take advantage of every opportunity presented to her. She spent three years as a working student at Beacon Hill Farm, which was owned and run at the time by Bill Cooney and Frank Madden. She

> In many ways, **Candice's interest in show jumping** is something that was **ingrained in her from birth**, and as a young child, she continued to surround herself with all things horse-related.

had the opportunity to ride many of the sales horses, which was a great experience for her. During her time at Beacon Hill Farm, she also rode many of the junior jumper prospects with famous riders like Michael Matz, Rodney Jenkins, and Norman Dello Joio. McLain Ward's father, Barney, was also instrumental in Candice's development. Candice's final year as a junior rider was particularly remarkable because it was the same year that she began riding in Grand Prix competitions. That year was also an Olympic year, and Candice had the tremendous honor of riding in the Olympic trials.

THE TURNING POINT

In 1989, Candice moved back to Los Angeles and purchased a pair of young horses with the support of her cousins, Larry and Connie Dinovitz, who owned a ranch. She acquired an English-bred mare named Carroll from Gerhard Etter's barn in Switzerland. Though Carroll was neither careful nor competitive, working with the mare was a great learning experience for Candice.

Her next horse, Trademark, was particularly difficult, which made him affordable. Though Candice was initially hesitant to work with Trademark, today she credits this horse with helping her break into the international scene. At 18 years old, thanks largely to Trademark and another new mount named Kodiac, she qualified for the Spruce Meadows Masters Tournament. After the Masters, however, it became clear that Trademark lacked the 1.60m scope needed to succeed in international classes. Candice, Larry, and Connie then traveled to Gerhard Etter's sales barn in Switzerland, where they purchased Wula. This allowed Candice to do her first International Grand Prix. Wula gave generously of herself, and Candice is quick to credit her with playing a critical role. The two became an extremely successful team. In 1989, Candice started her

GRETCHEN ALMY

Candice and her buddy finish in the money again and are elated to do so at the Old Salem Show (Spring 2011).

own business—a barn called Ranch del Puma in California.

In 1990, when she was 20 years old, Candice made the decision to declare herself a professional. For Candice and those who knew her at the time, it was not so much a life-altering decision as it was a natural progression. Her talent was obvious at this point, and numerous interested parties wanted to train with her. This year also marked the first time that Candice wore U.S. team colors, and it was the first year of the computer ranking system. Candice was one of the highest-ranking women on the list, which enabled her to be selected for the Nations Cup Team for the U.S. Candice's teammates were Margie Engle, David Reposa, and Chris Kappler. Together, they competed at the Royal Winter Fair in Toronto, Canada, where they placed second and jumped-off against Canada. Candice rode against Ian Millar mounted on Big Ben. Ian and Candice were both clear. Candice's little mare Wula was very competitive, and the experience was very exciting for Candice.

Candice fondly remembers what it was like to travel to Sweden in 1991 for the World Cup. "It was unbelievable; spectators packed in, not an empty seat in the stadium. When Jon Whitaker, riding Milton, came to his first jump, the entire grandstand lit up with flashes from every camera in the place. The lights, the deafening noise; these are moments you never forget... it was like a rock show."

LIFE ON THE ROAD

Candice went back on the road, this time accompanied by her fiancé (now husband), Brandon King. Candice says that these days were tough, and she did not feel confident enough to contact barns and ask whether they needed trainers or working professionals. The couple moved around, settling first in Colorado and then in Kentucky at a hunter and equitation barn. In 1993, Candice became the resident professional for Dan Lufkin in Millbrook, New York. In this junior phase of her career, Candice spent time with many professionals, including Jolene Labour, Tommy Lowe, Susie Hutchinson, Sheri Rose, Ronnie Beard, Hap Hansen, Joe Fargis, and Conrad Homfeld. Many who worked with Candice at the time liken her to a human sponge: she was thirsty for knowledge and absorbed it fully in every way she could.

In the summer of 1994, Brandon and Candice started their own business, Esperanza Inc. Though it was initially established in Southern Pines, North Carolina, the couple soon moved it to Wellington, Florida, where it is permanently anchored today. Candice and Brandon married in 1996, and three years later had their first child, a daughter named Alexandra. Alexandra rides and recently acquired her first jumper. Candice says, with a touch of bemusement, that her daughter is primarily interested in soccer, and Brandon serves as Alexandra's soccer coach. Candice and Brandon's encouragement of and involvement in their daughter's passion call to mind the relationship between Candice and her own parents. Candice is unbelievably dedicated to her family and maintains that they are her ultimate support system, a fact for which she is truly grateful.

LIGHTING UP THE INTERNATIONAL STAGE

In 2001, Candice made another important USET squad, this time competing in the World Cup Championships in Gothenburg, Sweden, where Candice rode a horse named John, E. M. Though she was competing against seasoned pros like Ian Millar on the legendary Big Ben and John Whitaker on Milton, she held her own and placed fifth in the World Cup standings overall and earned first place as the top American athlete.

Candice went on to **win the Queen's Cup** that same year, a **victory that an American woman** had not achieved in nearly **30 years**.

In 2001, Candice was understandably selected to be on the USET Developing Rider Program, a very prestigious invitation that provided her with even more critical international experience.

Today, Candice continues to make great strides in her career. In 2004, she won a six-bar competition in Rotterdam with her prized neat grey horse, Skara Glenn Davos. She took Davos to Kentucky and also to the World Equestrian Games in 2010 as the United States alternate or fifth team rider. Candice made the trip to Rotterdam again in 2010. There she helped the U.S. as a member of the winning Nations Cup team that anchored the U.S. performance in the Super League, where two critical clear rounds by Candice propelled them in the standings. Davos remains her top prospective Olympic hopeful for London in 2012. Candice also rides a young mahogany stallion named Toronto. (I joke with her that Toronto is my stallion because he is so handsome, and I have often threatened to steal him away.)

Candice remains eternally grateful to all of the owners that she has worked with throughout the course of her career and attributes much of her success to them, saying, "Ever since I was a kid, I had the horses nobody else wanted. Now that I have more support, I try to bring along younger horses and help them get to the bigger classes. It has become clear to me, as my career has developed, that I really enjoy bringing along the young quality horses. I have the patience, and I love living with the resulting quality. Of course, that patient and mature approach has been made possible because I've been fortunate to have those kinds of patient owners."

> Today, you would be hard-pressed to find a single athlete, trainer, or spectator on the circuit that has not been touched by Candice's kind and generous personality.

Candice has ridden for her country, competing in numerous World Cup Championships, the World Equestrian Games, and more than 15 Nations Cups. Yet she remains humble, grounded, and as eager to learn as ever. I have, on multiple occasions, watched her stop and spend time with a child who chases her down in the midst of horse show chaos seeking a word or an autograph; in fact, I've never seen her refuse anyone. This super person and superb athlete has a long career in front of her, and while I can't help but think an Olympic moment is on the horizon for Candice, she is already a champion in the eyes of legions of her loyal fans.

GRETCHEN ALMY

Candice shares some love with her partner.

More than 15 Nations Cup career appearances for the USET

Queen Elizabeth II Cup at the Royal International Horse Show, Hickstead

AGA record-placing 1st to 4th at the Merrill Lynch Grand Prix, Cleveland

Candice King
& Toronto &
Skara Glenn Davos

2010: Member of the winning all-women USA team at the Nations Cup, Rotterdam

2010: Team USA alternate at the World Equestrian Games, Lexington

2004, 2006, 2010: Team USA rider on the Samsung Super League Tour

2004: Winner of the Six Bar Competition at CSIO Rotterdam on Davos

2001: Top-placed U.S. rider at the World Cup finals, Sweden

Ch. 5

Margie Goldstein Engle & Perin

Asking Margie Goldstein to name her favorite horse is like asking me who's my favorite kid. With her many superb equine partners over the years, she is one of the top winning U.S. riders. She has captured nearly 200 Grand Prix wins, ridden on the U.S. Olympic Team, and been named AGA (American Grand Prix Association) Rider of the Year ten times. I am certain that is a record no other rider can claim.

"I've been fortunate to have had a lot of nice horses," she says. It is hard not to notice that she's regularly been paired with horses of the extra-large variety, which makes it all the more amazing to see this petite powerhouse of a rider in the saddle. She says it just happened that way, even

TONY DE COSTA
Margie with Hidden Creek-Jones.

though the horses seem impossibly big for her 5'1 stature. Margie's physical size should, however, not be confused with any thoughts that it limits her talent.

"Size is not what I look for," she says. Large horses just find her. Like many top show jumpers, she has ridden a myriad of clients' horses. "My ideal was more like Saluut's or Laurel's size [16.1 to 16.2 hands]." Years ago, when Margie did not have the investors she has today, she would take the horses that were sent to her, and they were all large horses. Maybe it all started with the first horse she was part owner of, DayDream.

DayDream was huge, and I am sure people assumed Margie wanted to ride big horses. "I started to think this is ridiculous for me to get something this big, but I just fell in love with him. It's not like a car where you can put your order in and get exactly what you want!" she observes. I have yet to see a horse Margie couldn't ride to success.

MARGIE DISCOVERS PERIN

In the long line of high performance horses, it was the super-sized bay horse with the kind eye that captured a special place in Margie's heart. It did not happen just because Perin was pure raw talent, but because he was like an enormous lap dog. Margie and Perin have the kind of special bond this book is all about. They just belong together.

As Margie recalls, she was looking at horses in Europe in 1998. Margie had been buying horses from Peter Nagel Tournout for a very long time, beginning with Carosa, who she showed internationally 25 years ago. Peter is located in Germany and is internationally known for breeding and showing top horses. At first, Perin was not for sale. Max Faninger, the dealer, wanted Margie to get on him and jump him a bit. Margie had purchased several horses for clients from Peter before, and he wanted her to sit on Perin so he could

GRETCHEN ALMY

Margie hanging out with now retired "best-est" buddy Perin (2011).

see the horse perform. Peter was originally going to keep the horse for himself and show him internationally. However, he got so caught up with breeding, stallion approval, and selling horses that he never got a chance to ride much. Peter and Perin had competed in less than ten horse shows. The horse was eight years old at that time.

"I thought when Perin first came out that he was not my type at all. He was huge, and he wasn't that fit. He stood 17.1 at least and was very big-boned. He looked like a big cart horse, but he had a very appealing face and really kind eyes," Margie reflects. He was not the type of horse for someone of Margie's size. Then Margie sat on him and realized his unbelievable ability. He was very green, but when he got to a jump, he tried to jump it clean regardless of the size. He had very raw talent, scope, and more explosive power than any horse Margie had previously ridden. Margie told Peter that if he ever wanted to sell Perin to contact her first, and she would try to get someone to buy the horse.

PERIN IS BROUGHT TO THE US

About a year later Margie, found out that Peter was willing to sell the horse because he did not have the time that he had hoped to show Perin himself. In the year that had passed, he had done less than a handful of shows, and the horse was starting to get older. Due to the fact that Perin had so little experience, it was difficult to get someone interested in buying him. Peter had a feeling that the horse was going to go on to great things, so he was asking a good price. I am sure the same would have been true with any dealer in possession of this horse.

Margie approached the deal cautiously with her business partner, Mike Polaski, who owns Hidden Creek Farm. Mike bought half of the horse. She said she would work with Perin and see what he could do. She would either try to find someone to buy him or get someone to buy the other half. Perin moved to Hidden Creek Farm and began to train with Margie.

Many of Margie's top horses are from Hidden Creek Farm. There is a breeding farm for Hidden Creek, located in Wisconsin. The show barn element of Hidden Creek is right next door to Margie's own farm, Gladewinds. This 32-stall barn, near the Palm Beach Equestrian Center, is named after the farm in Miami where Margie rode as a child. She dearly loved the family that owned it and named her own farm in their honor. Much of this is chronicled in a book Margie's mother published several years ago, *No Obstacle Too High*, which tells the story of Margie's life (it is a great book which I highly recommend).

Perin was no exception to Peter's reputation in the industry. The Westphalian gelding by the stallion Pagano is from impeccable breeding lines. Breeding is important to a point, but it is no guarantee. I know many people with offspring from famous mares or stallions that never amounted to anything. It is very much like raising kids; the environment, training, care, and people in a horse's upbringing have the greatest effect on their ability in the end.

I am sure Perin's life with Margie was the secret ingredient that cemented his international stardom.

In September of 1999, Margie brought Perin to the United States. It had been almost a year since she had seen him. She first brought him to South Hampton, and Perin was so out of

Margie flying high (2011).

BOB LANGRISH MB
EQUESTRIAN PHOTOGRAPHE

shape he could barely do anything. She remembers cantering him once around the ring, and he was huffing and puffing. When Mike first saw Perin, he thought Margie was crazy for being so interested in the horse. He was overweight, and he jumped very high straight up in the air, mainly because he did not get much opportunity to jump.

POLISHING THE RAW MATERIAL

Margie worked with Perin, trying to get him fit and progressing with his flat work and listening skills. She did very few shows with him. She could not keep shoes on him because he would get so high up in the air that he would grab his front shoes right off. It was obvious he was not going to go to the indoor shows that season, so Margie brought him home and dedicated a great deal of time to putting some polish on the raw material. She took Perin trail riding around Palm Beach, which he loved.

Margie worked diligently on the flat and started jumping him over small jumps because he was over-jumping everything. She taught him the basics, which included shaping that large, athletic body. She focused on making him more agile so he could not only jump up high, but could also find the right take-off and landing point and continue on to the next jump. One of the biggest problems, she said, was that it was very hard to rate his stride.

When riders walk the course before a competition, or when they set up jumps for schooling, they measure the line to a jump in what is equivalent to the horse's stride. Accomplished riders can help the horse compress or expand the stride, adjusting the horse to get to a fence in the ideal number of strides, or compensating for the approach by taking a longer or shorter stride. Perin had a huge stride with very little adjustability, but gymnastic training helped. Imagine the fine tuning and patience it took to get it right!

But Perin was a good student and very willing.

Perin was also very trusting, which is why he was so willing to do whatever Margie asked of him. He did not have much experience, but he did not have any bad habits. He wanted to please everybody—the rider and the people on the ground.

His time learning in Florida was well-spent, and at the Winter Equestrian Festival in Wellington he quickly moved up the levels to the Grand Prix by the end of February. At this point, Margie had many people interested in buying Perin. When he was in the intermediate jumper division, it was obvious how high he could jump with a lot of scope. Mike Polaski ended up buying the other half of him during the circuit that year.

> Perin came around very quickly, and what he lacked in experience he made up for in scope and ability.

HIS SWEET PERSONALITY

What was really special to Margie, however, was not all the power or athletic ability, but his kindness. "His sweet personality made you think he was a big pet. He was probably one of the sweetest horses I've ever been around in my whole life. He is a big lap dog. He doesn't know a stranger—he just loves everybody," Margie comments. "I think he was starved for any kind of touching as he wasn't the type of horse that came up to the door just for treats; he just craved human contact. He'd let you pet him, and he'd lick you like a big puppy dog."

Margie would like to say he has a special relationship only with her, but Perin seems to know no bounds. He loves everybody. He loves Craig, the groom who takes care of him and helps with riding; Margie's husband, Steve, who does the chiropractic work on him; and even new people who come by his stall.

THE 2000 OLYMPIC TRIALS

By spring and early summer of 2000, Perin and Margie were a formidable duo. They were ready for the trials that would lead up to the Olympics in September. The Olympics had been a long time coming for Margie who had the talent, experience, and resume. But, until Perin, she lacked the right horse.

They went to Gladstone, which Margie recalls as one of the hardest trials she had ever done—almost as stressful as the Olympics. Seventy or eighty horses started the last round, which was one of the biggest and most difficult tracks, and Perin won overall. He had been on the Grand Prix circuit for only three or four months, which makes winning at Gladstone an amazing accomplishment.

Although his rideability was improving, Perin should have been much further along in his jumping career at his age. For a horse to do what he did in such a short period of time was beyond remarkable—it was unnatural. Perin was leading in the trials by so much that when they went to California with the 11 other chosen horses, he did not even need to do the last phase. He was significantly ahead of all the other horses.

He improved by the day. Margie was the highest placed American finisher. According to Margie, "In the speed leg,

> The horses that perform the best at the Olympic trials tend to be the ones with the most experience. **Perin likely had the least.**

GRETCHEN ALMY

It doesn't get any better than this.

FOR PERIN, THE SHOW MUST GO ON. He loved all the attention and always tried his hardest.

we didn't know that much about going real fast yet, but in the Nations Cup, we ended up being the anchor." They were clean in the Nations Cup.

At the Olympics in Sydney, Australia, Perin's performance was stellar; however, the U.S. team did not come away with a medal. "We had the best score both individually and for the American team, and I had the highest individual score for a woman that year," Margie recalls.

> **The Olympics marked just the beginning** of an outstanding career for this horse that had just entered **his prime at the age of 11.**

Most horses need time to recuperate after an Olympic Games performance, so they start small and work back up to big events again. Perin came back from the Olympics and blossomed. He went on to win some big classes in Europe. He won Team Gold and Individual Bronze at the Pan Am Games. At Spruce Meadows, he was the anchor horse when the U.S. won the Nations Cup. There was only one other horse with a clean round, and that was Shutterfly. Shutterfly is Meredith Michaels-Birnbaum's superstar horse who has since gone on to win the World Cup. Margie recalls how the weather was a factor that day. "There was hail the size of dimes," Margie says. "There was water splashing in the water jump and hitting Perin on the neck. He could have had up to four faults without giving up anything competitively, and yet he went in and went clean."

As most of us know, having such a pleasing, laid-back

attitude in a large animal comes with a bit of a price. It is hard to keep the horse fit, as they need to be exercised twice a day. Margie would work him up and down hills when in Kentucky. "He was one that you had to tag team to work him enough. It didn't take much out of him, and he wasn't over-sensitive to ride, so it was a lot of work on the flat to make him work properly. When he jumped, he got quite interested."

> "There was never a course that I walked that I didn't think he could do."

THE 2004 OLYMPIC TRIALS

Margie, like most of the athletes we have examined, has had serious injuries. In 2004, she broke her hip riding one of her many horses and was still in recovery when the Olympic trials began. She wanted to try for the Olympics one more time with Perin.

"There are not too many horses I would have felt comfortable getting on, but I got on Perin almost two months early to try and do the trials in California. I literally couldn't get on by myself. I had to have someone put me on." I saw Margie ride during that period, and it was heartbreaking to watch; clearly, she was enduring a great deal of discomfort.

Perin needed to do a little extra because Margie could not do as much with her injury. He won the first trials. The committee told her to save any further wear and tear on her hip, they had seen enough and she could skip the remainder of the trials. Margie withdrew, even though the doctor told her she would be fine to ride by the time of the Games. She knew she would be doing a lot of damage by riding too early. She felt like she had a chance when the committee indicated to Margie that she was to be part of the team, but it was

Margie attacks the Fidelity Jumper Classic Course.

> "I knew as long as I could stay on, he knew what he was doing."

not to be. Margie wasn't selected, which from a distance seemed like a tremendous letdown given the heart of this courageous woman. I don't think I've ever seen that kind of raw determination more vividly on display than when she won the trial. It was terrifying to watch. I stood in total disbelief knowing how freshly broken her hip was.

For the next few years, Margie would win internationally with Perin again and again. It was a thrill to see the big-boned bay soar over the jumps that were higher than his rider, land smoothly, and come through the finish line clean with Margie smiling and leaning forward over his neck to pat and praise him. A couple of years later, she had a major fall at a competition riding another horse. I happened to be there, and I didn't think she was going to get up, stand, or walk out of that ring. But again, I saw her get on Perin the very same day to win yet another Grand Prix—bruised and bleeding.

PERIN RETIRES

The last Grand Prix Perin won was at the Hampton Classic, at the age of 19. In the last class Margie competed at South Hampton, he twisted his ankle in the jump-off. She said that he felt a little funny, but she didn't think about retiring him. Like in most horse-and-rider relationships, Margie hated to think about Perin's retirement, but in the same vein, she did not want to make him show if everything was not quite right. Perin was fine. He had done everything over the years, that was asked of him and more. He did not need to go anymore if he wasn't 100 percent.

At age 21, Perin is happily retired at Hidden Creek Farm,

and everyone loves him, including his owner, Mike Polaski, and Margie's parents, who were not originally horse people. Margie's mother, a retired school teacher and principal, has come to feel comfortable around Perin, who has achieved not only Olympic status but also treasured pet status.

> For a big horse to go so many years was amazing. For any Grand Prix horse to go to **AGE 19** IS **RARE.**

Perin still gets treated like a show horse. He is groomed every day, though he is barefoot. He is now best friends with another of her famous horses, Avaretto, who, Margie feels, was originally jealous of Perin. Perin is the kind of horse that hates to see his visitors leave. "Sometimes it's really difficult to leave his stall—I feel so guilty!" Margie says.

Margie never really leaves Perin. He is in her thoughts and heart wherever she goes. Perin carried her to the Olympics, and to win after win on the world stage. Incredibly, he carried her to their second Olympic selection trials when she could barely walk and somehow protected his fearless partner. Margie will protect him in kind wherever her journey takes her. You can rest assured that Perin, the horse that gave all, wants for nothing. Margie will see to that.

As of this writing, about to be the first rider to win 200 Grands Prix

AGA Rider of the Year 10 times

Member of 20 winning USA Nations Cup Teams

Margie Goldstein Engle & Perin

Numerous World Cup Final appearances for the USET

2006: Member of the World Equestrian Games and Samsung Super League USET Silver Medal Teams

2005, 2006: Led the U.S. World Cup League Standings

2000: Member of Team USA at the Sydney Olympics

1999: Member of the USET Silver Medal Team at the Pan American Games, Winnipeg

1992, 1993: Rolex National Grand Prix League Rider of the Year

1991: AHSA (American Horse Show Association) Equestrian of the Year

Ch. 6

Joe Fargis
Touch of Class,
Mill Pearl, & Edgar

In the 1980s, Joe Fargis achieved legendary status when he rode two fiery mares in back-to-back Olympic Games, winning Team Gold and Individual Gold on Touch of Class, and Team Silver on Mill Pearl. These two Olympic-caliber horses came along when Joe was riding at the top of the sport—this was truly something special. When Joe looks at photos of himself riding Touch of Class in the 1984 Olympics in Los Angeles and Mill Pearl in the 1988 Olympics in Seoul, he says wistfully, "I can't believe that was me." Named to the Show Jumping Hall of Fame in 2007 for his lifetime achievements, he recalls those halcyon days with fondness.

Janet Hitchen Photography
Joe Fargis and his Olympic partner Mill Pearl.

Joe began riding when he was seven years old and has probably been on thousands of horses in his lifetime. Each of those horses holds an equally special place in Joe's heart. Even when you ask him to tell you about Touch of Class, Mill Pearl, or Edgar, he does not like to single out one of them from the others.

"People ask me which is my favorite. I find that **we are the caretakers of these magnificent animals**, so why should we discard one because it cannot do what Touch of Class did? **They all provided something special in my life."**

Joe fondly recalls the first pony he learned to ride under the tutelage of Jane Marshall Dillon at her riding school in Vienna, Virginia. Dillon's riding school was next door to Joe's home when his family moved to Virginia in the 1950s from New York. The pony's name was Snow, which fittingly sounds like the name of a child's pony. "Snow was the sweetest creature," Joe says. "I still have good memories of how nice she was to me. She carted me around and stayed under me no matter what I did. I find it hard to say that Mill Pearl was nicer than Snow." According to him, all his horses did the best they could and cooperated enthusiastically once the saddle and bridle were on.

TOUCH OF CLASS COMES TO THE FARM

In the late 1970s, Joe and his business partner, Conrad Homfeld, were operating their business called Sandron in Petersburg, Virginia. Joe met Conrad on the horse show circuit. Janet Nonni from Virginia Beach arrived with a

Thoroughbred mare to board and train. That mare was Touch of Class, who had had a brief racing career and then did some jumping and training with Leslie Burr Howard. Conrad rode Touch of Class first and then Joe took over the ride.

Joe recalls how it was never his original intention to embark on an Olympic journey. But, as Touch of Class got better and better, so did Joe's relationship with her. The horse did everything she was asked to do in an agreeable way. She did not dazzle at any level; she simply did what Joe asked of her, jumping in a clean manner irrespective of the obstacle's size and width. She was solid, and Joe called her "nicely hot." This is a term riders use to mean naturally forward, implying that she had her own motor—you did not have to push to create her energy. Her first Grand Prix was Upperville, Virginia, where she ranked fifth. She jumped very well and was totally consistent.

THE 1984 OLYMPICS IN LOS ANGELES

Joe and Touch of Class qualified for the U.S. Olympic team. Conrad also made the team riding the great stallion Abdullah. Melanie Smith-Taylor, riding her beloved horse, Calypso, and Leslie Burr Howard, riding Albany, rounded out the U.S. team.

In 1984, the Olympics were held in Los Angeles, allowing the U.S. fans an opportunity to witness history in the making right here at home. What the huge crowds cheering from the bleachers saw was a compact little Thoroughbred mare with a tall, lean rider soaring over the Grand Prix jumps. When viewing the smooth, faultless rides on video, you wonder how the mare endured all the noise and excitement.

"I don't think horses are aware of the crowd except when there is loud noise and a packed arena," says Joe. We learned from Ian Millar that Big Ben thrived on the roar of the crowd, as did McLain's mare, Sapphire.

Joe recalls that when he first got to the show grounds at Santa Anita Park with Touch of Class, she seemed to remember the race track, a distant memory for a horse whose life started there. Santa Anita Park was a stabling environment, and Touch of Class became extremely fractious. They had arrived early enough to give her time to settle in, and under Joe's patient hand she became focused.

Team USA was unbeatable that year and into the history books they went. Touch of Class had the first double-clear round in Olympic history. She and Joe went on to win not only the Team Gold but also the Individual Gold at those Olympic Games. Touch of Class captured the hearts of America and was named USOC Female Equestrian Athlete of the Year.

Joe and his business partner, Conrad, vied for the Individual Gold medal on their famous mounts, and it was breathtakingly close as they tied for first place. Conrad Homfeld's equestrian ability is legendary, and it was a tremendous coincidence that he and Joe were first and second in the Olympics while operating the same business. The jump-off would determine that Joe would win and consequently Conrad took the silver medal. Today, Conrad is a Grand Prix course designer sought the world over. Joe's victory was made all the sweeter because his very first trainer, Jane Marshall Dillon, the woman who taught him so much about riding, was there to watch him in his most historic moment.

Touch of Class was owned by four partners after Janet Nonni sold her. "Janet was very proud of her and incredibly impressed. She was thrilled that she sold a horse she loved who continued to do well and exceed all our expectations," Joe recalls.

THE 1988 OLYMPICS IN SEOUL

Touch of Class' victorious career with Joe continued through the trials for the 1988 Olympics in Seoul, Korea. By then,

GRETCHEN ALMY

Joe studies a course while on deck.

Joe found himself in the unusual situation of having two outstanding horses. Touch of Class became his reserve horse while nine-year-old Mill Pearl was his 1988 Olympic mount.

It was a perfect overlap. The 1980s were wonderful for Joe Fargis. Mill Pearl was a very brave, clean jumper and an exceptional water jumper. Though Mill Pearl was about 17 hands high and Touch of Class was 16 hands, Mill Pearl's stride was shorter and a bit choppy. However, Mill Pearl was very aggressive and would always get down the line (meaning the horse would cover the related distances, such as four long strides between fences seven and eight).

Mill Pearl was coming up in 1985 on a winning streak. Again, like Touch of Class,

SHE EXCEEDED EVERYONE'S EXPECTATIONS.

She did everything her rider wanted her to do—she jumped higher and wider.

How Joe came to ride Mill Pearl is a strange story. Mill Pearl was an Irish Sport Horse by King of Diamonds, a legendary stallion thought of so frequently that "you could hardly have dinner without someone saying his name," Joe comments. The mare came from Noel C. Duggan at the Mill Street complex in Cork, Ireland. Joe had gone overseas to look for horses, and he saw Mill Pearl and liked her very much. He told the dealer he would get back to him if he could find a buyer.

A week later, when Joe was in San Francisco judging a horse show, Duggan, the dealer, called and said, "A lady just came through here—an old friend of yours named Jane Burr. I told her you liked Mill Pearl, and she bought her." Jane's purchase of Mill Pearl was truly serendipitous. In just a few weeks, Jane had purchased the horse for Joe Fargis to ride. Joe found his buyer without ever having to pick up the phone.

Before long, Joe was riding the big, solid chestnut mare from Ireland. As Joe remembers, "She came up through the ranks just like Touch of Class and did what was called, at that time, preliminary jumpers. [That language has since been eliminated. Today we would say a 1.40m open jumper class.] Amazingly, she won the first Grand Prix that she entered, which rarely happens in show jumping."

> **Mill Pearl won the Gold Cup at Devon**, a truly special moment that Joe considers himself lucky to have been a part of.

With both mares together at the Olympics in Seoul, it must have been a special time for Joe. "They were both wonderful in their stalls. They were like pets—everybody loved the horses but both were very active, very hot, and very aggressive when you put on the tack. They were comfortable with what you asked them to do," he says, admitting that he is "not very syrupy about what horses think." When Joe tells this story, however, you can see the affection on his face and his entire demeanor brightens.

Joe found the stabling, footing, and Olaf Peterson-designed courses to be to his liking in Seoul. The 1988 U.S. Show Jumping Team captured the silver medal, while Mill Pearl finished 7th individually. She had the best score in the Nations Cup rounds for the U.S.

THE HORSES RETIRE BUT JOE DOES NOT

A half interest in Mill Pearl was sold to Mr. and Mrs. Patrick Butler, big patrons and supporters of Joe and Conrad. They must have been thrilled to see the big Irish mare go on with her Grand Prix wins. In particular, I remember Mill Pearl winning the Grand Prix of Hickstead, England, and Zurich, Switzerland. She continued to compete until age 20 or 21.

Then she retired to an Ocala, Florida farm and lived to be 33. By show jumping standards, Mill Pearl was considered exceptional, as it is unusual for Grand Prix horses to have the capacity to compete past age 18 or 19 in the big rings.

Touch of Class, who was several years older, was retired to River Circle Farm in Tennessee, at the home of one of her four owners, Mr. and Mrs. Brownlee Currey, Jr. after an injury at the Tampa Horse Show in 1989. "We decided she had done enough—she didn't hurt herself badly, but enough that we decided she's done enough for all of us and she deserves a nice retirement," Joe explains. Foaled in 1973, she died at the age of 28, and had "three ordinary foals. She lived a great life," Joe says. The mare was inducted into the Show Jumping Hall of Fame in 2000, a year before she died.

Joe has had **great success** with mares, but likes **all his horses equally.**

Joe says he tried to retire once in the late 1990s, but patron Mary B. Schwab kept him in the Grand Prix ring by presenting him with another special horse with great ability: Edgar 12. Mary B. purchased Edgar in late 1998, when he was nine years old. He was very strong and competed without any interruption until age 19. Edgar won many classes and Grand Prix and retired in the spring of his 20th year. Edgar is now retired in the field on Mary B.'s Stoneleigh Farm in Middleburg, Virginia, and is very happy. Joe, who frequently checks in on his old friend, tells me that Edgar looks wonderful.

Joe exhibits classic form (2011).

Joe's careful, methodical way of training and hands-off approach to riding are the result of his lifelong experience, and he continues to encourage young horses and riders to learn and do the best they can. Joe will tell you he works slowly and methodically and does not rush through things. As Joe points out to me, "I'm slower than most people. Once I get going and I know the horse, then I will gallop and move forward." Most of the horses he rides typically go out twice a day, with the afternoon ride more of a casual walk. Careful, methodical, tenacious, dedicated, and incredibly smart are all words that come to mind when describing Joe.

Joe continues to compete successfully on a new crop of horses, defying the stereotypes of age. Show jumping is a sport in which athletes can compete at the elite level for decades. Many riders manage to stay on top of their game for most of their lives. He names two of the horses he's currently riding: Lariat and Last Dance. "I

> A good rider **passes what he has learned and experienced onto a new generation** of riders, who are grateful to have the guidance and teaching of successful show jumping legends.

have fun with them and they do well," he says. "Who knows how far they will get?" Of course it comes as no surprise that he continues with Grand Prix wins; I learned as this book goes to print that he and Lariat won the Grand Prix at the 2011 Swan Lake show.

Joe reflects back on the three, however, who were so consistently winning and made the '80s and '90s exciting for him and everyone who enjoys the sport of show jumping. In his understated style, he says, "These three were pretty darned good at jumping. Of course, there were bad days, but I've blanked them out."

Joe, like so many of the athletes I've introduced you to is somebody to look up to, not just for what he has done, but for who he is.

Joe now lives on Mary B.'s farm, still in the heart of the horse country where he grew up and first rode Snow at Mrs. Dillon's riding school in Vienna, Virginia. "It provided a wonderful start for me and a good environment through my junior years. That was in the late 1950s and early 1960s, and life was different then," Joe recalls. "The big show was shipping to Harrisburg or Devon for two days." As most of the great riders will tell you, they are profoundly influenced by their own trainers. After his early start learning to ride with Mrs. Dillion, Joe went to Frances Rowe in Crozier, Virginia, and worked for her for a long time. He also trained with Bert De Nemethy. "I've been surrounded by marvelous people my whole life, and I can't tell you how fortunate I feel," Joe says.

Joe would not say he did it very well, but anyone who follows the sport knows the truth. Like one of his Olympic mounts, Joe Fargis has been a touch of class in the world's most beautiful sport.

Grand Prix wins in Hickstead and Zurich; American Gold Cup; Hampton Classic; Ox Ridge; Mary Rena

Served on more than 30 winning Nations Cup Teams worldwide for Team USA

AAU's Sullivan Award Nominee–Given to the America's Top Amateur Athlete in any sport

Joe Fargis &
Touch of Class,
Mill Pearl, & Edgar

2003: Winner of $175,000 Cargill Grand Prix of U.S. on Edgar

1988: Team Silver medalist at the Seoul Olympics

1987: Leading International Rider in the National Horse Show at Madison Square Garden

1984: Team Gold medalist at the Los Angeles Olympics

1984: Individual Gold medalist at the Los Angeles Olympics on Touch of Class

1975: USET Team Gold medalist at the Pan American Games, Mexico City

1970: Team Gold medalist at the Nations Cup on Bonte II, Lucerne

JOE FARGIS & TOUCH OF CLASS, MILL PEARL, & EDGAR

Ch. 7

Debbie Stephens & Cosequin's CEO

Debbie was born on June 7, 1950 in Illinois and moved to Syracuse when she was three. From a very young age, Debbie gravitated toward horses, and whenever she was in a store, she went straight for the horse-related merchandise. Around the age of five, she started asking her parents for riding lessons. Her parents were not "horsey" people and were unsure what to make of their daughter's newfound interest.

Debbie continued to pester her mom and dad, pleading with them, "I want to ride!" When she was six years old, Debbie's mom bought her a coupon book entitling her to 12 riding lessons at a discounted rate under the watchful eye of Johnny Vass. The local stable was about 20 minutes

Debbie and Cosequin's CEO at Spruce Meadows.

from her house, and it was nothing special. Debbie is quick to point out that in those days, riding was not as expensive as it can be today. There were not a lot of equestrian events in the area where Debbie lived. Syracuse was not an easy place for a young person to get immersed in the equestrian world. The biggest nearby venue, at the time, was the New York State Fair, which hosted a small horse show.

DREAMS AND DETERMINATION

Debbie soon exhausted the opportunities in Johnny Vass's barn. Her parents bought her a pony which she named Strawberry Shortcake because he was a strawberry-colored roan. Shortly after she began riding Strawberry Shortcake, Debbie became the number one rider in Johnny's barn. That success was all the motivation she needed to push forward. Debbie moved on to her first horse, named Son Imp, who was an exceptionally good performer.

Neither Debbie nor her parents realized the incredible journey on which they were about to embark. Her dad was successful in the oil and gas business, and he wanted Debbie to pursue

> **By the age of nine,** this firecracker was **competing** in the hunter and jumper divisions **with the professionals**. The lower-level child classes simply were not challenging enough.

a profession and explore other options. Her parents wanted her to be well-educated. Debbie went to college, but her passion for horses remained with her.

Although Debbie's father did not at first consider riding horses to be a viable career for his daughter, he was entirely supportive when it became clear that this was her chosen path. Just as Debbie was gaining confidence as an equestrian, Johnny Vass received an extremely generous offer and subsequently sold the farm. The land was promptly turned into a golf course and restaurant, leaving a hole in Debbie's heart. Debbie was ready to move anywhere to continue the pursuit of her passion, but her parents nixed the idea of moving the family out of state.

Luckily, the Firestones were friends of her parents. Debbie's dad made arrangements for her to ride at the Firestones' private farm, where their professional trainer, Adolph Mogavero, would teach Debbie until they could locate another facility. The name should be a familiar one to those involved in the sport. Ring 8 at the Winter Equestrian Festival in Wellington is named in honor of Adolph Mogavero.

In the spirit of supporting her fully, Debbie's parents built a big stable in Cazenovia, New York. Today, this is the site of John and Beezie Madden's famous base of operation. Now, Debbie was in horse country.

The stable was named DE HECHT Stables, or D. He Stables for short. Her parents were now 110 percent behind her riding. They were allowing Deb to become her best by fully supporting her.

Just as the stars were beginning to align for Debbie, her dad had a heart attack. They were forced to sell the farm, along with the horses. Debbie moved back to a local stable. "I suddenly and completely lost my affluent lifestyle at age 16," she says. Deb worked as a groom at Cold Creek Stables to pay for lessons and go to shows. She did everything from riding to mucking stalls. She was far and away the best rider in the barn. Debbie was now training with Ted Ralston, who was at the later stages of his career. She showed locally at this point and had many wins to her credit.

Debbie in Florida (2010).

FROM BAD TO WORSE

Debbie then entered Cazenovia College which is now a big equine studies school (where Debbie has since been asked to lecture). Then, her dad suffered a second heart attack. Deb said that she was at a show competing when she got the awful phone call, and although she rushed to get home, her dad passed away before she arrived. Debbie's dad was only 52 at the time, but he had an unhealthy lifestyle. Debbie says he was a heart attack waiting to happen. Unfortunately, his death left Debbie and her mom in financial trouble. They ended up owing money to many of his business associates. Debbie said that it was only then that she fully understood why her dad wanted her to be well-educated.

Debbie and her mom did not know anything about business, and, because they were too trusting, they were often cheated. These were really rough times. When Deb was 19, they ended up penniless. The only real asset they had was the house, but even that was not enough—the IRS had come down on them, only adding to the mounting pressures. Debbie decided to finish college, picking up where she had left off at Cazenovia. She did indeed get the education her dad wanted for her, ultimately finishing at Syracuse University. Through all of the hardships that Debbie faced, she never once lost the drive to ride.

At the age of 23, Debbie made the worst decision of her life. She was introduced to a man in Buffalo, and shortly after meeting, they wed. Her new husband was in the industry and made loads of promises about horses, support, and taking care of her, but in the end, he revealed himself to be a bad character. He was verbally and physically abusive. It took Deb three years to find the courage to get out of the relationship, which was one of the hardest things she ever had to do.

BACK ON TRACK

Once Debbie regained control of her personal life, her riding career began to get back on track. It was at this point that she was paired with her first superstar horse: Abdullah. Deb quickly became a leading rider with him. Abdullah was the springboard for her international jumping career. Debbie went to Rome, the World Cup, and many other venues. Abdullah had gone to the Olympics with a foreign rider earlier in his career. A big part of this horse's career was his work as a breeding stallion. The family that owned him relied on his stud fees for a major part of their income. The family bred him and sold his offspring, while Deb handled the riding and worked around Abdullah's breeding responsibilities.

From 1979 to 1982, Debbie and Abdullah made frequent appearances wearing the colors of the United States Equestrian Team. Debbie's career was skyrocketing, and other horses were coming into her life. Debbie moved to Philadelphia and rode with Michael Matz for Vintage Farm. Her learning and passion continued to grow with Michael's help. At Vintage Farm, Deb met Bill Glass, who became her business partner. Together they founded Centennial Farms, which Debbie still operates today.

Debbie was a full-time international jumper at this point in her career. She and Bill were in the business of buying and selling horses as well as training both horses and students. At the same time, Debbie was concentrating on being on the

Riding Rocky Raccoon, she became the record holder for the **HIGHEST OUTDOOR HIGH JUMP**, clearing 7 ft. 8 in. and winning herself a BMW in the process.

U.S. team, and George Morris was coaching her. He believed in Debbie; she is very grateful for all George taught her. Other horses came into Deb's life, Volan and Rocky Raccoon of particular note.

> Her **PASSION FOR HORSES** is an integral part of who she is. Debbie says it is just in her blood.

The trust Rocky placed in Deb during the outdoor high jump was staggering when you consider that she asked him to gallop straight toward a wall he could not see over; it was, after all, taller than he was.

Finally, after the death of her father and the collapse of her abusive marriage, Deb seemed to be back on track. Riding was her backbone—it allowed her to keep fighting through those turbulent times, until finally her life began to come together.

A SETBACK IN SOUTH FLORIDA

In the winter of 2003, Deb went to South Florida to attend the Winter Equestrian Festival, where she opted to take a catch ride on short notice and entered an open jumper class in the international ring. Catch riding is a practice where individuals come to professionals with young, developing horses who have behavioral issues. For a fee, a professional rider will take the horse into a class for the experience or for rehabilitation. Deb is an experienced catch rider, and when she was approached that morning, she quickly agreed.

Deb was about halfway around the course with the horse, figuring him out as she showed him the way. As they picked up steam and she aimed her mount toward the 16 feet of open water (from one side to the other, a difficult obstacle common at the Grand Prix level), she sensed that the horse was reluctant to approach the water. Deb, being the experienced rider she is, felt his reluctance and urged him to continue and complete the class.

Tragically, the horse suddenly stopped, refusing to go over the water, and throwing Debbie off in the process. Deb lay unconscious in a heap on the floor of the international arena, her neck broken. A medevac helicopter was called, and Deb was transported to the Delray Trauma Center where her injury was confirmed. It soon became clear that she was paralyzed.

Things at Delray progressed from bad to worse. Debbie's condition worsened, and she received surgery to remove a "stinger," a broken bone in her neck. Fortunately, Deb was transferred to the Miami Project to Cure Paralysis, which made a vital difference in her recovery.

As Debbie tells me, "I would have died if I had stayed at Delray. All of the nerve damage worsened, the swelling in my spinal cord worsened , and when I did make the decision to leave, I was released in very bad shape." She was also suffering from a serious concussion, which added nausea and poor vision to her rapidly expanding list of symptoms. "It was extremely fortunate I didn't die there," she says.

> **Debbie proved to be the fighter everyone thought she was.** She was determined to return to the sport as an athlete, not as a wheelchair-bound spectator.

At the Miami facility, she immediately began treatment under the care of Dr. Bartholomew Green and things began to take a positive turn in relatively short order. She pushed the medical team to move fast. At this point, they conducted extensive tests, and the doctors wanted to remove several of the broken bones in her neck. However, the recovery time required of such an

Debbie and her best friend, Picture Perfect.

extensive operation would be extremely long. The alternative was to live with the risk of some moving bone fragments, and to begin therapy concurrently. Debbie opted for the shorter path and threw her remaining strength into her rehabilitation, explaining, "Surgery would be risky, and I would be out a year. A year without riding was inconceivable to me. I took the therapy route and attacked it with everything I had, making the hospital staff a bit crazy, constantly pushing them to let me work longer, quicker." Six weeks later, Debbie was up, walking, and out of the hospital. She was soon back at ringside in Wellington, but still recovering. Two weeks after her initial return, she began riding again.

> "I had to decide: **was my life worth living if I couldn't ride?** I decided for me, it was not."

BACK IN THE SADDLE ON COSEQUIN

Ninety days from the moment Debbie left the international ring via helicopter, she reentered it, ready to compete. The doctors were amazed and concerned, but understanding. Her family was frantic, but Debbie was very much in charge, and, while her body was a bit broken, her spirit soared as she trotted back under that famous Wellington foot bridge, ready to make her comeback.

Debbie reentered the ring on a horse she bred and raised from a foal. Her new horse was named Cosequin's CEO in honor of his sponsor, the equine joint supplement company. Debbie and the horse had history, trust, and love, qualities that make all the difference when it comes to riding. Debbie knew Cosequin was going to care for her and that he would not let anything happen to her. Because of this, she trotted into the ring with total confidence. Deb was not focused on her accident; she was in the ring to win. The memorable chestnut with the big white blaze on his face did what Deb knew he would do. Deb and Cosequin not only jumped the water jump that caused her accident, they jumped clear, they jumped fast, and they won! Her ten-year-old chestnut partner must have sensed the importance of the moment, as we know horses do. The results are the stuff of legend.

"To be honest, the only reason I was able to get back in the ring was that I had so much confidence in Cosequin," Debbie explains. "Not only did he bring me back to the international level, there was nothing in my eyes he could not do. The bond with this horse was incredible. Not just because I bred him, but from the minute he was born, there was good chemistry. I looked at him, and I knew. I also believed he was destined to be great. I had to ride for him, for Cosequin. I simply had to."

A writer for the *Palm Beach Post* interviewed Debbie after the victory. She asked Debbie if it bothered her that the water jump was positioned in exactly the same place as it was when she had her accident. Luckily, the interview occurred after the class and not before, as this question might have planted a seed of doubt in Debbie's mind. Deb responded honestly, saying that the thought had not crossed her mind. It was all because of who she was riding. Deb won the first Grand Prix she and Cosequin ever did together in that same ring.

COSEQUIN WAS HER PEGASUS,
even though he had all the wrong physical attributes for horses born and bred to jump.

TONY DE COSTA

Debbie at the Hampton Classic.

Debbie had managed Cosequin's life and career very carefully up to this point. She always thought of him as an amazing horse, but many others did not. His build and body type were all wrong for the traditional thinking of the sport. He was too big, and his hind end was higher than his front end—he was built downhill, so to speak. As a result, Debbie wisely did not start training him at serious levels before he was nine, much later than is typical. She let him grow into himself. He was big and awkward as a young horse. Debbie knew if she held him back and worked him he would blossom. He was eight when he started jumping competitively and was a star by the time he was ten. So Debbie rode through the discomfort and pain, working extra hard to get her own body fit and ready to take her partner to the top of the sport. Why let a little thing like a broken neck slow you down?

At this point, Deb and her amazing partner assumed they were living the Cinderella story they deserved. Sadly, that is not the way it played out.

After additional wins and further demonstrations of their mutual trust for one another, Cosequin began to experience trouble with his feet, as is common for large horses. Wanting only the very best for him, Debbie took him to the finest equine clinic in the area, where his feet were worked on in a manner designed to give him full relief from some quarter cracks and ensure his comfort and performance from a long-term perspective. Her crackerjack partner was largely recovered, and Debbie visited him at the clinic every day. She began riding him again, bringing him back to competitive form.

SAYING GOOD-BYE

Disaster struck when a strain of equine herpes virus struck Florida. It infiltrated the clinic where Cosequin was stabled at the time, carried by a horse imported from Europe who was thought to have an innocent fever. It spread through the barn, eventually infecting Debbie's soul mate, who never recovered. Cosequin died at 11:00 AM on December 10, 2006. He had to be humanely put to sleep, and a part of Deb died with him that day.

As Debbie explains, "We were going to bring him home, but he had a temperature. We did not know he was sick at this time. We waited a couple of days and then got the news. It was a good move, although tragic, not to bring him home, as he would have infected all the other horses in the barn. I knew it was the best thing for him. He had extremely sensitive skin. He had very fine hair, and his coat was that of a redhead. So when he contracted this virus, I knew he would overreact to everything. My heart was breaking; I just wanted to make him well, but I could not help him. I'll never forget how helpless I felt."

Deb tells me she had two days of mourning—a total shut down. "I didn't want to see anybody or do anything—I wasn't sure I wanted to ride ever again," she admits. In the end, Deb remained a very positive person. She picked herself up, motivated by her desire to forge a career that honored Cosequin's service to her. The woman who spent her life committed to the sport she loved forged on, now dedicated to preserving the memory of that very special once in a lifetime horse.

ANOTHER FALL

But the story does not end there. A day before my first interview with Debbie was scheduled, she suffered another bad fall. This one was nothing short of a freak accident. She jumped a fence in the schooling area while warming up, and the horse caught a toe. He tripped, and his front legs buckled, causing him to go down with Debbie. Deb broke her pelvis in several places. I got a call from the hospital where she had just gone through hours of surgery to fix her pelvis. Unbelievably, Debbie got back to me from her hospital bed, saying, "I'm a bit doped up today, but I can get on the phone as early as tomorrow if they give me back my phone. It is very important Cosequin's story be told. I don't want this mishap to get in the way."

I talked to Deb a few times to complete this chapter. In

just a week's time, she was out of the hospital, being driven around the Winter Equestrian Festival in a golf cart, unable to walk or drive herself. I talked to Debbie at the ring where she was teaching from that uncomfortable perch in her golf cart, and she confidently assured me that she would be riding again in eight to ten weeks.

> This woman exemplifies the term **CHAMPION**. Champions are made of a very special mettle that makes them unbending in their devotion to their tasks and their will to achieve. **Debbie is a force unto herself that cannot be denied.**

On a much happier note, along the way, Debbie met and married the true love of her life, Steve Stephens, in 1993. Steve is an accomplished equestrian in his own right, and one of the sport's most sought-after course designers, having built everything from the American Invitational to the Olympics. They are a very happy couple, and, despite all of the challenges Debbie's life has presented, she is, in my experience, relentlessly upbeat, dedicated to her horses and students, and immensely passionate about the next phase of her ongoing career.

As a footnote to the parents reading this, it is true that at the top level of the sport there are dangerous spills, and frequently a physical toll is extracted. I have been forthcoming about the risks of this sport from the first chapter. The dangers are not as great in the amateur levels of the sport, and, even with all the physical bruises acquired along the way, the strength of character that is built is a life lesson that cannot be denied.

2008: Winner of the Kentucky Summer Grand Prix

2007: Winner of two $25,000 Haygard Grands Prix

2005: Winner of the $25,000 Grand Prix–Kentucky Horse Park Summer Shows

Debbie Stephens
&Cosequin's
CEO

2003: Winner of the $25,000 Grand Prix–The National Horse Show

2002: Winner of the Canada One–Grand Prix Spruce Meadows

1994: Winner of the American Gold Cup–Grand Prix

1993: Winner of the American Invitational Grand Prix

1992: Two Team Gold medals for the USET at the Nations Cup

1990: Team Gold medalist for the USET at the Pan American Games, Havana

1989: Winner of the Grand Prix, Zurich

Ch. 8

Nona Garson & Rhythmical

Athletes come in all shapes and sizes, but in the sport of show jumping, most equine athletes are tall and powerful. They come from exclusive breeding backgrounds and generally are bought and sold for hefty sums. Equally impressive and unique are the riders who partner with these creatures. Nona Garson is a powerful force in the sport, a legendary horsewoman who rode in the 1998 Olympics, the 1995 Pan American Games, and the World Championships.

Nona began her equestrian career at the age of six. She grew up in New Jersey, the legendary home of the United States Equestrian Team (USET), and had a notable junior career. Nona opened The Ridge Farm in 1970 along with her father. She began competing at the international level in 1995.

ESI Photography
Nona and Rhythmical win the Fidelity Investments Jumper Classic.

The story of her career with the little Ritmichny, known in English as Rhythmical, is atypical to say the least. He and two other horses were hauled from a remote government breeding farm in Russia via open truck to Finland and traded for 150 used washing machines. Hardly a classic champion's story. Nona, who rode him all the way to the 2000 Olympics, says she would like to see him immortalized in a major motion picture on par with Secretariat and Seabiscuit to showcase his great athletic ability and his show-off personality. Her admiration for the little horse with the big heart is well-founded. Although Rhythmical was not Nona's only great horse, there definitely was something very special about the little chestnut with the massive jump and attitude to match.

A ROAD TRIP WITH GEORGE

Nona first saw Rhythmical in 1994, when he was ten years old. She remembers, "When I was at the World Cup finals, he was competing in the Junior Jumper classes in Finland, ridden by a little girl. He was an intriguing horse; he was fast, he was impressive in his jumping technique, and he was wild. There were a lot of people trying him, but they all passed on him. I did not try him at that point."

At that time, Nona was competing internationally with her white horse, Derrek, and the pair went on to the Pan American games the following spring. After that, they were slated to go to Europe, touring with the U.S. team, when George Morris called from Finland about the little horse. George thought Nona should try him. When George Morris has an opinion, smart people listen. It is widely known that the legendary coach of Team USA is a genius in the sport of show jumping.

Nona remembers her road trip with George, recalling the moment she decided to buy Rhythmical. "George and I went on a trip to Finland, and this time I rode Rhythmical for two days. He was erratic. When I cantered him, he would swap his leads all the way around and was so unpolished on the flat that you could not tell if you were on the left lead or the right lead. George pointed out, 'Are you here to buy a jumper or a horse in the under-saddle class you can ride on the flat?' So I laughed and said, 'I guess you're right, I'm here to buy a jumper.'" Nona bought the horse with her neighbors, the Kamine family.

Before shipping Rhythmical to the United States, Nona brought him to Luxembourg for her first international competition with him. Before Rhythmical arrived, however, the grooms who were waiting to settle the horse in received five full pages of instructions from his previous owners, spelling out exactly

> When they opened the van, they saw a **TINY CHESTNUT HORSE.** They called him the **TASMANIAN DEVIL.**

what not to do. It was like a warning label on a power tool. Nona recalls the list said things such as "do not turn him out," "always put a lead-line on him when you are in the stall," and "keep the halter on him at all times." The international grooms at the horse show were expecting a big, scary horse. At 15.2, he was just a hand higher than pony-size, and a 5'5 rider could easily look down on his back. Nona herself is 5'2 so it was not a bad match. Rhythmical and Nona have eclipsed their physical stature and become legends in the sport of show jumping.

Nona explains, "Some horses are a big 15.2, and some are a small 15.2. I could sit on Rhythmical and pat his head and his tail from the same spot. He was a compact horse. He wore a small cob bridle and tiny little shoes." He was Nona's version of My Little Pony—a fire-breathing one at that.

GRETCHEN ALMY

Nona and her loving friend.

RHYTHMICAL'S RUSSIAN HERITAGE

Rhythmical is a Budyonny horse, a Russian military breed named for a general. "The government-bred Russian horses are mostly chestnut and are bred for speed, soundness, and agility," Nona notes. "They were fast war horses, and in Russia, the Budyonny horses actually race against Thoroughbred horses. They could have a little Arabian in them. They are not big horses. They range from about 15.2 to 16.2. Rhythmical was bred by a famous Russian horse called Reis, who was a medal winner in the Moscow Olympics—that was the year the U.S. boycotted."

"Times were tough for Russia as it went through so many changes," she says. "Russia was broke. They had an incredible breeding program, and they were proud of it. But when the Soviet Union came apart, they had huge government stud farms going broke, and unfortunately, many of the great horses were sold off like cattle—even some for meat."

The lure of Russia as an undiscovered treasure box for horses became strong for Nona, and she purchased Susdal, another Russian horse. She showed Susdal to Grand Prix levels and then sold him to her student, amateur jumper Katrina Woods. "He is probably the most successful amateur jumper in the world," Nona says of Susdal. "He won practically every major class —Wellington, Lake Placid, Old Salem—everywhere Katrina chose to go."

Russia still has an active breeding program. "I've been to Russia many times looking for another Rhythmical," Nona says. "It is not practical to bring back only one or two, and many of the horses test positive for a blood disease due to the mosquito infestations. I'm still talking with the breeder. They're breeding direct descendants of Reis, Rhythmical's father, but it is a difficult place to do business."

Rhythmical's breeding was showcased with the expert

guidance of Nona, even though they had a moment of doubt while competing at their first show in Luxembourg. "The first class I showed him, he stopped [at a jump], and everyone was horrified. Then he turned around and jumped it. He won a class in France, he won at Rotterdam, then the last show in Royan, France. I was the leading lady rider on Rhythmical, though I was also riding Derrek at the time—my Nations Cup horse."

> At that point, they were calling Nona the **fastest girl in the world**. Show jumping was still predominantly a man's sport in those days. That is clearly not the case today. Show jumping may be the only Olympic sport where men and women compete against each other as equals.

WINNING STREAK

All the way through Europe, Rhythmical was a big winner. He was billed as the fastest horse in the world.

Nona and Rhythmical rode their first Grand Prix on U.S. soil in the Hampton Classic, where they captured second place in the smaller Grand Prix. Nona brought him to the indoor shows that fall and won a class in Washington, D.C. The pair then arrived back in Wellington, Florida, for the Winter Equestrian Festival, where Rhythmical won his first major Grand Prix in the United States. After his first year in the Grand Prix circuit in 1995, the pair went on to be on many victorious Nations Cups teams and won on the legendary field at Spruce Meadows.

Their wins earned them the opportunity to compete in the Olympic trials in 2000. Nona remembers being named the leading rider at the conclusion of the Olympic trial at the Oaks in California. She was asked to introduce the singer Jewel before her concert, and Rhythmical was named the

1999 American Grand Prix Association Horse of the Year. Nona and Rhythmical were on a roll at that point. Not bad for a horse paid for in used washing machines.

BORN SHARP BUT ALLERGIC TO HAY

Nona and her crackerjack horse were headed to the Olympics. Along the way, the horse who was such a natural jumper continued to improve. "He always trained me," Nona says. "He was a strong-minded horse who needed to be ridden in such a way that you were protecting him from himself." Nona did all of this in order to keep him aggressive and confident. He was a tiny horse who jumped over his head all the time. With many horses, when you get ready to go into the ring, you want them to rub the jumps in the schooling area to get a little sharper. Rhythmical was born sharp, so you always wanted to keep him comfortable and content. Any sharper and this malcontent may not be ridable.

Nona said he had the ability to go fast and jump up and round all at the same time, a skill not possessed by most horses. He would crouch down and disappear in front of the rail before he jumped it. This must have taken a lot of getting used to and a lot of guts. Nona suggests that from her perspective as the rider, everything she jumped was made to look bigger. If you are sitting on a small horse, galloping to a very tall jump, and that horse crouches down to spring up and over, it must feel like you are jumping out of a hole.

"He doesn't have a huge canter. He's kind of like an Arabian, and you have to hold him back a little bit. He's such a tiny horse that nobody realized how little I am." Nona showed me a photo of Rhythmical jumping a water jump. She says, "Look at his size in relation to the jump." A 15 ft. water jump is very hard for a little horse because of his short body extension. Some of the bigger horses just stretch their long legs, but Rhythmical had to fly across the water.

Nona said Rhythmical was as sensitive as he was sharp. She says, "You cannot change his footing, and you cannot change his bit a half a notch. Any change in his tack upsets him."

One time in Wellington, Nona got a call from her groom that the vet had been to see Rhythmical because they were getting ready to take him out of the competition and move him for possible colic surgery. Nona came to look at him and said, "Why does he have a tail wrap on him?" (A tail wrap covers the top of the tail where the hair is easily broken if the horse rubs against anything). They took it off, and he walked around the stall, shook his head, stomped his feet, and then settled down and started eating hay. He was so sensitive that the pressure of the tail wrap irritated him.

Rhythmical was also allergic to hay! He had to eat denghi (a chopped, specially treated hay), which Nona had shipped all over the world when they were at a show. However, he had no problem flying on an airplane. His passport was stamped so many times he was issued a second one!

His sensitivity, feistiness, and speed made Rhythmical a very special ride. He was one of those horses who was never really trying to get you off; he was just explosive. According to Nona, "He would have been horrified if I fell off." For all of the unmanageable elements to this fireball's personality, it is clear Nona and Rhythmical were a perfect show jumping team.

2000 OLYMPICS IN SYDNEY

Sadly, his stamina and surefootedness were shaken at the highest performance of their lives when, at the 2000 Olympics, Nona and Rhythmical were competing on the first all-women U.S. Show Jumping Team.

The only time Rhythmical ever lost his footing was in the Olympics. He was very sensitive to the footing —he worked off the ground more than a bigger horse, so if it was slippery or dug-up, it was a real problem for him. Unfortunately, in

TONY DE COSTA

Nona riding for the U.S.

Nona and Languster getting it done.

the first round, the footing was not very good. The first rider in the ring broke a bone in his neck and had to be taken out in an ambulance. Many horses were not good, or were uncomfortable, or slipped, or almost fell. Unfortunately, Nona and Rhythmical fell. Nona knew that Rhythmical was rattled. It was not the way she wanted the two of them to go into the biggest event of their lives.

Because Rhythmical had to go fast to jump the larger jumps, good footing was even more crucial. He was such a little guy he needed speed to gain enough power for many jumps, and the footing is much more critical when you are using 110 percent of your body.

A Cow-kick in the Hip

Rhythmical won his last Grand Prix at the age of 19 at the Fidelity Investments Jumper Classic in New England. He is retired at Nona's Ridge Farm in New Jersey and is still ridden six days a week even though he is in his mid-20's. "He's amazing—he's still sound and strong but his face is greyed out a little bit, his blaze has extended itself around his muzzle, and his back is a little lower. I wish all my Grand Prix horses could be as sound as Rhythmical," Nona says. Some days he will only let me get him in from the field. He will not let any of the grooms catch him; he plays with them, torturing them for hours on end."

Nona's love for Rhythmical as her equine partner allowed her to overlook the little biting and kicking habit he still has. I saw it at one or two shows—this little horse was like a cross between a land shark and a mule. Nona recalls, "He was the kind of horse the rider could run to get a leg up on in the jump-off, and he would cow-kick you in the hip as you were getting on him. He is so athletic most horses cannot even kick you there. He'd turn around and bite your foot. You had to keep him in line at all times."

He was a very competitive horse. He would stand at the in-gate and his knees would shake. When people would cheer, he would bolt or play around and take off at the end of the course just for fun. He was such a fast horse that in the jump-off, you could leg him to go forward and win a class early in the jump-off, and then settle in and jump the last few fences carefully because he started out so lightning fast at the beginning.

"He was the **FASTEST HORSE I EVER SAT ON**, the fastest horse I've ever seen jump at that level. You had to hang on a bit extra with your thigh and balance. Sometimes he would **JUMP A FOOT OR TWO HIGHER** than the jump. You had to be ready for that."

He was from a field in Russia, bartered for washing machines, too small, unbroken, too difficult—but for Nona, who believed in him from the very beginning, Rhythmical was the soul mate of a lifetime.

I chose to add Nona and Rhythmical to the list of partnerships memorialized in this book for several obvious reasons: her career success and their journey to the Olympic Games. What makes this particular partnership particularly interesting is Nona's unshakeable faith in Rhythmical and his complete and total trust in her, which, despite the odds, put them on top of the exhilarating sport of show jumping. It is this spiritual bond, faith, and undeniable love that is the heart and soul of *Unbridled Passion*. I can think of no better example than Nona and Rhythmical.

Winner of the Fidelity Investments Grand Prix

$100,000 Grand Prix Winner Jaguar Gold Coast Cup

Three-time recipient of the Leading Lady Rider Award–La Baule, France, 1997; Aachen, Germany 1999; Helsinki, Finland 2000

Nona Garson & Rhythmical

Samsung Super League and Nations Cup team member–Drammen, Norway; Aachen, Germany; La Baule, France; Rotterdam, Holland; Dublin, Ireland; Spruce Meadows for USET

2000: Winner at the Grand Prix of Florida

2000: Member of the Sydney Olympics on Rhythmical

1999: Budweiser/AGA Show Jumping Champion

1998: Cosequin Grand Prix winner

1998: Member of the World Champion team on Rhythmical, Rome

1995: Winner of the Pan American Games selections trials on Derrek

1995: USET Team Bronze medalist at the Pan American Games

Ch. 9

Norman Dello Joio & Glasgow

When you talk about Norman Dello Joio, you must begin
with a reference to his father in order to put the story of
the son in context. His father was born Nicodemo DeGio
in New York City to Italian immigrants. Norman and his
father have both achieved considerable celebrity in their
respective specialties. Norman Dello Joio, Sr. was a famous
musician and prolific composer who won the Pulitzer Prize
for Music in 1957 for *Meditations on Ecclesiastes* for string
orchestra. He also won an Emmy for his music composed
for the television special *Scenes from the Louvre*. In 1958,
CBS featured him in a one-hour television special, *Profile of
a Composer*.

TONY DE COSTA
Norman puts in another clear round.

Norman Dello Joio, the equestrian, would compose his own life's opus as one of the most decorated and capable equestrians in the United States. Norman grew up in New York City and started riding rather late in life, at the age of 15. I say late in life because many riders of Norman's stature started much younger. Maestro Dello Joio, of course, wanted Norman to become a musician, and Norman took piano lessons because that was the track that all Dello Joio men took. His family hoped Norman would follow in his father's footsteps and become a composer, but that job went to his brother. A career in music was not for Norman. Fortunately, Maestro Dello Joio was willing to support Norman in whatever path he chose, as long as he worked hard, was happy, and did his job well. Prior to Norman's interest in show jumping, his father had no exposure to any equestrian sports.

Norman chose a non-musical path and **followed his own star**—and a star he became by anybody's standards.

Norman wanted to get out of the city, so he got a job at Glenview Stables on Long Island, owned by Ralph Caristo. It was a nice change of scenery for Norman. He worked as a groom, mucked stalls, and did anything he was asked to do in order to be close to the horses, eventually trading his labors for lessons. He fell in love with what he was doing and it soon became clear that horses would be Norman's passion. Norman skipped the pony phase and the short stirrup beginnings that most expert equestrians go through as children. He started riding horses for other dealers at the age of 17, taking every opportunity to ride anything presented to him.

Has anybody risen to greatness in this sport without, at one time or another, receiving help from George Morris?

Norman trained, throughout his career, with Victor Hugo Vidal, Ronnie Mutch, and George Morris. He began his Grand Prix career rather quickly. After only five years of riding, he became a Grand Prix athlete, which is virtually unheard of. The normal path to elite status in the sport is 10 to 15 years made in a slow progression among the most talented up-and-coming younger riders. Norman, as you will quickly see, earned his moniker "Stormin' Norman."

His last year as a junior proved to be a life-changing experience for Norman. He won the Junior Amateur Jumper title, which was awarded at the American Invitational. As part of his prize, he received a two-week training session with Bert de Nemethy at the USET headquarters in Gladstone, New Jersey. Norman took in everything he could during these sessions, which further ignited the flame that drove him to Olympic glory.

HIS FIRST BIG BREAK

His first big break came with a horse named Narcisis, Norman's first really talented jumper. Narcisis won the high jump or the Puissance at Madison Square Garden. (The Madison Square Garden event was the ultimate show jumping venue at that time. That event has now rolled into the Winter Equestrian Festival in Wellington, Florida.) The Puissance is the opposite of a limbo competition—instead of going lower with each pass, in each successive round of the Puissance the horse and rider leap increasingly higher over a single solid wall built of blocks until only one horse and rider is left. Norman and Narcisis jumped 7ft. 3in. Can you imagine? At this height, neither horse nor rider can see the other side.

Norman was the leading rider in Harrisburg and Washington that same year on Narcisis. I questioned Norman about this horse's odd name and got a little chuckle. Norman assured me the horse came with his name. "He was a useful horse, and I could really rely on him."

ALLEGRO AND JEANNIE ENTER THE PICTURE

In 1975, Norman bought Allegro from David Hopper. This turned out to be the deal of a lifetime for Norman; he got a great horse, but, more importantly, he met his wife, Jeannie. At the time, she was working for David's family as a nanny, and she also rode. Jeannie, a rider to this day, is Norman's partner in life and work.

Shortly after meeting, they started a business together buying, selling, and training horses. They married in 1985 and had two children, Daniella and Nick. Norman and his family call Wimbley Farm in Wellington, Florida, their home base.

Norman knew that Allegro had a great deal of potential. They went on to win the American Invitational in 1978 and Team Gold at the Pan Am Games in Puerto Rico in 1979. Norman's teammates were Melanie Smith, Michael Matz, and Buddy Brown. Norman made the Olympic team in 1980, but that was the boycott year so he did not compete. Fortunately, they had substitute games in Rotterdam. The 1980 Olympic team consisted of Norman, Melanie Smith, Michael Matz, and Denis Murphy.

1992 BARCELONA OLYMPICS AND IRISH

His second Olympic experience was in 1992 in Barcelona. The team at that time was comprised of Michael Matz, Lisa

GRETCHEN ALMY

Norman delights in seeing his son, Nick, getting it done.

Norman in perfect form.

BOB LANGRISH MBE
EQUESTRIAN PHOTOGRAPHER

Jaquin, and Anne Kursinki. The team did not win a medal that year, but Norman won the bronze in the individual competition. This was a surprise. Norman will tell you he just had a good day. "Everyone was crashing that day. The course was huge." Norman had one of those "What am I doing here?" moments. He and Irish were able to perform and they won the bronze. It was a memorable moment in show jumping history.

Norman had a typical Olympic experience and cherished

every moment he was there. Norman enjoyed living in the Olympic Village with the other athletes from all over the world and sharing the common bond and the camaraderie that elite athletes share, regardless of the sport. Norman supported other athletes from other sports and went to as many venues as he could. Show jumping was last on the schedule of events. Overall, he loved the Olympic spirit and being a part of it.

Irish had a lot of heart, and the partnership between the horse and rider in this case was broad and deep. I have heard people say it was **as if Norman felt the horse's heart** —the two of them were that much in tune.

On the podium that day, his thoughts were about how incredible the experience was. "The horse gave it all. There were a lot of other riders who were more talented and qualified than I. In one sense, Irish was over his head, but he rose to the occasion. He had a very good day." Talk about understatement! A good day for Norman and Irish would be a moment of a lifetime for the rest of us.

GLASGOW

Norman met Glasgow in England. He was looking for horses and doing business at this time with Robert Smith of Birmingham, England. They heard about a nice gelding, a Dutch-bred horse in Scotland. Norman tried him, and he and Robert both loved him. Norman returned home to get a syndicate together to buy the expensive seven-year-old. Norman was able to raise the money and brought Glasgow home. His first time showing with Glasgow was in South Hampton in late 1980. From the first time they competed, the horse was solid. Glasgow would continue to win through the late 1980s, almost ten years of competitive partnership, all of it well spent.

> Norman won two American Invitational classes, **20 YEARS** apart—the first with Allegro and the second with **GLASGOW**.

Glasgow was cued up for the Athens Olympics in 2004 when he was about 12. He went to the trials in California and won the first two trials. Unfortunately, due to a suspensory issue, Glasgow did not make it through the trials or to the 2004 Olympics.

After a rest, Glasgow went on to win several big classes. He won the 2001 King George Cup in Hickstead, England, one of two Americans to ever win this event. He was first in the World Cup Qualifier in Oslo, Norway, in the same year. In 2002, Norman and Glasgow were the Leading Jumper Rider and Horse at the National Horse Show in Wellington, Florida. On two occasions, he placed at the Masters Tournament at Spruce Meadows - 2nd and 4th. During this period, Norman acquired several other good horses including Auriel, Peace Train, and Mila.

Norman was beginning to feel Glasgow's age. He was getting older, but Norman knew he could still be useful. Norman turned Glasgow over to his owner, Judy Richter. Her son, Philip, is still riding Glasgow in amateur classes to this day. In fact, Philip won the 2010 High Amateur Grand Prix in Wellington and was the Champion at Devon in 2010. Glasgow still shows about five times a year.

NORMAN AND HIS FAMILY

In addition to being a talented sportsman, Norman is a wonderfully dedicated husband and father. His youngest child, Nick, is an up-and-coming rider who has enjoyed a

GRETCHEN ALMY

Norman's son, Nick, looking strong (Spring 2011).

---

great deal of success thus far. Norman is coaching his son and says Nick is starting to catch on to the sport.

Nick was an all-around athlete in school and traveled around the world with his dad to all of the greatest events in show jumping. Nick started riding when he was 15 years old. Nick is learning all of the side issues that go along

GRETCHEN ALM

Team Mexico's Coach Norman, using positive reinforcement.

with the sport and is immersed in his training. Norman is very proud of Nick because he is a good, solid person. In Norman's mind, that should come first. "Nick has his feet on the ground."

His daughter, Daniella, on the other hand, wanted nothing to do with the horse business. "I am very proud of my daughter," says Norman. "She is very focused and is working in New York City, doing what she loves." Norman considers himself very blessed.

TEAM MEXICO

Norman is currently the coach of the Mexican Jumping Team. When he first started working with the Mexican team, they were somewhat disorganized. "They were very talented individually, but they needed some pulling together," Norman explains. "There are amateurs involved, but with real heart and talent." He greatly enjoys training the team.

Overall, I am awestruck with what a great horseman Norman is. He continues to get better with time. Although he has worked hard his entire life, it is Norman's integrity and character that are so amazing. He is kind, thoughtful, and clearly focused on who he is and what he does.

Norman has had a lot of support particularly from his wife and two children. He received additional support from Rob Spatz and Tammy Rubio, Glasgow's former grooms, and of course, all the individuals who were and are part of his syndicates: Judy Richter, Ira Kapp, Tony and Judy Weights, Danny McGil, and Lisa Silverman. Norman's students include such notables as Jeffery Welles and Peter Wylde. All in all, this is a man of character who loves his family, his horses, and his sport. He is the first to volunteer help or assistance.

If show jumping is the world's most beautiful sport,

ESI PHOTOGRAPHY

Norman in action at the Fidelity Jumper Classic.

perhaps that is in part true because of people of this caliber who are the leaders in our sport. One thing is certain; the symphony of Norman's life has been beautifully composed by a man who has left a powerful legacy. Maestro Dello Joio, I am sure, looks down on his son with pride and happiness; he raised a very fine man.

Currently Chef d'Equipe for the Mexican Show Jumping Team

Leading rider titles numerous times on different horses at Washington, Harrisburg, Madison Square Garden, and the Royal Winter Fair in Toronto

Norman Dello Joio & Glasgow

2002: Winner at the American Invitational for the second time on Glasgow

1992: Equestrian of the Year, Whitney Stone Award winner

1992: Individual Bronze medalist for the USET at the Barcelona Olympics

1983: World Cup Champion on I Love You

1983: Winner at the Spruce Meadows Masters on I Love You

1980: Qualified for the Olympic Team USA (boycott year)

1978: Winner at the American Invitational Grand Prix

1978: Team Gold medalist for the USET at the Pan American Games, Puerto Rico

CH. 10

The Amateur Equestrians

It is important to tell the story of amateurs working hard to attain what professional riders have achieved. Amateur riders are just starting their journey. We can relate to them a bit more as they seem less superhuman. They are at different stages in their riding careers, but share the same goals and aspirations of experienced stars. Show jumping is not for everybody. It is difficult, seemingly endless work. Riders fall, have their share of bruises and broken bones, and fail many times before they succeed. Such is the case for each of the following three amateur riders. Each has achieved notable success with great difficulty. Though some riders have more financial backing than others, this does not guarantee success. The paths of show jumpers are strewn with the marks left by their struggles, mistakes, and incremental progress. Opportunities in the sport are of the rider's own making.

Victoria Birdsall
& Little Lady d'Elle

Like so many aspiring show jumpers, Victoria Birdsall began her riding career at five years old. She made it clear to her mother, Karen, and her father, David, that all she wanted for her birthday was riding lessons. On Victoria's fifth birthday, her parents brought her to a local barn in Ipswich, Massachusetts. She was introduced to her first ride, an old black pony named Ebony who was 20-something years old. Ebony, like a lot of school ponies, had taught hundreds of children. On this day, he was only too happy to take Victoria through the introductory paces. A star was born that wintry day in New England.

I know Victoria and the Birdsall family well. I share a barn with them at their farm, Silver Oaks Equestrian Center,

FLASHPOINT PHOTOGRAPHY
Victoria and Lady on course at the Fidelity Jumper Classic.

which doubles as the home of the Fidelity Investments Jumper Classic. Victoria is one of the top junior jumper riders in the United States. Her career is truly a family affair, and unlike some situations I've witnessed, Victoria's parents support their daughter every step of the way. Victoria also has a very involved older brother, Nick, who adds to her support system.

David Birdsall is rarely called by his name. In the equestrian world, he is "Victoria's Dad," a title that he proudly accepts. David hauls Victoria's horses all over the country: Florida, Kentucky, New York, Michigan, and New Jersey. If Victoria is in a show, her dad is with her, horses in tow. Karen is a constant presence wherever Victoria's competitive travels take her. Karen takes on multiple tasks: travel agent, barn manager, psychologist, and, above all, just plain Mom.

Vic, as her close friends call her, moved on from that winter morning on Ebony to her first pony, Melody, with whom she did all the childhood short-stirrup things kids do. Melody was followed by Jazzy, a small pony hunter on which she won the Mass Mini-Medal finals, an equitation final held in Northampton, Massachusetts. Kids under 18 compete, usually on their horses, not on a pony like Victoria did. At eight years old, Victoria was the youngest rider ever to win on her small pony, Jazzy.

Victoria's dad told me, "When I saw how **CALM** and **FOCUSED** my daughter was just before the final round, I realized this horse thing might go on for a **LIFETIME**."

About this time David and Karen bought Victoria two larger ponies of her very own, Jack and Annie, a bay and a white pony, respectively. They worked with Vic through all the pony accolades, winning on both the local and national levels. In 2004, Victoria won the Pony Medal finals. Vic told me she would ride every pony that she could, regardless of the challenge. Recently, Jack and Annie have moved on to help other children aspiring to walk in Vic's footsteps.

VICTORIA'S EARLY CAREER

By age 11, Victoria had acquired her first horses—Bambino, her first equitation horse, and Maxim W, her first jumper. Vic was starting to step it up. Patti Harnois at Holly Hill Farm was training Victoria. Patti is a great teacher, trainer, and overall superior horsewoman. Patti has done a fine job with Victoria, just as she has for so many other young riders.

A defining experience in Victoria's career happened in 2006 at the Prix de States jumper competition at the Harrisburg horse show. She was competing with Maxim and had a difficult first round. The levels of the jumps were bigger and more technical than she was expecting. Max was bought as a children's jumper, and this course was simply built bigger than Max was used to. Victoria made it through the first three fences, but Max simply could not cope. It was more than he could handle and the pair was eliminated for multiple refusals. When a horse stops or refuses the rider's command for forward motion before a fence, the rider is penalized four faults; two such disobediences in any one round results in disqualification. Victoria was rattled, shaken, and uncertain; Max was feeling much the same as his rider—he had to be thinking, "Are you kidding me, kid? Have you seen the size of these fences?" The disobedience in the first round caused Victoria to be spun off and, in that round, gravity won.

Between rounds, Patti took Victoria aside and had

Victoria and Lady in Florida (2011).

one of those critical coach-to-student conversations. Patti convinced Victoria that she could put the doubt in a different place and go into that ring and get it done. Victoria, in an effort to please Patti, managed to get back in the ring. Max, however, wilted at the same third fence. But Victoria kicked him forward and over the fence in question, and they completed the rest of the course with a clear and graceful finish, which was a victory in itself.

Victoria admitted that this frightening and soul-searching experience was a turning point for her, as it taught her to believe in herself. In times of pressure, she often reflects back on those moments to get herself through the current demands. I think all athletes have that kind of life-altering moment. Victoria to this day credits Patti and Holly Hill for getting her through this career-changing moment. Victoria is also quick to point out that Max dug down deep and got it done for her, even when it seemed impossible.

2008 began with Vic winning the Christy Conrad Perpetual Trophy for Equitation excellence. The year continued with the Shallano Style of Riding Award at the Devon Horse Show and the same award at the Hampton Classic Horse Show, followed by the East Coast Show Jumping Hall Of Fame Junior Year End Championship. Victoria also placed second in the Maclay Finals, fourth in the USEF Talent Search Finals, and finished up 2008 on the 4th place team in the Champion Prix de States.

FINDING HER ROMEO

By 2008, Victoria's stable included Romeo, her equitation horse of a lifetime. Romeo is one of those drop-dead handsome members of the equine species, incredibly affectionate and giving. The partnership with Romeo put Victoria on the map. She won the George Morris Horsemanship Award at the Winter Equestrian Festival with the best junior riders in the country under George Morris's direct supervision. This is a grueling weeklong clinic she had been participating in for multiple years. Accomplished junior riders are invited to this clinic after winning a major final or Prix de States, or by being in the top five equitation rankings for the country. Victoria has been invited three years in a row.

Victoria finished the bulk of her equitation career to this point with help from Andre Dignelli and Heritage Farm. Much like her experience with Holly Hill, her time with Andre was extremely important to her. In early 2009, as Victoria's focus shifted almost entirely to the jumpers and the Grand Prix ring, I introduced the family to John and Beezie Madden. John and Beezie entrusted Vic with the development of a chestnut mare named Little Lady d'Elle they had bought as a sales prospect. Lady is a quick, catlike, French-bred mare. When Victoria took over she was working in the Low Junior Jumper Division.

> Through their chance meeting, Vic has perhaps discovered her horse of a lifetime, and the **LOVE**, **TRUST**, and **MUTUAL DEPENDENCE** between the two has become obvious.

Victoria, with the help of the Madden family, has worked through the Low to High Junior Jumper Divisions and on to the Grand Prix ring with this mare.

Victoria was winning throughout 2009, including the Circuit Championship for the High Junior Jumpers at the Winter Equestrian Festival and the United States Equestrian Federation High Junior Jumper of the Year. Victoria rode in several of her first Grand Prix events, placing eighth at the Fairfield Hunt Club Grand Prix, and tenth in the Fidelity Investments Grand Prix that year. Victoria also won the Carolex Show Jumping Derby in 2009.

Show jumping can be a costly sport, and Victoria has not had an unlimited pool of personal horses to draw upon, so she has often leased horses. Through this important period, Karen and David leased two jumpers: Jeremy, a spirited, hot-tempered gelding, and Hot Wheels, another very talented horse. It is amazing how a horse's name sometimes perfectly describes his or her character. Jeremy was leased for two years and Hot Wheels for one. When Hot Wheels first came to the barn, he came with special mounting instructions. She could not mount him in the traditional sense, but had to lie across his back before she sat up in the saddle—that's how hot he was. Victoria made good use of the two feisty, difficult horses. These partnerships advanced her place.

Victoria also owns Tiffany. She is a beautiful snow-white German-bred horse, whom Vic adores. Tiffany has been prone to heartbreaking injuries that have slowed her progress, but Vic has made do with some leased and some borrowed horses to supplement her own. She has also ridden more difficult horses that other juniors were not suited for. These issues have not kept Victoria from winning, however. In 2009, Victoria won the William Steinkraus Style Award, named after one of the famed U.S. Olympians. Victoria also placed first in the High Junior Amateur Owner division at the Syracuse Sport Horse Invitational indoors in Syracuse, New York, on Jeremy (the High Amateur Owner's is only a few inches short of a Grand Prix).

MAKING SACRIFICES

Victoria has made many personal and social sacrifices to pursue her sport. She has forfeited many of the typical experiences of a young teenager. As Vic puts it, "I missed most of the sleepovers, the movies, the dances, and all the school trips. I see my friends infrequently during the Winter Equestrian Festival, since my time is spent with tutors and independent study. I have to be disciplined about delivering my reports to Pingree High School." As Victoria explained the sacrifices, she recounted them with a quiet, steady sense of purpose. "I am the weird kid, and I like that. I like the fact that I am different and don't enjoy some of the things that other girls do. I just love my life in show jumping." Aspiring to compete at a world-class level comes with all the rigors one might expect, and young people in the sport give up a great deal in order to succeed.

A typical day in the life of Victoria Birdsall includes three hours of weight lifting and cardio work at the gym. Time in the gym is followed by several hours of riding her own horses and catch riding for other people who recruit her for help. She also attends six hours of school when she is at home. Late in the day, Victoria's work with her tutors or on self-directed projects begins and continues into the evening.

Victoria has a special way of working with young horses or problem horses who have lost their confidence. Victoria understands horses, and, while she demands their best, they invest in her as she invests in them in an uncanny way.

Despite innumerable successes, things haven't always been rosy for Victoria. She had a bad fall on Tiffany while warming up for the Sunday High Junior Classic at the Winter Equestrian Festival. They flipped over a fence, and Victoria got up slowly, bloody and bruised, with a splitting headache. It was the kind of fall that would be enough to end the dream for the weak of heart, but in her usual fashion, Victoria shook it off, went in the ring bruised and bloody, and won!

In 2010, Victoria won the George Morris Excellence in Equitation Award and the North American Equitation Championships. She placed sixth in the USET finals.

GRETCHEN ALMY

Our dynamic duo in good form.

WHAT'S NEXT

During the 2011 Winter Equestrian Festival, Victoria and Lady took the big step into the Young Riders Competition in West Palm Beach. The Young Riders are comprised of the best young men and women in the sport, riding in classes from 1.40m to 1.50m. It is big, technical, and demanding. I have witnessed over and over again how

GRETCHEN ALMY

Best friends at the Birdsall Family Farm in Wellington, Florida.

Victoria has shown incredible determination, poise, and talent. Victoria and Lady competed so fiercely that she has been selected to ride for the USET Young Riders Tour in Europe in the spring and summer of 2011, with stops at big shows in Germany, Belgium, Sweden, and Austria. Representing the USET in Europe is a big honor, and I know she considers it a privilege as well. She is deeply humbled and thrilled to meet the challenge.

Like many other young competitors, Victoria owes much of her success to her trainers, in particular Frank, John, and Beezie Madden. Victoria's groom, Baldo, has been an important friend and has helped tremendously in the caring for all her various mounts over the years. He works many long and tedious hours to ensure her success along the way. Baldo is both a caregiver to the horses and a big brother to Victoria wrapped in one person. He has become something like a second son to Karen and David.

> "They do their very best for me because I give them my very best every day, and that is as it should be."

On top of her busy riding schedule, Victoria is also a dedicated student. She graduated cum laude in 2011 from Pingree High School in South Hamilton, Massachusetts. Though Victoria sacrificed being at her high school graduation with her classmates and friends to be with Lady in Europe riding for her country, she has no regrets. Victoria describes her horses as her best friends and explains there is no fear, no mistrust, and no lack of understanding in these relationships. There is only mutual devotion and friendship.

Victoria is the very best, and I am proud to know her. She is an amazing young woman, whom I will continue to enjoy watching for years to come.

Victoria has been accepted at Boston College, for the fall of 2011, as well as several other notable schools, many offering her academic scholarships. She is attending Boston College because of her desire to remain within an easy commute to the family farm. She is a shining example of a young rider balancing school with the pursuit of her equestrian dream.

Victoria dreams about the Olympics, just as many of our past subjects did at her age. Vic is very humble about it and admits it is many steps away, but this was once the case for Beezie, Leslie, Margie, and others who made it. Speaking for myself, I believe in fairy tales just as much as I believe in Victoria Birdsall, and I eagerly wait for her Olympic moment.

2011: Selected as a member of the USET European Young Rider Tour

2010: Making of the film *Heart of the Equestrian*

2010: 1st place at the George Morris Excellence in Equitation Championships

Victoria Birdsall
& Little Lady d'Elle

2010: 1st place at the North American Equitation Championships

2009: 1st place at the Syracuse Invitational High Junior/AO Final

2009: 1st place at the Carolex Show Jumping Derby

2009: 8th place at the Fidelity Investments Grand Prix

2009: USEF High Junior Jumper of the Year

2008, 2009, 2010: Invited to participate in George Morris Clinics

2008, 2009: Winner of the East Coast Show Jumping Hall of Fame

Alexandra Cherubini & EquiFit Pozitano

Alexandra Cherubini, or "Al" as she is known to me, started riding when she was 12 years old, which is a bit older than most women who are immersed in the horse world today. Alexandra became exposed to horses through her friends Lana Bilzerian and Marisa Fiumara. Marisa brought her to the barn where she first rode in Weston, Massachusetts. It was there that Marisa got Alexandra to ride Farnley Bow Bell, and she even cantered and jumped that first day. Alexandra had no idea what she was doing, but Bow Bell stole her heart. She began taking lessons and, after a while, leased Bow Bell. She competed in local unrated horse shows and wanted to be at the barn all day long. Her parents were not thrilled about this, but did not object. Her family was

JAMES LESLIE PARKER
Alexandra and Pozzi on course.

not involved with horses—in fact, her family owns a large medical supply company in the Boston area, AliMed, Inc. Like many young riders, once Alexandra fell in love with horses, she was hooked for life.

Alexandra went on to train and ride with Tracy Gardner. Then she trained for several years with Cookie Desimone, the Equestrian coach at Dana Hall, a prestigious boarding school in Wellesley, Massachusetts. Today, Cookie is partners with Greg Prince and part of Woodridge Farm, where Greg is the resident rider and coach. By the time Alexandra's riding had become serious, she landed at Holly Hill Farm with Patti Harnois. Alexandra rode with Patti during the end of her junior career and during summers in her early adult years. While training with Holly Hill, she would travel to Florida on weekends during the winter circuit.

At this time, Alexandra attended a private high school, Buckingham Brown & Nichols, located in Cambridge, Massachusetts, not far from the Harvard campus. She spent the winter months of her senior year in Florida and would fax her assignments back to school. Her school was not terribly supportive, as she would often miss Mondays and Fridays due to travel for her equestrian duties. She had to participate in other team sports to keep the school happy. Her parents, on the other hand, were supportive, as long as she kept her grades up and was aware of what a privilege it was to be involved in equestrian sports.

THE EARLY YEARS

Alexandra continued her studies at Bates College in Lewiston, Maine. She took a break from riding after her senior year of high school for almost two years, but during this break, she was never really at peace. She started riding again and bought her first equitation horse, Baccarat, who also served as hunter and jumper. Baccarat, who went by the barn name Jax, had been very successful in his earlier career. He was older, however, when Alexandra acquired him and blind in one eye. But because he was the ultimate teacher, he was affordable. She brought Baccarat back to school with her.

Alexandra graduated from college in 1999 with a B.A. in Anthropology. After a brief stay in Boston's North End, she moved to New York City and did not ride much right out of school. One day Alexandra received a call from Patti Harnois who was in Europe at the time. Patti told Alexandra that there was a great jumper she wanted Alexandra to see. He came with the barn name was Max, but Alexandra chose All That as his show name. She bought him as a hunter prospect, but showed him only twice, then sold him. He went on to compete on the show circuit with other riders. This purchase, however, moved Alexandra back toward her equine destiny.

Alexandra was always tuned into the latest fashion trends, so it seemed only natural that she took a job working in public relations for the fashion industry. (Not that I would know anything about it. My personal style can best be described as frumpy and a bit wrinkled, usually accented with horse manure.) This experience was a personal version of *The Devil Wears Prada*. Alexandra was working hard and enjoying her life in New York, but she wanted to get back to riding no matter what it took. She had to figure out how to make her job fit her equestrian ambitions.

> The best possible outcome would be to combine her public relations experience and marketing acumen with horses and her background in the family medical supply and manufacturing design business.

"SHOULDERS BACK"

Alexandra decided to leave her job in fashion but remain in New York. Rather than getting another job working for someone else, she developed her first product called ShouldersBack™, an all-elastic, vest-like garment designed to help improve posture. She developed the concept from her early years of riding, involving a technique familiar to many riders—a trainer would have her place a crop between her elbows to assist with her posture, which is crucial in riding. The product gives the rider the support they need to sit up straight. The name ShouldersBack came from hearing her coach constantly yelling, "shoulders back!" Production began on ShouldersBack in Dedham, MA and was then shipped to Alexandra's New York apartment, where she would package it and make a trip to FedEx every afternoon. Often Alexandra and her future husband, Camilo Alvarez, would cut out the boards that the product was packaged on themselves. Alexandra was the entire marketing end of the company. She was an amateur rider determined to make her own way and did it from a single idea. The product was an absolute hit from the beginning.

Alexandra was at a New Jersey horse show selling ShouldersBack when a magazine editor from a high fashion teen magazine picked one up, and wore it herself to help improve her posture. From there, other magazines soon picked up on it, like *W*, who reviewed the product and said it was the most inexpensive "boob lift" a woman could have. ShouldersBack was also featured on Home Shopping Network. Another magazine, *Beverly Hills 213*, reported that Julia Roberts wore it in the movie *Erin Brockovich* and that Catherine Zeta-Jones wore one as well. Alexandra concedes that though the exposure was wonderful for business, it is unlikely that either Julia or Catherine wore one. Nonetheless, the publicity was great and the company took off.

ShouldersBack was actually part of an exhibit in the **Metropolitan Museum of Art**, titled Extreme Beauty.

EQUIFIT

EquiFit's protective horse boots are the industry standard.

Alexandra recalls sitting at her kitchen table in Brooklyn, picking a tack store in Arizona out of a phone book, and cold calling them. She gave a sales pitch over the phone and the store ordered six units of ShouldersBack. She had all the encouragement she needed and was off and running. This was her first official tack store order.

BUILDING HER BRAND

Today, EquiFit, Inc. is an extremely successful company. They have produced nearly a dozen innovative products that solve common problems for horses and riders. Best-selling items include the T-Boot Series™, T-Sport Wrap™, and the AgSilver line of antibacterial and antimicrobial products. Virtually every high-end performance athlete we have talked about in this book uses EquiFit products. EquiFit is an industry standard and a brand recognized throughout the equestrian world.

Alexandra was able to combine her love of horses, her fashion know-how, and her knowledge of manufacturing materials to make it her life's work. Her family's business continues to play a role and serves as a platform from which to launch her products. Alexandra recalls how, at a very young age, she developed a keen understanding of the different materials her family used to manufacture their products. EquiFit's success was no accident.

Alexandra has always possessed a keen business sense. When she was about 11 years old, she and her friend Lana started a store in her attic. The store's name was Tiffany 2, and they sold Alexandra's grandmother's old costume jewelry. Her grandmother, Rose, was a bridal gown designer, and the jewelry was from one of her stores earlier in her life.

TRANSITIONS

Alexandra married Camilo, the love of her life. She was commuting back and forth between Boston and New York, and Camilo was working hard in the art world. They decided after 9/11 to move back to Boston together. Camilo's art gallery, Samson Projects, named in part after the couple's dog Samson, opened two years after they moved to Boston. Prior to starting his business, he worked at the MIT List Visual Art Center and held art-related positions.

Alexandra was now transitioning as a rider and becoming even more serious in the sport. She began to ride with Jimmy Toon of JT Farms. Alexandra bought a horse called Tiny Toon, who was, as she describes her, like a sports car, quick and finely tuned. She also had Omar at that point, or Good Night & Good Luck, a wonderful Amateur Owner hunter. Tiny won the Adult Jumper Classic at the Washington International Horse Show. Alexandra explains that they were wait listed, but went at the last minute and won.

JAMES LESLIE PARKER

Pozzi – very handsome.

A Chance Encounter

The story of Alexandra finding her important equine partner is a story of coincidence that really makes you to think about fate. While in Washington after she won the Adult Jumper Classic on Tiny Toon, Alexandra was having dinner with a friend, and they were trying to decide whether or not to watch the Puissance. They decided to go. Alexandra had been chatting earlier with Lee McKeever, Manager at McLain Ward, Inc. She asked him what horse McLain would ride in the Puissance, and he answered "Pozzi." A friend who was with Alexandra at the time, Vandy Lipman, said she should see the horse. Her daughter Emma had ridden him at the barn and said he was lovely. At that point, Alexandra didn't think much about the suggestion.

That night as they were entering the stadium, Alexandra recalls seeing McLain aboard a beautiful jet-black horse that had an incredible amount of presence. For those who are unfamiliar, the Puissance is like limbo in reverse. The class consists of a single wall that is raised with each successful round. If you knock a block off the wall, you are eliminated. If you clear it, you move on until one horse and rider are declared the winners. McLain and Pozzi, his winning mount, cleared 7ft. 2.5in. Not record-breaking, but enough to win. Alexandra was impressed.

Alexandra went to the Royal Horse Show in Toronto for work, and while there, joked with Lee about "her" black horse. After returning to Boston, Alexandra received a text message from Stepping Stone Farm. They had just tried this amazing horse, and they thought Alexandra would love him. After going back and forth a bit, Alexandra realized it was the same horse she had been admiring. She went out to Stepping Stone and rode Pozzi, otherwise known as Pozitano.

IT WAS LOVE AT FIRST RIDE.

MEETING HER MATCH

Alexandra had never jumped anything bigger than the Low Amateurs and suddenly she found herself sitting on a horse that won the Pussiance. She managed to scrape together every cent she could muster and bought Pozzi in 2006. Alexandra then started riding in bigger classes. Not just slightly bigger—a lot bigger. Pozzi took her to the high Amateur/Owner classes in Florida, which is the deep end of the pool: 4ft. 6in. in height with very wide oxers and technical distances.

Pozzi, who was nine years old at this point, was a scopey horse that had been passed around a bit prior to Alexandra's ownership. Bob Kraut rode him at Spruce Meadows and several other venues. Pozzi was not very mentally focused, and quite spooky though not in a careful way, which made him accessible to Alexandra as an amateur. If he were stronger mentally, it is likely that he would have continued to do the bigger classes with the pros.

Pozzi was a difficult horse, and Alexandra has had a lot of ups and downs with him. The relationship, however, has been mutually beneficial to both Alexandra and Pozzi. Despite his talent, Pozzi himself decided once that he was finished jumping and showing, and needed a long break. People told Alexandra that Pozzi was done, and would never make a comeback. Still, their partnership has allowed her to progress as a rider and has given Pozzi the time to mentally catch up with his athletic abilities. Regardless of his tendency to misbehave, he always greets Alexandra with a whinny and a toss of the head. He is very sensitive, and

JAMES LESLIE PARKER

Alexandra, looking mid-air for the next fence.

those who know him always joke that he "hears voices" in his head.

BALANCING BUSINESS AND SHOWING

Since EquiFit has become a household name on the show circuit, Alexandra is spending most of her time working and promoting her company, and riding and showing when she can. EquiFit's success is making Alexandra's equestrian pursuits practical.

Alexandra's successes as a businesswoman and a rider have put her life on exactly the track she envisioned for herself. She now keeps her horses close to home, and meets her trainer, Margie Engle, at shows. Alexandra has a new jumper named Carlos, an eight-year-old grey gelding, acquired in Florida last winter, thanks to Margie's educated eye.

Al tells me she has much more to accomplish before her riding career peaks. Having made it through the high Amateur/Owner courses in Florida, she is not far from the Grand Prix level on her best days. Meanwhile, as her own company continues to grow and prosper, Camilo's art gallery has become an international success. Despite her achievements, Alexandra remains one of the most grounded and kindest personalities you will ever meet. Nothing has come easily to her, but she has used her tenacious efforts to forge her path in the life she has chosen. I am proud to call her a friend and anxious to watch the next chapters of her equestrian pursuits unfold under Margie Engle's guidance. Who knows where she will go next? Perhaps one day Al will make it to the Grand Prix ring herself. I wouldn't bet against her.

EquiFit T-Boot selected as Official Performance Horse Boot and Leg Wear of the USEF

2010: 1st place in the M&S Adult Jumper Classic at the HITS Thermal

2010: Champion Adult Amateur Working Hunter at the Lake Placid Horse Show

Alexandra Cherubini & EquiFit Pozitano

2007: Champion Adult Amateur Hunts at the Florida Classic/WCHR Spectacular

2006, 2007: Puissance Winner on EquiFit Pozitano

2006: Champion Adult Jumper Finals at the Washington International Horse Show

2005: Debut of T-Boot EXP at the World Cup Finals on Sapphire (ridden by McLain Ward)

2005: Reserve Champion Adult Working Hunter at the National Horse Show

2002: ShouldersBack featured in Metropolitan Museum of Art exhibition, "Extreme Beauty: The Body Transformed"

2001: ShouldersBack featured in *W* magazine

Paige Johnson & Beach Bum

When Paige was about seven years old, she saw a cartoon called *My Little Pony*. In the cartoon, the ponies could fly and always seemed to save the day from the villains. Although these ponies were not ridden by humans, they stimulated Paige's interest in ponies, and she asked her mom if she could have a pony to ride. Her mother was reluctant at first, like most parents who did not grow up with horses in their lives would be. But after weeks of begging and pestering, her mom gave in. Paige can be quite persuasive. She is articulate and persistent, an effective combination.

Paige's mom took her to Meadowbrook barn outside of Washington, D.C. This barn still exists as a training facility and stabling complex. Paige began taking riding lessons. She

James Leslie Parker
Paige with good form and determination.

showed sufficient talent to catch the eye of the lead trainer, Art Combs. Paige's folks bought her first pony, Sailor, whose show name was Fox Hollow Sailing Star. He was a great one though a little stubborn. All ponies are a bit lazy.

Paige often fell off of Sailor because he would stop short and put his head down. Paige would fly off and hit the dirt. Young Paige was as stubborn as Sailor though, and always got back on, insisting that Sailor yield to her will. Sailor's behavior was just what Paige needed to get the fire burning inside of her.

"Even at a young age, **I always knew what I wanted** and would do anything to achieve it. At this time, I had probably just turned eight years old. I fell in love with ponies and knew this was something that I wanted to do competitively, and **nothing was going to stop me.**"

PAIGE'S MANY HORSES

Throughout the years, Paige has had many amazing ponies and horses, from Sailor, where it all started, to her second pony, Mikey (Midget's Lad), to an amazing small pony named Elfie (Himself the Elf). "[Elfie] was the cutest grey pony with freckles around his nose and eyes," Paige recalls. "He had adorable floppy ears." There was yet another pony in the mix at one point, Lizzie (For Kids Sake), Paige's first fancy medium pony. When Paige was still on small ponies and transitioning into mediums, her trainer had some conflicts he had to overcome, so he generously put her family in touch with Bill Moroney who became Paige's next trainer. Bill trained Paige for 13 years. He was into hunters when he first started training Paige during the pony era. When the decision was made to transition to the jumpers, Bill brought in jumper trainer Chuck Keller, who entered the mix and co-trained Paige for nine years.

Paige's first jumper, J.D. (Rebel Without a Cause), was like Paige's personal body guard. As Paige remembers, "He was the sweetest jumper I could have hoped for. Then I had Puffy (Sweet Diamond), my second children's jumper who would run out to the left. My trainers would keep tally to see how many times Puffy would 'win' with running out or I would 'win' by making him jump the fences and complete the course. This type of horse makes you a tough rider, a rider who rides every inch of the course and takes nothing for granted. Good horses are honest, and boost the rider's confidence." Puffy was a good horse for Paige, and he knew what he could get away with. If Paige did not control him, he did as he pleased. Paige also had a horse named Flirtatious that she bought from Elisabeth Salter who had shown her in Geneva in 1996 at the World Cup finals.

Flirtatious was tough. Paige either fell off or won. Flirty, as she was known, was a tiny mare, only about 15 hands plus a bit. "I would school her without stirrups and jump verticals as tall as five feet. She would not stop when I had no stirrups because I had her in a death grip with my legs," Paige explains. " I was holding on for dear life! My greatest accomplishment with her was winning the Washington International Horse Show Junior Jumper Classic when I was 12 years old. I was the youngest in the class. It was a proud moment because of how difficult Flirty was." Overcoming all those ups and downs is what makes winning taste so sweet. What Paige went through with a number of ponies and horses is what every amateur rider goes through. Rarely do you find the perfect match without this kind of character-building experience.

Paige tells me she had many amazing junior jumpers. She gives credit to Dominique, Reddy Teddy, Just Dreamin', and Beach Bum, the last of whom became Paige's horse of a lifetime. Beach Bum took her from those early pony years all the way to the Grand Prix ring.

> Although he didn't have a conventional style, Beach Bum was one of those horses that comes around once in a lifetime and **teaches you how to believe in yourself and your talent.**

BEACH BUM: PAIGE'S MISSING PUZZLE PIECE

As soon as Paige sat on Beach Bum, it was love at first sight or first ride, if you will. The deal was done in a virtual heartbeat. Horses like Beach Bum don't grow on trees. "Beach Bum is my heart, my soul, the first thing I think about in the morning and the last image I remember before falling asleep at night," Paige says. Beach Bum came into Paige's life when she was 13 years old, and Chuck Keller, her trainer, was watching the high amateur jumpers in Florida. The high amateur jumpers in Florida are a couple holes shy of the Grand Prix level. Paige's trainer watched Beach Bum put two strides in a one-stride combination and clear it. That is not typical and takes a bold, willing, and overly generous horse. (I have done that with Roxett and I know how special that is.)

Paige quickly went on to win the High Junior Jumper Stake at Devon with Beach Bum when she was just 14. Paige and Beach Bum started to do Grands Prix from Lexington,

JAMES LESLIE PARKER

Jumping high and wide.

Virginia, to Lexington, Kentucky, from the Cincinnati Night Class Grand Prix to Lake Placid, and eventually to the Saturday 1.50m classes in Florida. "Beach Bum taught me how to do the next level, from juniors to the open divisions," Paige notes. "Competing against the top professionals at 14 and going around usually with no more than four faults and sometimes a great clear. At such a young age, you can imagine how this horse became my hero." Beach Bum went in a hackamore so he had no bit in his mouth. "He has a funny mouth so when I would get close to the fence, I would have to let go of his mouth and hold on to his mane. This

JAMES LESLIE PARKER

Beach Bum, Paige's horse of a lifetime.

allowed him to follow through with his hind end. This kind of horse also teaches you how to adjust your ride for each horse so you can ride them the way that will most benefit the horse and you in the end," she explains.

After witnessing the two-in-one stride in and out performance, a trial was set up with Joe Fargis of Olympic Gold fame who would become Paige's next trainer. Joe Fargis came into Paige's life when Chuck Keller retired when Paige was 19 years old. Joe has been a tremendous asset to Paige, and she speaks of him in the most respectful and thankful terms, noting "Joe is always a positive influence and a great person to have on your side. He is now my solo trainer."

Beach Bum continued to show at the 1.50m level until

he was 19 or 20. He is one of a kind and has a big personality. "He talks to you, he licks you, and I swear he understands English. He is so intelligent—it is unbelievable. He is like a pet, and he has a home for life."

Paige, like all of our accomplished athletes, did not get here on her own. All these athletes are quick to speak in generous terms about their grooms who have been with them for years. Juan, Agustin, Sergio, and Rob Jones, her barn manager, have been with Paige for many years. "A barn is nothing if you don't have a good support system; this starts with the grooms and ends with the rider. It's truly a group effort to get the rider to the ring and make sure the horses are on their game," Paige explains.

One of Paige's favorite accomplishments is winning the Calvin Klein Derby on Dominique. During that time, Paige was training with Laura Kraut. This was a great win for Paige because she was the only clear round over the first course so there was no jump-off.

MOVING UP TO THE GRAND PRIX LEVEL

One of Paige's first Grand Prix horses was Lancier 4, who was bought from Jimmy and Danielle Torano. Paige tells me he was an amazing horse and teacher. She remembers being second with him in the Sunday Grand Prix in Florida behind Chris Kappler's Olympic mount, Royal Kaliber. This has to go down as one of any young rider's favorite Grand Prix placings. Paige went on to place in many top Grands Prix with Lancier 4 in Florida, Lake Placid, Lexington, and Spruce Meadows. I was surprised to learn Paige had ridden in the Queen Elizabeth Cup in Calgary, also on Lancier 4, which is about as big as it gets. Paige remembers going clear until fence 12, then having three down. She is sure that was because they were both exhausted and the jumps were huge. Nonetheless to have a respectable round as a young 19-year-old athlete in a huge caliber class was a great accomplishment.

"I have many more goals that I want to achieve," Paige assures me. "In riding, there are ups and downs, and right now I don't have the Grand Prix horses that I need in order to compete at that level. I hope to put together a great string in the next couple of years so I can represent the U.S. in overseas competitions and earn my red team coat." No doubt the determined and talented Paige Johnson will do exactly that.

Looking to the future, Paige is quick to recognize the help of those who have made her rise possible. "I want to thank Kent Farrington, who used to ride a horse named Gera for me who then went to Michael Morrissey," she says. "Kent has been a friend and fellow competitor for years, and he helps me when Joe is unavailable. It is always great to have a good team of people surrounding you." Paige also expresses gratitude to Debbie Stephens and Jeff Wirthman, who trained her for a time, as well as Laura Kraut.

> "With great success comes great sacrifice, and I feel that no matter what you do, most everything has its pros and cons. I'm just lucky enough that I found something that I love. If you love something, then it doesn't feel like a sacrifice at the end of the day."

BEACH BUM STEPS DOWN, PAIGE MOVES ON

When Paige decided that it was time for Beach Bum to stop showing, it was not a decision she had to go to great lengths to make. Beach Bum got hurt, and at his age Paige decided there was no reason to push it. "He has done so much for me and owes me nothing," she says with affection. Beach Bum is the

JAMES LESLIE PARKER

No challenge too big.

cover boy on the 2010 SmartPak annual catalog pictured in a blue and white sheet looking younger than his 24 years. Beach Bum still gets ridden almost every day. He is not the type of horse that you just turn out in a field, forget about, and let him enjoy his retirement. He is a true show horse and wants his treats and his bath and lots of attention from his people. Paige admits that riding is time-consuming and requires complete dedication and focus. So as a child she missed out on normal things like her senior prom.

Paige is a grounded, dedicated, talented athlete. She has

been blessed with a number of talented horses, but Beach Bum is her soul mate, her once in a lifetime.

Obviously, the bulk of Paige's career is in front of her, and the heights she may reach are yet to be determined. It is clear she has made many sacrifices, but has benefited from supportive parents, trainers, and staff getting to this notable point in her career. Who knows what the future holds?

Young riders and parents reading this chapter: I can tell you with certainty the three notable amateur athletes I have described here will lead by example both in sport and in life. These are young women of tremendous integrity, courage, and heart. I could not be more pleased to bring you this terrific trio not only as athletes, but also as role models to emulate.

Won the High Amateur Owner Classic two years in a row, Harrisburg

Won the High Amateur Owner Classic two years in a row, Washington, D.C.

Made it to the 1.50m Grand Prix Ring on Beach Bum, Florida

Paige Johnson & Beach Bum

2nd place at the Grand Prix on Lancier 4 (2nd to Chris Kappler on Royal Kaliber), Wellington

2nd place at Eight-Year-Old Championships on Monopoly, Florida

2007: Winner of High Junior/Amateur Classic on La Martinee, Charlotte

2006: Winner of High Junior/Amateur Classic on La Martinee, Charlotte

CH. 11

Laura Kraut & Cedric

The story of Laura Kraut and her rise to show jumping's elite begins with her mother, Carol, who gave Laura her first riding lesson. Carol set in motion something larger than anybody could have foreseen at the time. Laura vividly remembers her early experiences with horses when she was only three years old. There is a real family story behind Laura's successful career.

Laura was born in Atlanta, Georgia, in November of 1965. She and her sister, Mary Elizabeth, shared an interest in horses. Mary Elizabeth remains a central part of the management of Laura's show jumping operation to this day.

When Laura was 13 years old, she owned her first pony,

BOB LANGRISH MBE, EQUESTRIAN PHOTOGRAPHER
Laura and Cedric attack the Olympic Course in Beijing.

Polaris Smarty. Laura and I had a good laugh remembering the candy with the same name. The pony and the sugar high from the candy created much the same childhood euphoria. Laura had great fun with that pony, teaching him to step up on the stairs to her mounting block and attempting to enter the house with him on more than one occasion. An interesting tidbit about this first pony is that he had only four riders in his life. Each of these riders went on to Grand Prix, if not to Olympic success. What are the odds of that? Laura was the first owner, followed by McLain Ward and then Aaron Ballard, of Canadian fame. McLain would become Laura's Olympic teammate. Smarty clearly was quite a pony to have inspired such riders and such fantastic careers.

Laura's sister, Mary Elizabeth, is a driving force, a powerful personality, and a serious organizer. Mary manages Laura's horses, staff, and barn, leaving Laura free to train, teach, and compete. These young women are naturally symbiotic and family-aligned in a common and mutually passionate way. Like all of the super stars of the sport, Laura is blessed with a talented and dedicated team. Nobody arrives at the pinnacle Laura has reached without the reality of a high-quality support system.

Ashley Yanke is another long-standing member of Laura's support system. It's obvious how much affection, respect, and support Laura benefits from having Ashley on her team. Another key player in Laura's network is Johanna Burtsoff, who is also a dedicated and important member of the team. Laura says Johanna is Cedric's "co-mother" and longtime groom. You cannot talk about the family nature of Laura's operation without touching on her son, Bobby, who was born in 1999. Bobby has literally traveled the world with Laura and has more recently begun to follow in Laura's footsteps (including several wins in Wellington, Florida, beginning in the winter of 2009).

Laura is universally known for her positive outlook,

ASHLEY YANKE

Cedric and Mom, a quiet European moment.

good sportsmanship, and high regard for the sport. These characteristics come naturally to Laura—it's just who she is. This fact is well-codified through her receipt of the Jack Kelly Fair Play Award by the Olympic Organizing Committee in 2003. This award recognizes key character traits of athletes in all Olympic sports. Laura's resume is long, deep, and incredibly global. She chooses to compete as much in Europe as in North America and wins equally on both sides of the pond.

2004 OLYMPIC QUALIFICATION

While a member of the United States Equestrian Team (USET) team at the Pan American Games in the Dominican

Republic, Laura's horse suffered a slight injury that did not cause the horse to fail the required veterinary inspection, but which might have affected Laura's performance in the competition. In order for the U.S. to qualify for the 2004 Olympics, the team needed to do well in the Dominican Republic. Laura made the difficult decision to withdraw and allow the alternate to join the team. Instead of returning home and maximizing her time and programs, Laura remained in the Dominican Republic and became a passionate cheerleader and a source of inspiration and support for her team. This selfless act sums up Laura Kraut.

Show jumping is the world's ultimate team sport and the only one where there is not a spoken word that need be exchanged for the magic to happen. It's **heart to heart** and **spirit to spirit,** and as fanciful as that description may seem, it is as real and pragmatic as communication in the huddle in an NFL moment.

The U.S. team went on to win the gold medal in the Dominican Republic, which enabled them to qualify for the 2004 Olympics. They ultimately secured the Olympic gold medal in Athens, aided in no small part by Laura Kraut.

One of the unique aspects of Laura's success is her ability with many different horses. Laura is able to get the most out of different types of horses. She has enjoyed championship success with Anthem, Miss Independent, Allegiance, Liberty, Quickstar II, Athletico, Milano, and Simba Run, several horses that come to mind before her fortunate connection with Cedric.

LAURA MEETS CEDRIC

We could write as much about Laura and Anthem as about Laura and Cedric. I've chosen to focus on Cedric as he is her most recent partner.

Laura was in Lummen, Belgium one spring a few years back. She had some time before her next competition in La Baule, France one afternoon and was in the company of notable horse dealer Emile Hendricks. Emile was the dealer from whom Laura acquired Liberty, Anthem, and Miss Independent. No wonder Laura chose to spend that spring Sunday afternoon with Emile (Ian Millar also acquired the legendary Big Ben from Emile).

Emile suggested they watch the Grand Prix, which Laura rarely gets to do because usually she is competing herself. This was a bit of a break. Laura was not focused on the Grand Prix. Instead, she was thinking ahead to the competition in France where serious challenges awaited her the following week. The Grand Prix that Sunday in Belgium was on a large field, and midway through the class Laura's attention began to drift. She turned and began to watch the action in the small ring behind her where young horses were jumping. Laura spied a dark, dappled grey horse which was being ridden by Michael Vanderveluten, the son of Eric Vanderveluten—another top international rider. Laura watched him jump a half dozen fences and grabbed Emile by the shirt sleeve demanding that he find out about this horse. Even though she had caught little more than a glimpse of him, Laura asked Emile to do whatever he could to identify the horse that had caught her experienced eye.

The horse was none other than Cedric! Early the next morning, Laura rode Cedric. They jumped less than a dozen fences, and she knew that this horse was hers. To buy him, she knew she would have to put a syndicate together, but she had done this before with horses she had bought

TONY DE COSTA

Laura and Cedric at the World Equestrian Games.

from Emile Hendricks. He always gave her time to put the deal together. Laura took a big breath, shook hands with Emile, and had Cedric put on a plane and sent to Spruce Meadows. After the Grand Prix in France, she would join Cedric in Calgary.

After making the journey to Calgary, Laura ran into Peter Wetherill and showed him a digital picture she had snapped of Cedric. "Here is your next super star!" Laura told him. Laura had a long-standing, trusting relationship with Peter Wetherill, an owner of Laura's horses. Peter and Laura were partners on another horse Laura was selling, and Peter had half-joked, "I suppose when this one is sold you'll be coming to me with the next prospect." Peter is one of those owners who, when you have a bad class, he will be the first to slap you on the back and make you feel better or, when you win, he will scream and yell with wild enthusiasm. After some good-natured kidding about Laura's new find, Peter agreed to anchor the syndicate and become an owner along with Laura and others.

CEDRIC SURPRISES

Shortly after this chance meeting with Peter, Laura rushed to the stabling area and threw open the stall door, anxious to be better acquainted with Cedric. She stood, dumbstruck, staring at what looked like Polaris Smarty reincarnated. Based on the way she rode and jumped, Cedric had created the impression of a much bigger horse than the diminutive Smarty look-alike standing before her in the stall at Spruce Meadows. Cedric was seven years old, but he would never grow in stature to meet Laura's immense vision of him harbored in her imagination. When Laura and Cedric cantered into the North American ring later that week, he seemed all the more Smarty-like in the vast space of the venue.

Every trip around a show jumping course is a test of the team, a demonstration of the harmony between horse and rider. **Success or failure is measured in fractions of a second** where a single rail knocked to the ground can shatter a dream or leave one questioning the sanity of the sacrifices you have made to get to the in-gate.

It did not take long for Cedric's jump to erase all concerns about his size. In the early stages of their partnership, Cedric jumped Laura loose or off several times. After one such fall, with ring sand still in her teeth, Laura lamented to her colleague Ashley Yanke how difficult it was to stay on this super jumper. Ashley related to Laura that she and her husband, Paul, were working on a product which used an interesting combination of magnets placed in the stirrup irons and in the soles of the rider's boots to better secure the rider on the horse.

These magnets became a product manufactured by the company now known as Ontyte. I use this product on all my saddles, and I cannot imagine why anybody would ride without the magnets. Sometimes circumstances cause you to depart your equine partner, and the gravitational force of your body overrides your artificial connection, causing you to fall. Despite that risk, such a scientifically engineered bit of extra contact can be the difference between winning and losing, finishing and ending, walking and limping.

Not to be deterred by his small size and propensity to jump Laura loose, her emotional connection with the small spitfire Cedric developed quickly. Cedric was endearing to her from the beginning. He was as much a pet, clown, or source of entertainment as a teammate and athlete. Laura says when she is on the road, she will sometimes put a chair outside Cedric's stall and sit with him for hours. These quiet moments further the bond between them and help reduce her homesickness. The trust and close personal relationship with Cedric is critical to Laura.

2008 OLYMPICS IN BEIJING

In 2008, when Cedric was still very much a youngster in age and experience, Laura made the ambitious decision to enter in the Olympic trials. Although she did not think they had a shot at ending up on the team, the decision to enter the trials was as much for the experience and seasoning as it was for her sense of duty to Cedric. They not only qualified but led the way, winning trial after trial in the Olympic selection process.

These stories are truly special. **Show jumping is not simply the light-hearted beautifully artistic picture it sometimes appears.** There was real danger and high anxiety in the decisions Laura made to enter Cedric into the Olympic trials.

The confidence Laura had then and enjoys today with Cedric is pivotal to their amazing success and the Olympic gold. A rider's investment in this kind of partnership is utterly complete. It is not just Laura's investment—Mary Elizabeth, Ashley, Johanna, and the entire staff are also stakeholders. Success or failure is entirely balanced on the bond that is built between the horse and rider.

Like all of our Olympians, I asked Laura to be candid about that special, less public Olympic moment for her and Cedric. Standing on the Olympic podium with Cedric behind her and "The Star Spangled Banner" playing conjures all kinds of emotions. Laura told me, "I've had a lot of really great horses in my life, but I don't think I'll ever have another one like Cedric. He's extra special. He's got tremendous heart and the ability to match, which is not often the case. I'm a lucky person to get to have him, and I'm going to enjoy every minute of it."

For Laura, looking back on her Beijing experience, there is a deeply personal side to these Olympic moments. After the medal ceremonies, there was a party back at the hotel. Her longtime friend and ally, Peter Wetherill, was in classic form. He was perhaps the happiest person at the party. Laura recounted for me that Peter had the Olympic gold medal around his own neck for a time, and she is certain those were among the happiest moments in Peter's life with horses.

Peter Wetherill's tragic death was sudden and unexpected. For Laura, that personal Olympic moment with Peter will live in her memory in an extra special way. She is all the more proud of Cedric who, in her words, "did not put a single foot wrong during the Olympics, as if he needed to get it done for Peter." Not only that, Cedric did it at the tender age of ten which is very young for an Olympic mount.

Laura and Cedric soldiered on after the Olympics, continuing their winning ways. Peter's family inherited Peter's share of Cedric. The Wetherills wasted no time letting her know, in no uncertain terms, Cedric would never be for sale. Cedric competes in the memory of Peter Wetherill.

WELLINGTON, 2011

The Winter Equestrian Festival in Wellington, Florida, concentrates in a single place the very best the sport has

BOB LANGRISH MBE
EQUESTRIAN PHOTOGRAPHER

Laura and Cedric perform at the Super League.

to offer for three months during the winter. As a result, the competition is fierce. Understanding the quality of the field they are contending with, course designers set very stiff tests for the winter Grands Prix. Laura's win at the Spy Coast Farm $150,000 Grand Prix in 2011 demonstrated that her relationship with Cedric was very much in force. Following this big win, Laura had interesting things to say about her now 13-year-old Dutch partner, Cedric: "He is equal parts heart, speed, and smarts, but always heart first. I seldom walk a course, no matter what challenges it poses, without understanding there is a formula for Cedric to add a stride here or leave one out that will allow him to get the job done." Following Laura and Cedric's win at Wellington, McLain Ward was heard to say, "Man, Cedric's going to be a pain in the neck for the next few years! I can see him at 17 still clocking around like that."

Much of show jumping is mental. If you can visualize the right things happening when you walk a course and if you have faith and trust in your horse, you are going to enter the ring inspired with confidence. The inverse is equally true. If you, the human half of the equation, have doubts and begin to ride defensively, then stride lengths change, pace and rhythm suffer, and the relation between horse and rider unravels. When we talk about great partnerships like Cedric and Laura, it is a compounding equation that breeds powerful results.

Laura tells me she expects Cedric to be her Olympic partner in London in 2012, and another World Equestrian Games is not out of the question. Starting as early as he did, being as small as he is, Cedric seems to stress his body less than the bigger horses. Bobby, Laura's son, loves Cedric and wants to ride him now. Laura says that is not going to happen any time soon. That's the Mom talking. "Bobby is 11 years old. Maybe when he is 18, if he has done his homework," jokes Laura.

Cedric has earned a special place alongside the string of famous horses Laura has ridden to championships the world over. These include Anthem, Simba Run, Liberty, Allegiance, Miss Independent, and a longer list we can look forward to watching as Laura moves forward in the world's most beautiful sport.

1st place at the Grand Prix on Cedric, Hachenburg

1st place at the Samsung Nations Cup Royal Winter Fair on Anthem, Toronto

2011: Winner of the $500,000 FTI Grand Prix on Cedric, Wellington

Laura Kraut
& Cedric

2011: Spy Coast $150,000 Grand Prix on Cedric, Wellington

2010: $150,000 CN U.S. Grand Prix on Cedric, Wellington

2008: 1st place at the $500,000 Grand Prix on Anthem, Charlotte

2008: 1st place at the Olympia Grand Prix on Miss Independent, Geneva

2006: Team Silver medalist at the World Equestrian Games, Aachen

2005: Gold Medal Team on the Samsung Super League Tour

2000, 2004, 2008: Olympics in Sydney, Athens (Gold), Beijing (Gold)

Leslie Burr & Howard S'Blieft

Leslie Burr Howard's competitive spirit emerged early in her life. When she was just four years old, she started carrying a stopwatch to time each lap around the track in her yard. It was all her own idea; she had no one to teach her to ride. In no time, she was blazing around the track, despite the confines of her Western saddle. She exhibited unusual interest, enthusiasm, and discipline from the start. Leslie is not called "Leaping Leslie" for nothing. The woman is fearless and has a special kind of competitive fire that really drives her in the ring.

From her earliest days in the saddle, she loved to ride at top speed (or as fast as a pony could go). Thankfully, her parents recognized her love for horses early.

Gretchen Almy
Leslie Howard the queen of speed in action.

If Leslie has a better idea for doing something, you'd better listen because she is probably right and won't put it to rest until she has been heard. She is also the first one to compliment you when you get it right. Leslie is a perfectionist in everything she does, which I have observed directly at the Fidelity Investments Jumper Classic, where she has often helped me improve the show, and with tips she has given me for one of my horses.

AN EARLY START

Leslie's parents had no experience with horses. Leslie thrived on speed and has always looked forward to a challenge. Leslie's parents decided when she was six that it was time for formal lessons. Within a mile of where she lived was one of the top pony farms, Highfields Farm. At Highfields Farm, Leslie gained access to great ponies and fine teachers, particularly Sharyn Hardy-Cole and her brother, Thom Hardy, who rode for USET. Maybe she got lucky and fell into the right situation, or maybe it was nature's way of separating the ordinary from the extraordinary. Leslie was unstoppable.

She soon saw the wisdom of riding in an English saddle. She was a natural, but you do not get to the top tier of international athletes just because you are a natural. You get there because you are willing to work harder and take chances when you have a chance to win. Leslie had many horses, but the one who would change her life did not come along until after she had claimed both gold and silver medals at the Olympics. He was still the horse she singled out. To understand her love for S'Blieft, it helps to know how Leslie rode her way to the top.

Not every aspiring junior rider has the opportunity and talent to train with the legendary George Morris. At 14, Leslie was securely under his wing at his farm in New Jersey. A year later, she won the 1972 ASPCA Maclay

Leslie loves all her horses as individuals.

Finals at Madison Square Garden. To win the Maclay is to be crowned the top young rider in the United States. This equitation foundation has served most of the great Grand Prix athletes well, including McLain Ward, Beezie Madden, and Chris Kappler.

ALBANY AND THE LOS ANGELES OLYMPICS

Fast forward a few years—Leslie was on course to the Olympics with a talented horse named Albany. He belonged to one of her students, Debbie Dolan, and would partner successfully with Leslie. Albany captured the title of AGA (American Grand Prix Association) Horse of the Year in 1983. The following year, Leslie would be named AGA Rider of the Year, and Albany would once again be Horse of the Year, a prelude to the golden year of 1984.

"Albany was a young, brilliant horse. He was very scopey and brave," Leslie said of the Thoroughbred. American Thoroughbred horses are not the norm in the world of show jumping. Show jumping is dominated by European breeds from warm bloodlines whose offspring tend to be bigger, more heavily muscled, and better suited to show jumping than Thoroughbreds.

> Show jumping is a **sport of lifelong passion,** and riders do not disappear after claiming the ultimate championship. **They go back for more,** year after year.

In 1984, Leslie and Albany made it to the top level of the sport through the Olympic trials and onto the U.S. show jumping team at the Olympic Games in Los Angeles. Two of her teammates, Melanie Smith and Conrad

Homfeld, were also students of the legendary George Morris, who was Chef d'Equipe (equestrian-speak for coach). Also on the team was Hall of Fame rider Joe Fargis who claimed Individual Gold on the unforgettable Touch of Class. That 1984 team was a sensation, winning the gold medal as a unit.

Leslie had begun a HOT STREAK that would last her lifetime.

Leslie had already made a solid name for herself around the world, but there was still no stopping her at this level. In 1986, she won the World Cup Finals in Gothenburg, Sweden, riding a horse named McLain (no connection to rider McLain Ward). Leslie was then given the opportunity of a lifetime when she was paired with the "World's Greatest Horse," Gem Twist. So extremely notable was this magnificent animal, that he was cloned in 2008, several years after his death, in an effort to continue the lineage that had died with him.

GEM TWIST MAKES HIS MARK

Gem Twist had already won Horse of the Year twice with his rider Greg Best, but when Greg was injured, Leslie continued his competition year. The pair had instant success. "Taking over Gem Twist was not easy. He had only been ridden by Greg Best before me, and it takes a while to get used to a horse and the horse to get used to you. You can adjust, and I did. You often have to do this. You're not really at your comfort level until you've ridden the horse at least six months, and it can take two years to build a solid relationship." He was her ride, and she was up to the challenge, no matter how early in the relationship. They won the 1993 Budweiser/AGA Championship and with it,

BOB LANGRISH MBE
EQUESTRIAN PHOTOGRAPHER

Leslie at the 2011 Winter Equestrian Festival in Florida.

Gem Twist's record-setting third Horse of the Year title.

In 1994, the pair represented the U.S. at the World Equestrian Games in Holland. That same year, she rode Charisma and Gem Twist to a first place tie in the USET. Show Jumping Championship at the Bayer/USET Festival of Champions in Gladstone, New Jersey.

"Gem Twist just had everything. He was a winner. That's probably his biggest asset. He had the talent, he was careful, and he was such a competitive horse." An American Thoroughbred, Gem Twist was from the Bonne Nuit line. The legendary Frank Chapot, himself an Olympian and a

USET coach, bred the magnificent stallion Good Twist to his mare, and Gem Twist would forever make his mark. Twist was owned by Michael Golden, ridden by Greg Best, Leslie Howard, and then Frank's daughter, Laura Chapot.

The winning horses in most equestrian sports are the fiercest competitors. They have fire in their eyes and strong, volatile behavior. They are that way by nature, not nurture. Like racehorses, the show jumping horses that win have plenty of heart. It takes a rider of equal heart and a lot of determination to ride them and win. Leslie has had many exceptional horses to match her extraordinary abilities.

In 1996, Leslie found herself on her second U.S. Olympic team. She rode Extreme, a horse belonging to Jane Clark. Along with Leslie, riders Peter Leone, Michael Matz, and Anne Kursinki captured the Team Silver medal in Atlanta.

"I've been fortunate to have had a lot of great horses over the years. Probably the most famous horse I rode was Gem Twist, who was obviously a lovely horse and a great powerhouse to sit on. But I have to admit my favorite horse, and with the best personality, was a horse called S'Blieft."

S'BLIEFT: THE HORSE OF A LIFETIME

This may be a name that dedicated fans will recall. S'Blieft took Leslie to the top of the sport. Early in their career, they won the du Maurier, the world's richest Grand Prix event (now the CN International) with a million dollar prize at Spruce Meadows in Canada. They were among 12 U.S. Equestrian Team horse-rider combinations competing in the inaugural Samsung Nations Cup Series, now known as the Super League. In the Super League, U.S. riders take on the powerhouse European nations.

"That would have been in 1997," she says, speaking in a dreamy tone as she recalls the most significant memories of her nine-year relationship with S'Blieft.

"He was a funny-looking horse," she says of the superbly bred chestnut-colored Dutch warmblood. The son of the famous, stately stallion Burggraaf, he was one of several successful jumping progeny which also included Roelof Bril's Burggravin, Peter Wylde's Kuno, Piet Raijmakers's Now or Never, Thomas Frühmann's Procobs Dumbo, and John Whitaker's Peppermill. Burggraaf's offspring also succeeded in the very disciplined and elegant Olympic sport of dressage.

S'Blieft was only five when Leslie found him in Holland, where a partner in Europe saw him competing in some young horse classes. Leslie vetted him and brought him home, where he settled in well for a five-year-old. Leslie took S'Blieft up through the ranks. It is as if the plan she had for him from the beginning was totally committed to muscle memory. He was first named Aalst U Blieft, which means "please" in the Dutch language, but sounds like S'Blieft when said quickly. S'Blieft was used for the partnership that was formed by his owners, Leslie's husband and two long time friends, now called the S'Blieft Group.

"S'Blieft is my favorite horse. He was an amazing character, feisty, smart, and he did funny things that made me laugh.

"I taught S'Blieft to bow in his stall and chase carrots down the aisle."

It was easy to teach S'Blieft to bow. Carrots are amazing things. Food meant a lot to him," Leslie laughs. "He could buck, play, leap, and pin his ears to demonstrate emotion." Leslie has a legendary laser stare, and she is also feisty and smart. It makes sense that Leslie and S'Blieft would be especially close when horse and rider are so much alike.

GRETCHEN ALMY

Another trip to the winner's circle (Spring 2011).

S'BLIEFT LIKES TO PLAY

Just thinking about S'Blieft makes her smile. Many riders and horses are very serious when they are schooling, exercising, and especially when they are competing in the Grand Prix field. It is easy to forget that, with these high performance horses who are so focused on their jobs, there is a special personality that connects them with the person on their back. Those are the horses that indulgent riders adore.

"You'd be trotting S'Blieft out in the Grand Prix field and

GRETCHEN ALMY

Leaping Leslie flying high.

---

all of a sudden he would fall to his knees and eat grass! He was a real clown," Leslie says. "He did other funny things as well. At Spruce Meadows, they have parades where every country is represented. The riders follow a little girl who is holding the flag of the country they represent. S'Blieft would walk up behind the little girl carrying the American flag and try to pull her scrunchie off her ponytail, not biting, just nibbling. Unlike other horses who would get terrified and do stupid things, he would come out and look around as though everybody was there cheering for him. Because he was so successful in the international ring at Spruce Meadows, a good portion of the time they *were* cheering for him." You could see the mist in Leslie's eyes as she remembered the playfulness of this magical horse.

S'Blieft would also play with Leslie. He would walk behind her and put his head right on top of her hunt cap (this was back in the days when there was a little knob on top of the cap the rider wore). He would bite the little knob and pull her hat off. He would play with zippers and do silly things that might have annoyed some riders, but Leslie enjoyed his teasing. These were some of the stories she clearly cherishes. The wins were wonderful too, but did not rise to the same level of distinction as his playful disposition.

THE HORSE AND RIDER PARTNERSHIP

Leslie never took S'Blieft to the Olympic trials. During the eight years she rode him, he could have done two sets of trials, but at the time of the first set he was too young and at the next set he had a leg injury.

Leslie's sense is that the relationship with a Grand Prix horse is a very different relationship than you would have with a racehorse, where the person that actually races the horse rarely rides it on a daily basis. Racehorses are ridden by the exercise boys, and then a jockey rides the horse for a couple of minutes. There is no serious relationship formed like that of an equestrian show jumper and the horse he or she works with every day of the year. You have to know your horse, and the best partnerships are those where thousands of hours are spent together over many years.

There are many facets to the development of a young competition horse beyond physical training. There is also a relationship that takes a great deal of time to grow and requires commitment from the rider. The relationship continues through the years in the competitive ring. The horse usually is not ready for the Grand Prix until he or she is eight or nine. Often, the best partnerships are formed when you take a horse who is five or six years old and bring him or her to the Grand Prix level. Leslie has done this many times in her career.

Then there is the task of moving the young horse up through the ranks. Keeping the horse at his or her comfort level is a carefully honed skill, unique to each individual horse and rider. "Like any athlete, you cannot be performing at your peak all the time. You must know when to peak, when to let them down, and when to bring them up again, mentally and physically. Some horses do better with a lot of showing and some with not much showing at all. You have to get to know each individual horse," Leslie explains.

S'Blieft kept a pretty steady pace of wins and delighted Leslie for nine years. "He was not a powerhouse horse, so he had to build with lower classes early in the week, then by Sunday, he would have the scope, power, and his confidence level would be there for the Grand Prix," Leslie says.

No one but Leslie rode S'Blieft, except on occasion Molly Ashe Cawley, who worked for Leslie for a while. Molly has become a star in her own right. Leslie is a teacher of champion riders as well.

In 2004, after winning the Atco Midstream Challenge for the third time at Spruce Meadows, Leslie said, "Every day from S'Blieft is a blessing. **If you're going to jump, you may as well jump to win."**

She has left a lasting imprint on the fabric of the sport, not just as an individual, but also as a teacher who has repeatedly seen her students rise to the top. Nicole Shahinian Simpson is another student of Leslie's who went on to succeed in the sport. Other notable examples are Judy Garafalo Torres, Christine McCrey, and Kent Farrington, all of whom owe elements of their style and success to Leslie.

Leslie once scolded me at a horse show: "Glorydays [my horse] is too heavy—take some weight off her, Jeff." I thought I knew my horse inside and out, and in many ways I did. Leslie was right, as usual, and we did get Glorydays down by about seven percent of her body weight. She is now performing better than ever. Leslie sensed all this from across the ring while doing three other things simultaneously.

S'BLIEFT LOVES TO SHOW

Despite Leslie's careful riding and S'Blieft's joyful personality, injuries and illnesses wove their way through S'Blieft's competitive life. However, he would always rebound and do great things.

Leslie put S'Blieft back to work after an injury in January of 1998. Leslie thought, "Since he is feeling good, we'll go into the Queen Elizabeth II Cup next week." And they won it! She always put his well-being first and let him tell her if he was up for the next challenge. He loved the show circuit and loved to travel.

Leslie claims that S'Blieft was always super on grass fields. He won a lot of classes at Spruce Meadows. At that time, she had some other horses, but they fade in and out of memory by comparison to her special friend. In his prime, he was by far the best horse she ever had. Then, as S'Blieft was aging, Priobert de Kalvarie was coming into his own.

The two horses competed at the same level for about two years, but Priobert was not as great on grass. He would become Leslie's indoor and sand ring horse, while S'Blieft was good on grass and did the outdoor classes. The international stadium at Spruce Meadows, which is the North American Mecca for the sport, was and always will be

Leslie cools down after jumping another clear round.

GRETCHEN ALMY

grass, so it was a great place to be comfortable.

"S'Blieft had tons of animation," recalls Leslie. "He was quite strong, bouncy, and very aggressive in his way of going. He was just hysterical. He really would attack a course. He always was unruly in the schooling area and hard to get to the jumps in the ring, not because he didn't want to jump, but because as soon as he knew he was going to jump, he would go as fast as he could. Once he got into the ring, he would sort of settle into this nice rhythm. He liked to go with a nice gallop. He was fun."

REINING IT IN

By the age of 15, S'Blieft let her know that he was not able to keep up the pace any more. The injuries had caught up with him, and there were soundness issues. She made the difficult decision to retire him. He lives happily on a farm in Aiken, South Carolina, his devilish personality very much intact and frequently on ample display.

Leslie took a framed photo from her desk to show off the star that had once shone brightly with her in the Grand Prix spotlight. In the photo, S'Blieft stands without any tack, unrestrained, quietly posed in a spacious grass field. Sitting on his back is a two-year-old girl, safe, smiling, and gently steadied by her mother as the three look into the camera lens. Imagine that this great and powerful horse would be so trustworthy.

There are lots of great horses in Leslie's life. Her barn is star-studded with her current mounts, Lennox Lewis and Jeans Glove Varnel among them. In the past, there was Nick of Diamonds, another overly-animated, incredibly fast little grey stallion. Leslie won many speed classes on Nick. I once saw Leslie turn so fast in a jump-off with Nick of Diamonds that she caught her knee against the jump standard on the way over, and the crack it made left you wondering not only how she stayed on, but how she dismounted afterwards and limped away.

Leslie loves her horses and is overjoyed when they win the big classes together. She is not biased, however. She pulls back the stall door to reveal a little guy, a hunter named Zipzoo. "He is funny because he's always in trouble, doing the wrong thing at the wrong time. I like the ones that have a little personality," she says.

Beyond everything else, Leslie is a competitor, a horsewoman, a partner, and soul mate to her beloved champions, be it S'Blieft, Priobert, Nick of Diamonds, Lennox Lewis, Gem Twist, or any of the others upon whose backs she has ridden to greatness. For those of us who know Leslie, we all benefit from her love of the sport. As for her horses, they receive the best gift of all—her love for them as individuals.

Rider of the AGA Horse of the Year, Gem Twist

AGA Rider of the Year

Two Queen Elizabeth II Grand Prix wins at Spruce Meadows

Leslie Burr Howard
& S'Blieft

2005: Chrysler Classic Derby Champion at Spruce Meadows

2005: Animal Planet Sport Horse Cup at the Syracuse Sport Horse Invitational

1999: Team Silver medalist at the Pan American Games

1998: Runner-up at the $100,000 Budweiser/ American Invitational, Tampa

1997: Recipient of the Whitney Stone Cup Award

1997: Du Maurier Ltd. International Grand Prix at Spruce Meadows

1996: Team Silver medalist at the Atlanta Olympics

1986: World Cup champion, Gothenburg

1984: Team Gold medalist at the Los Angeles Olympics

CH. 19

Judy Garofalo Torres & Oliver

Many of us can look back to a favorite animal—the dog who was always with us when we were playing, the cat we snuggled with and told our secrets to, or the pony who opened up the whole new world of riding for us. For Judy Garofalo Torres, that special animal was Oliver. For ten years, this special horse was her partner, her confidante, and her horse to ride whenever the rides on other mounts were difficult. Oliver is a Swedish warmblood stallion whose breeding is Irco Marco (the same as Leslie Burr Howard's famous speed horse Nick of Diamonds). Oliver was Judy's loyal Grand Prix champion. He was, to quote the song, "the wind beneath her wings."

BOB LANGRISH MBE, EQUESTRIAN PHOTOGRAPHER
Judy and Oliver, a lifelong love affair, here in action.

213

Most competitive riders get their start as early as age six. They learn to ride the ponies, go up the levels as juniors, and finally become adult jumpers. Getting to the Grand Prix level takes the right combination of experience and opportunity, as well as an extra special horse. Judy Garofalo had a lot of catching up to do when she started riding competitively at age 17. Growing up in Long Island, she had taken riding lessons and had competed in local shows. When a friend introduced her to the famed Olympian Leslie Howard, she was hooked. Judy trained intensely with Leslie for eight years, sometimes riding a half dozen horses a day. She loved riding with Leslie, who put a great deal of effort into training Judy and helping her progress to the adult jumper classes. Five years after Judy started working with Leslie Howard, she was riding in her first Grand Prix—yet another testimonial to Leslie's skills as a teacher and trainer.

After some successes on other Grand Prix horses, Judy was ready for a horse of her own. She and Leslie made the trip to Sweden to try a few horses owned by Svante Johansson. She describes the memory of finding Oliver with some irony. "It was funny because at Svante's farm, you had to go out of his barn and walk down a street to get to the ring. They were riding Oliver to the ring for us to see, and suddenly, two mares from somewhere in town, not Svante's farm, got loose and ran up behind Oliver. Here he was, a stallion with two mares chasing him down

Oliver had a short stride. Judy learned she almost always had to add a stride when riding him to the jumps. When other riders measured five strides, she would measure six strides. That **little anomaly** made a **big difference** on the day Leslie Howard and Judy tried Oliver for the first time.

the street. He was looking quite wild at the time, and I did not know if I could handle it."

Judy describes how on that first day, "Leslie rode him and jumped a combination, but did not walk it. When she tried to jump it, Leslie and Oliver fell down. It was so dramatic! It was awful! The jump was set at the wrong distance. When they put the jump back up, Leslie walked the proper distance and got back on. They came back to the jump and without stopping or spooking, Oliver went over perfectly. At the end of the trial, Leslie said, 'Okay, we're buying this horse,' and I said, 'Why? He's crazy, he's wild, he just fell down,' and Leslie said, 'No, he is perfect.' I owe all of the credit of finding Oliver to Leslie. He was the selection of a lifetime." What Leslie saw was a horse with enough heart to pick himself up off the ground and gallop back to a jump where he had just fallen.

Judy competed with Oliver in Holland before bringing him home to Leslie's barn in Connecticut. A partnership and bond was formed. When she brought him home, the learning curve began in earnest. "He was a fantastic horse from the beginning. I knew how to jump a big jump, but I did not know how to put it together with the balance needed."

In the early days, nobody realized what a powerhouse Oliver could be. Everybody thought that he was quiet and easy-going. In fact, he had a great deal of energy, and, when she was training with Leslie, Judy would ride him for 45 minutes before a class.

At Leslie's barn, Oliver gradually took the place of a couple of older Grand Prix horses Judy had shown previously. She fondly remembers the fantastic Montrachet. Oliver was Judy's first competitive horse. The 16-hand bay appeared to be small, almost pony-sized in his stall. Even though Oliver was on the shorter side, he was built like a weightlifter: fit, very compact, and powerful. Being small in stature herself, Judy and Oliver were well-matched.

THE OTHER MAN IN JUDY'S LIFE

Though Oliver has always been the main man in Judy's life, he made room for Judy's husband, who came along several years later. While Oliver is jealous of other horses, he does not seem to mind Judy's husband, Pedro Torres. Pedro has ridden on the Grand Prix circuit, but is now too busy serving as President and CEO of Millbrook Ventures. He occasionally rides Oliver to exercise him in the field. Pedro brings a great deal of riding experience, and he understands what it means to have a horse of Oliver's caliber.

THE MAIN MAN IN THE BARN

Oliver had done a few national Grand Prix classes in Sweden with Svante and some derbies. Judy knew he was going to be a good first Grand Prix horse for her but did not realize he was going to be a great international horse. Judy rode Oliver over a period of ten years in the Grand Prix ring. Not many people can say they rode a horse at the top level for that many years. Oliver was consistent; he jumped well and was happy in the game of show jumping.

Oliver wanted to be ridden in the big classes, even when Judy had other plans. One time, Judy thought she would give Oliver a break and do the smaller classes with Priobert, also a fantastic horse. Oliver performed poorly when Judy rode him in the lesser classes after Priobert. Oliver had done one or two of the smaller classes, when Priobert's career ended suddenly because of an injury. Oliver went back to being the main man in the barn after that.

Oliver was always best at the big shows and the big occasions. "Oliver loved a horse show and is much happier when he has to put his mind to work," Judy says. "At home in the fields, Oliver does not pay attention, and he is all over the place, but at horse shows, he knows his job and is a perfect gentleman," according to Judy.

"He taught me a great deal in big classes. In one Grand Prix, I remember everyone I had worked with jumped in a certain class, and there was a wide water jump at B of the triple. All these riders were experienced jumpers, and they were falling off! I went in with Oliver, and he made the water jump without a twitch."

Judy knows she has Oliver to thank for it. You might say he put the polish on her riding.

Judy would always start her day riding Oliver. "Every day I woke up and executed Oliver's plan," she says. "I learned from Lauren Hough to have a plan for the year as to what I was going to do with my horse." In Florida, she tried to ride Oliver outside the ring as much as possible and would take him on the trails along the canals. When Judy would ride him at home, he always preferred the morning. If she rode others before him, he would be screaming in his stall and pacing back and forth. He wanted to work first. He did not want to get turned out first.

> What Judy learned from Oliver gave her a new edge for competing at the Grand Prix level. **He boosted her solidly into the elite tiers of the sport.**

TAKING IT UP TO THE NEXT LEVEL

Their consistent performances inched them up the computer list and qualified them for the 2004 Olympic trials. A number of good riders were going to the trials in California, but Judy decided to back off. "That would not have been good for Oliver. There would have been too many big jumps in a row, and it would not have been fair to him," she notes. Instead, they had the honor of riding in the Samsung Super Leagues for the U.S. Equestrian Team.

JACQUELINE KNUTSON

Handsome Oliver retired and living the life at home.

Judy toured all over Europe, and it was like a dream come true for her. "It was amazing and a lot of fun. I'm very happy to have had that under my belt," she says.

True to his nature, Oliver's tendency to be silly outside the show ring gave those who did not know him some doubts when Judy and Oliver were training at Olympic Chef d'Equipe, Henk Nooren's farm. When they were schooling, Oliver was acting up and not paying attention. Oliver did not want to practice. Henk formed his own impressions after he saw the horse knock down some jumps. But at La Baule, the first Grand Prix on the Samsung Super League tour, Judy and Oliver were clear, and America was third at the Nations Cup. When they came back, Henk confessed he had been really nervous because he did not know if Oliver could jump that class. Obviously, he could jump at that level when it counted.

OLIVER PUTS HIS FOOT DOWN

They competed heavily on the East Coast of the U.S., sometimes every week, consistently without injury. Only once did Judy worry that Oliver may have had a serious problem. "It was a funny thing that happened when we were in Florida one year," she recalls. "He was such a good horse. He always tried to do the right thing. One day, there was a skinny white wall that was cutout underneath and with a blue cap or line on the top of the wall. We had been riding three or four years by then, and I was training with Lauren Hough. We went in the class, and all of the sudden, Oliver stopped at the wall. I could not believe it. In a million years, he had never stopped at anything. We came back again, and he stopped again. Oliver never does that. He just said, 'No! I'm not doing it!' He did not go up to it and slam on the brakes; he just stopped as he was coming out of the corner and did not want to go forward, or anywhere close to the wall in question. We came out of the class, and I was convinced he was sick. For three weeks, we did all this testing. We thought Oliver was tying up, and everybody wanted to make sure he was okay [a horse tying up is an expression used when a horse has muscular cramps due to lactic acid build-up and is unable to perform]. This was the first time in his life he had done anything bad."

All sorts of blood tests were conducted over a couple of weeks. Judy babied him and had no idea he was just being a horse who simply did not want to jump the skinny wall. It was the only thing he did not want to jump—a wall that has no standards and a cutout underneath. It is scary because the horse can see through it. It is the only jump Oliver ever objected to on the Grand Prix circuit. That is an amazing thing, given some of the scary jumps I have seen Judy and Oliver accomplish at Spruce Meadows. After this incident, whenever Judy approached a similar jump with Oliver, she had to encourage him a bit more. Otherwise, Oliver was a perfect jumper over water jumps and derby banks. He was totally reliable.

The Super League tour in 2008 went to Rome and then Lucerne, and though that was supposed to be the last competition for Judy and Oliver, they were asked to stay on. They went to Rotterdam with the team, then Hickstead, Dublin, Falsterbo, and Barcelona. There are eight competitions in the Super League, and the only one they did not compete in was Aachen. "It was the dream of a lifetime," Judy says. "I was young, and it was so exciting. I never in a million years thought I'd be where I was, competing with the people on my team—the people I looked up to my whole life. I hope to get back there one day. But I've got to find the right horse that I think will get me there."

STILL SHOWING AT 19

In 2009, Judy and Oliver showed at the CN International,

Whenever they had a rail or two down, Judy says, "It was my mistake. I'm so grateful to Oliver that he didn't hold it against me. We got better as a team. **He trusted me, and I trusted him.** He could jump clean the biggest Grand Prix in the world. Oliver was not the fastest horse, but he was fantastic."

a hotly contested million dollar class. They were clean in the exciting first round. At the Hampton Classic in 2009, they were double clean. Riding at the famed show grounds on Long Island had been a dream for Judy as a child. Oliver had taken her to the Hampton Classic in 2006, where they captured 6th place at the Grand Prix. Oliver loved jumping off the grass. The Grand Prix in 2009 was to be even more memorable. At the advanced age of 19, Oliver showed how magnificent a horse can be when he rode in this class against Olympic gold medalists McLain Ward and Sapphire.

It was with some awe and reverence that Judy walked the course with McLain Ward. When McLain suggested she do five strides after the water jump to the combination there, she automatically factored for Oliver's short stride and said, "No, I'll have to do six." Then, Judy says, "McLain looked at me and said, 'Do five.' I said okay." Even though she knew Oliver jumps well off of a short stride, she took McLain's advice and did the five strides. To her amazement, they ended up in the jump-off with the world-renowned McLain Ward and Sapphire.

McLain has that kind of genius. He had never ridden Oliver, but from casual observation, he gave her the right advice. It was an unforgettable moment. It was only McLain and Judy in the jump-off. "I had a plan to go around nicely and make Oliver jump a double clear and be happy with that." In Judy's mind, there was no way they could beat McLain and Sapphire. Judy thought Sapphire probably had double the size of Oliver's stride and twice the experience. Judy was happy and content to be where she was (and she had a nice check for her efforts, too!).

OLIVER RETIRES

Judy and her barn manager and head groom, Maggie Mulligan, decided in late summer of 2010 that Oliver should retire. Maggie came to work for Judy about two years after Judy acquired Oliver. She helps Judy with all the horses and ponies at Higher Ground Farm in Millbrook, New York to ensure that they are in top performance condition.

Maggie also had a lot to do with another special horse that held the record for the longest career, For the Moment, who belonged to Lisa Jacquin and retired at 21. Maggie had worked for Michael Matz, the Olympic show jumper who now has Thoroughbred race horses. Michael has launched his new career with derby contenders like the famous Barbaro.

Few horses have had such a long Grand Prix career as Oliver has. At age 20, Oliver was still winning in the Grand Prix ring. The first time Judy had to plan her day without Oliver was very difficult for her.

Judy had always planned her work around Oliver. Where

"It may sound ridiculous, but I have known Oliver longer than I have known my husband. **My whole life revolved around Oliver for ten years**, as to what Grand Prix I was going to and where I was going to spend my summers."

her customers were going and what her other horses were doing all revolved around this one special horse.

Judy knew it was the right time to retire Oliver, but it was a very strange experience. In the last summer that they showed, they won the Giorgio Armani Welcome Stake at the 2010 Vermont Summer Festival. The famous duo of Judy Garofalo and Oliver went out on a high note.

Not long after that victory in Vermont, Judy came down with Lyme disease and had to abruptly end her 2010 summer season. The decision to let Oliver have a rest and step away from the show scene was appropriate. Judy began recuperating from the debilitating illness but remained uncertain about her health. As she gradually got better, she prepared for the winter season in Florida. She and Maggie decided to leave Oliver in New York as they headed south with the rest of the horses. She says it was agonizing to go to her first show without him. She was unsure of how Oliver would react to watching her and the other horses leave without him and not having Judy around every day.

Not long after retiring Oliver, Judy decided to have him checked out. She had the veterinarian, Amy Rabbanol, take a scanned image of his legs to see how they looked. Judy never had him scanned before. Many riders have their horse's legs scanned due to injuries or suspicious lameness. The vet told Judy that Oliver had the legs of a young horse—very clean and no issues. It was a rewarding discovery for Judy, who had babied Oliver through the ten years and spared nothing to ensure he was in good shape.

CHASING THE BUTTERFLY

Judy has a favorite story to tell about her partner: "When I decided last year I was going to retire Oliver, we put him in the paddock right outside the window of my house. I looked out and saw that he was running around the paddock, and

I was not sure what he was doing. I thought maybe he wanted to come inside or maybe he was disturbed because I was concerned he would be unhappy about not going to the shows. It really bothered me. He was not racing around, just running back and forth. I thought to myself, what is he doing?" She went out to investigate, as all horse owners do when a horse starts running. Judy says, "Then I saw a little yellow butterfly. Oliver was chasing the butterfly in the paddock! How a big animal like that could be having fun with a butterfly in his turnout was surreal. It is not like me to think of it like that; I'm not really emotional—it was just so nice to see, and it made me laugh." The butterfly episode gave Judy the assurance to go on and do her first competitions without Oliver, knowing he was happy at home.

Oliver is now the chief stallion in residence at Higher Ground Farm. Being a stallion, Oliver has the potential to have offspring that may exhibit some of his traits. As of this writing, Judy was looking forward to having his second foal on the ground in September 2011, and she plans to keep this one. Now that he is older, Oliver has grown into his stallion personality. He loves people and his mares at the farm. At the shows, Oliver was never crazy with the mares. He was always polite and respectful, but tuned into Judy while ignoring everything else.

Today, back at the farm, he has a lot of energy and is always looking for his mares to see that each one is accounted for. Judy remembers her favorite competitive moments with Oliver, and nobody can ever take away from them what they earned together: love, respect, admiration, and gratitude. Those are the sentiments that run through Judy's mind every day because Oliver is still first in her morning routine even if it is only a fond memory flitting through her mind like that little yellow butterfly.

Represented the USET in the Samsung Super League Nations Cups

Entered the Grand Prix Rankings and qualified for her first World Cup at age 21

5th place at the $50,000 EMO Grand Prix, Saugerties

Judy Garofalo Torres & Oliver

Member of multiple USET Nations Cup Teams

2010: Winner of the Giorgio Armani Welcome Stakes Class at the Vermont Summer Festival

2010: 3rd place at the $30,000 Vermont Summer Festival Grand Prix

2009: 3rd place at the $50,000 Garden State Grand Prix, New Jersey

2009: 2nd place in the $250,000 World Cup Qualifier Grand Prix at the Hampton Classic

2009: Winner of the For the Moment Open jump-off at the Pennsylvania National Horse Show, Harrisburg

Kent Farrington & Up Chiqui

HUMBLE BEGINNINGS

Over the years, I have had a lot of exposure to Kent Farrington, who has not only been a very regular supporter of the Fidelity Investments Jumper Classic, but has also been the singularly most decorated Grand Prix winner there, with three victories to his credit coming in 2006, 2007, and 2009. My exposure to Kent is not exclusively based on my management role in this horse show—it is because of his naturally welcoming demeanor that I've had a lot of chances to chat with Kent at various venues around the circuit. Kent is an open book, a gentleman, and a great ambassador for show jumping.

Bob Langrish MBE, Equestrian Photographer
Uceko and Kent on course at the Fidelity Jumper Classic.

Kent began riding at the age of eight in downtown Chicago in a stable that ran horse carriage rides. As his next step, Kent joined a small pony club filled with young riders, and, after experiencing success there, he progressed to the show jumping circuit shortly thereafter. Kent did not have the sport handed to him with an endless string of horses at his disposal during his junior career, but rather he developed a reputation as a young rider willing to hop on anything and improve upon an often difficult horse's collective experience and resulting demeanor. Kent's mom spent a big part of her days driving him out of the city to the barn, where she would patiently wait while Kent would ride several horses per visit, under the watchful eye of Nancy Whitehead. Kent was not picky; he rode whatever he could, and from a very early age, his commitment to excellence and hard work was apparent. Kent's work ethic remains very much intact today. You can call Kent at daybreak, he answers every time, and he is always at work.

HIS ROAD TO SUCCESS

Like so many other serious riders, Kent followed his early training with a classical equitation foundation early in his riding career. Kent got a serious taste of success during his equitation career when he won the Washington International Equitation Medal in 1999 and the equally notable Pessoa National Equitation Medal in 1998.

His winning ways continued when he competed at the Washington International Junior Jumper Championship. That milestone was followed by a Team Gold medal at the North American Young Riders Championship in 1999.

Kent turned professional very early by most standards. One of his first big wins came in 2004 with his then-partner, Madison, a spectacular mare, at the $75,000 EMO Grand Prix in Saugerties, New York. Madison was named the AGA

(American Grand Prix Association) Horse of the Year in 2005 and in 2006. Amazingly, this was followed by consecutive USEF (United States Equestrian Federation) Grand Prix Horse of the Year titles in the same years. Shortly after Madison's remarkable winning streak, Kent's career took off at a velocity seldom seen in a sport where a lifetime of training is required to obtain the consistency in performances that have been the blue print of Kent's success.

Kent credits much of his success in show jumping to the people who have helped him along the way. Early in Kent's professional development, he worked with Olympian Leslie Howard, a master teacher and rider. Kent was also mentored by British Olympian Tim Grubb. Leslie Howard fondly remembers how Kent was always extraordinarily anxious to learn anything and everything and how he never balked at any job she had for him within the business. Kent told me he never worried much about what he was being paid early in his career because he was far more focused on the learning opportunities. Before long, Kent established his own farm and business.

THE FORMATION OF A NEW PARTNERSHIP

Following his early success with Madison, Kent formed a critical partnership with a smaller chestnut gelding known as Up Chiqui.

> Kent and this athletic speed demon quickly developed a winning partnership and have **won more than 40 Grand Prix classes** together since 2005.

In the 2007 competitive season, they were all but unbeatable and finished off that year winning the National Show Jumping Championships. Kent and his copper-colored partner were part of Team USA, twice in 2008, once in the

Up Chiqui and Kent on course at the 2011 Winter Equestrian Festival in Florida.

World Cup Finals in Sweden and then again as part of the winning Nations Cup U.S. team in Wellington, Florida.

Kent and Up Chiqui won four World Cup-qualifying Grand Prix classes in 2009, leading the East Coast World Cup League and punching their ticket to what would be a second World Cup appearance for the United States in 2009.

To put Kent's talent into perspective, it is important to reiterate that at this point, Kent and Up Chiqui had 40 Grand

Prix victories. Their success came so incredibly quickly that even the most seasoned pros were surprised by it. There are very few combinations in the history of show jumping that have so frequently visited the winner's circle.

Kent describes the beloved Up Chiqui as **"A TOTAL PRANKSTER."**

Up Chiqui's playful demeanor also made their partnership unique. As Kent explains, "You might be headed toward the first fence, and he may rear up and spin around." This made Kent very aware of where the entry timers were in any competition as a way of avoiding elimination. "It's not that he was ever scared, but more of a clown, always playful. In the barn, his demeanor is like a Jack Russell Terrier; he bites, pins his ears, bangs against the bars of his stall." Kent tells me Up Chiqui bites at him almost every time he mounts him. Kent recounts all of this with amusement and affection, utterly devoid of the slightest hint of frustration or concern. After all, Up Chiqui's aggresive behavior is, to some degree, all an act. I remember trying to pin Up Chiqui with the blue ribbon one year at the Fidelity, and he pinned his ears at me. Up Chiqui could easily have left his teeth marks if he wanted, but it was, as Kent says, just the equine clown coming out.

THE 2011 AMERICAN INVITATIONAL

In early 2011, Kent added what might be the biggest win of his career to date when he and Uceko, a spectacular dappled grey, won the American Invitational. The American Invitational is to show jumping what the Super Bowl is to football. Gene Mische named it the Invitational for a reason—you cannot just show up and take your turn. It is the

TONY DE COSTA

Kent and Up Chiqui victorious at the Fidelity Jumper Classic, a hat trick for Kent.

only class in the United States where riders are not charged any entry fee. This was a field of the 30 best North American and international combinations doing battle for $200,000 in prize money and serious bragging rights. In addition to the fierce competitors, the course was also a force to be reckoned with. As Steve Stephens, the course designer, tells me, "I want riders to gulp when they walk this course; it needs to be as big a test as they ever face—[that's what] makes this class truly special." Kent emerged victorious.

Kent laid down a blistering pace in the jump-off, fully aware of who was coming behind him: show jumping heavyweights Ian Millar, McLain Ward, and Margie Engle. Kent later confirmed that he lost his stirrup with four fences left to go in the jump-off and somehow managed to ride on balance with only one foot in the irons. Despite adverse circumstances, Kent finished the short trek in an astonishing 36.34 seconds. Even McLain Ward, following on the lightning-fast Rothchild, finished behind Kent in 37.84 seconds, Ian Millar took the third spot with Star Power, and Margie Engle placed two seconds behind him.

Though it may be hard to believe, Kent's mount for that night, Uceko, had missed most of the last season with a collateral ligament injury. Clearly, the Dutch-bred dappled grey was back in prime condition.

THE FARRINGTON EXPRESS ROLLS ON

Shortly after racking up the biggest win of his career to date in Tampa, Kent and his stable of horses made the trip to Lexington, Kentucky for the Spring Classic series held in the incredible Kentucky Horse Park. There have been a number of headlines written about what happened next, but my favorite was sportswriter Kenney Krauss's column where he eloquently entitled the Kentucky Spring Shows as the "Farrington Express Rolling On." As of this writing, Kent has won four Grands Prix in a row with Uceko, beginning in Tampa and culminating with the $55,000 Mary Rena Murphy Grand Prix. I can't remember another time this has happened.

Ian Millar, who finished alongside Farrington in these same classes, jokingly tells me, "Kent is a wonderful talent and a great credit to our sport, but he is fast becoming a serious pain to deal with in these jump-offs." This is an aspect of our sport I truly love; everybody I've talked to is excited and happy for Kent even when they can't help adding a bit of ribbing. Not many sports boast that kind of camaraderie.

NOT JUST A HOT STREAK

While Kent's story would still be interesting if his success were attributed to a hot streak, it is his sheer talent that makes his story truly remarkable. At this point in his career, Kent has amassed more than 75 Grand Prix wins. While legends like McLain, Margie, Ian, and Leslie have experienced more visible results, few others in the show jumping circuit will ever experience the kind of superhuman success that Kent has. Kent Farrington's winning percentage is positively off-the-charts—he simply wins more often than he loses, and in a sport with so much room for error, this is rare indeed. It took some serious pestering on my part to convince Kent to let me tell his story in the pages of this book; he felt less deserving than his mentors in the sport.

Kent's humility is even more admirable when we list his seemingly innumerable successes. This is a rider that has scored two AGA Horse of the Year titles consecutively, won the Grand Prix of Devon, the American Invitational, back-to-back victories in the Prix de Penn National, has been a World Cup League winner, won the Fidelity Grand Prix three times, and won the President's Cup Grand Prix in Washington, D.C., the EMO Grand Prix of Ocala, in addition to many more. You

BOB LANGRISH MBE
EQUESTRIAN PHOTOGRAPHER

Kent and "The Prankster," a.k.a. Up Chiqui, attack another monster track.

have to take a large breath to recite Kent's victories in a single sentence—imagine the effort required to accomplish all of them. Kent and McLain Ward are the youngest riders to reach over a million dollars in winnings.

While it has been my intention throughout the course of this book to showcase the value of hard work when combined with talent, Kent is quick to point out that he has not achieved his success solely by his own efforts. He acknowledges the role Andre Dignelli played during the equitation phase of his training, and later when Kent ventured out on his own, Andre helped him start his business. Kent insisted on recognizing his owners, starting with the McNerney family (who own part of Up Chiqui as well as Valhalla, Zasira, and a new, young horse so recently acquired that the horse is yet to be named). Kent also extends his gratitude to the R.C.G. Farm, the owners of Uceko, who is a part of the Gay family operation and is looked after by the Gay family's equestrian daughters, Lara and Summer. He would also like to thank Craig Dobbs and the lovely Boone family, who complete the syndicate behind Up Chiqui. Alex Warriner, Kent's barn manager, has been an integral part of Kent's operation for nearly a decade. Kent makes it clear to me that he couldn't enjoy the success he now does without the help of people like Alex behind his operation.

While this factor is indeed out of our control, much of any **DREAM** is based on and controlled by the **PASSION** and **EFFORT** that propels it.

ON THE HORIZON

What's next for Kent? Kent will take a shot at the USET's Pan American team and the Olympic selection trials for London 2012, but only time will tell if he succeeds this time around. Kent doesn't think Uceko has any upper limits, so it becomes a question of remaining healthy and prepared. Kent comments, "The bittersweet truth is injuries happen to both riders and horses, and to some degree that part of the sport is out of our control."

As I sat and talked to Kent, he was preparing to head off to Europe, returning next for the summer Spruce Meadows tournament in Calgary, Canada. He has again tasted victory. Kent has undeniable talent and experience, but he has also star quality—that special champion ingredient that is hard to define and even harder to come by.

Two-time winner of the U.S. Open, the only CSIO five star, first on Madison, second time on Up Chiqui

Member of four Nations Cup USA teams

2011: American Invitational Grand Prix Winner

Kent Farrington
&Up Chiqui

2010: Winner at the New Albany Classic on Up Chiqui

2008: Winner at the $100,000 Upperville Grand Prix

2007, 2008: Winner at the Harrisburg Grand Prix

2006, 2007, 2009: Winner at the Fidelity Jumper Classic Grands Prix

2005: Winner at the Grand Prix, Devon

2005: Presidents Cup Grand Prix, Washington, D.C.

2004, 2005: Two consecutive AGA Horse of the Year titles on Madison

est d... Pferdesports

Ch. 15

Beezie Madden & Authentic

I first met Beezie and her husband John Madden when this dynamic duo helped me acquire a horse named Kobalt. Kobalt proved to be a spitfire of a Dutch Warmblood and quite a character. Oddly enough, these qualities also describe John and Beezie Madden. Based in Cazenovia, New York, John is the business end of John Madden Sales (JMS) and Beezie the Olympic show jumper. John has the more spitfire personality of the pair, while Beezie leaves her mark in the ring.

Beezie began riding at the age of three or four, having come by her interest naturally since her parents owned show horses. When she was six years old, her parents acquired her first pony, a cute hairball with the typical pony mind—a bit

---

of a brat. Beezie vividly remembers this first pony coming into her life. She continued to ride and became more serious during her school years. During high school, she was juggling schoolwork while competing on the Florida show jumping circuit. At that time, Florida was not the epicenter of winter equestrian sport, that it is today. Beezie went to college in Virginia and graduated as valedictorian.

> In my experience, high performing people achieve in all aspects of their life, and **Beezie is no exception to that rule.**

John and Beezie first met in 1987 at a horse show. John was apparently impressed with her talent and she went to work for him shortly after they met. Eleven years later, they were married, and they remain one of the sport's consummate teams. Beezie is the rider and teacher. John is the trainer, handles all of the business operations, and also teaches.

I've had a few lessons with John, who is a task master. At my first lesson, he laid down the rules which were specific and colorful. One of the Madden commandments was, "I talk, you listen. Do you understand?" I enthusiastically replied, "Yes, sir," which came quite naturally for me as an ex-Marine. John's response when I failed to follow any of his commandments was, "That will cost you a dollar." Monetary penalties for other infractions followed and became a great source of humor for John.

Beezie made her first Grand Prix appearance in 1985. Eight years later she was named the United States Olympic Committee's Female Equestrian of the Year. This recognition came shortly after Beezie led the United States Equestrian Team (USET) to back-to-back Nations Cup wins at the Washington International Horse Show and the National Horse Show. She also won the American Gold Cup, the Grand Prix of Rochester, the Grand Prix de Penn National at Harrisburg, and the Grand Prix of the I Love New York Horse Show.

HOW TEAM MADDEN DISCOVERED AUTHENTIC

Johan Heins, John's longtime business partner who was his eyes and ears on the ground in Europe, found Authentic and brought him to John's attention. Johan is a world-class rider in his own right. John got on the phone and put a call in to Elizabeth Busch Burke, and together with John Madden Sales, they purchased him. Later when Bud was nine years old, and just before the Olympic trials, the syndicate was expanded, but Elizabeth and John Madden Sales remained part owners. The larger syndicate included such generous and important owners as the Pattons, the Jacobs family, and the Wolf families, as well as Elizabeth Busch Burke and John Madden Sales's direct investment. Elizabeth Busch's heritage as the patron of the Anheuser Busch or Budweiser enterprise led to Authentic's endearing barn name, Bud.

His barn name Bud suits his personality. You can almost picture him with a "Bud" in hand. John has jokingly remarked, **"He sort of walks like he might have had one or two too many."**

THE 2004 OLYMPICS IN ATHENS

Beezie entered her first Olympic games in Athens, Greece, in 2004 and was part of the winning gold medal U.S. team along with McLain Ward, Chris Kappler, and Peter Wylde. Few folks ever get to the Olympics at all. How many bring

Gretchen Almy

Beezie and Bud.

home gold on their first Olympic appearance?

The Olympic trials were interesting. Another one of John and Beezie's horses, De Silvio, was in the lead, going into the last segment of the trials. Unfortunately, he was injured in the second-to-last trial, and his Olympic dream ended. At this time, Authentic was sitting in fourth position. Beezie persevered with Bud. They had to come from behind to qualify. With the pressure on, Beezie and Bud jumped clear, in fact double clear, putting in two flawless rounds on the last day of the trials. In the end, Bud was two rails better than any other horse in the trials.

Every little girl who dreams of show jumping has dreamed of being Beezie Madden. Team Madden, Clark Shipley, Bud's longtime caregiver, John, and a host of other supporters boarded the jumbo jet for the test of a lifetime. Imagine the excitement, the anticipation, and the awesome responsibility of carrying your team and your nation's hopes and dreams into competition against the world's best show jumpers. John's and Beezie's parents had followed them to Athens. Like everybody sitting in the Olympic stadium at the opening ceremonies, they were thrilled to hear the Olympic anthem for the first time and filled with anticipation and pride.

TRAGEDY STRIKES!

After the horses arrived and the training began, just 24 hours before the opening round, tragedy strikes Team Madden: Bud is sick! He was thrashing around in his stall, not behaving like himself at all. A call was sent out early in the morning from Clark Shipley to John and Beezie, who arrived within minutes to witness Bud obviously in stages of intestinal distress. The equine digestive track is clearly a weak link and every equestrian's worst fear.

If Team Madden is forced to aid Bud with a routine dose of Banamine (horse aspirin) in an attempt to relieve his discomfort and arrest the situation, Authentic will be banned from Olympic competition. The dream will be forever shattered. Bud is adjacent to the veterinary facilities needed for emergency surgery. If surgery is required, Team USA as a whole will be affected. The alternate will show in Beezie's place, shattering all of their dreams. Particularly Beezie's.

John, Clark, and Beezie try hand walking Bud, having him lunge on a small circle and jump a few shavings bags in an attempt to end the colic. Nothing works. Hours pass. The moment when the Olympic horses need to appear before the officials for what is known as the jog is fast approaching. The jog is an official demonstration of horses in hand trotting to allow a visual inspection of their fitness and health. A horse in the midst of colic cannot complete the jog with success.

John and Beezie were filled with stress and alarm, thinking about the nightmare they were living through. John thought of his aging mother's journey to Athens, Beezie's parents, and all of the owners in the Madden syndicate, sitting in the Olympic stadium on the edge of their seats. None of them were aware of the drama being played out in the stabling area. It looked more and more like the end of the dream.

Two hours before they were to report for the jog, Team Madden was forced to think of Bud's life first and foremost; clearly, he was their priority. From the start of the crisis, Bud was put on the intravenous fluids, which are allowed in competition. He was never given any form of drugs of any kind. The big decision in the end was simply to take him for another walk and let him roll. A horse in colic distress always wants to roll, but it can make it better or further entangle the intestine, requiring immediate surgical intervention in such cases. John and Beezie took Authentic out of the stable into the sunshine of the warm Athens day for a moment of reflection and peace. Walking horses in colic is typically called for and provides some comfort. Tears streamed down Beezie's face. John was also terribly upset.

Bud – On a Roll

About this time, Bud decided to lie down, frightening John and Beezie further. This is not a good sign. Bud began to roll. He rolled left, then he rolled right, then he flipped all the way over from side-to-side and suddenly sat halfway up. Bud looked at John and Beezie and exhibited a rousing and audible demonstration of flatulence, leapt to his feet, and shook hard. Minutes later a completely at-ease Authentic is standing ready to lead the team into the Olympic Games. Minutes from disaster, the Olympic dream is rekindled. Team Madden, with one typically cocky nine-year-old Dutch gelding, proceeds to the jog and is declared good to go.

Game on. Bring on the world.

Bud's opening Olympic round was flawless, one of only a few horses at the Olympic Games to post a zero on the score card. His first clear round was day one, earning him the anchor position for the Nations Cup the next day. Authentic posted two more clear rounds on day two in the Nations Cup, and Team USA earned the silver medal. The Germans won the gold.

The German team was later stripped of the gold medal when a German horse tested positive for a banned substance. Equine testing can pick up miniscule trace amounts of any number of banned substances. These determinations can be less clear-cut than the performance-enhancing drugs in human sports. Either way, innocent or not, intentional or not, the German controversy left the United States in undisputed possession of Olympic Gold in show jumping for the first time in many years. Show jumping had, for decades, been dominated by the Europeans, specifically the German and Dutch teams, but that has since changed.

In recounting their experience at their first Olympic games, John explained what the gold medal meant: "Authentic's owners and caregivers raised this horse and went through years of preparation intent, not on money, but on medals. This is what we worked and planned for. Bud's career was designed for the minutes he would spend in two Olympic rings for an entire nation. Not for me, Beezie, or his owners, but for his country." It is rare to find this special kind of dedication; country and team first, personal gain deferred.

> Show jumping desperately needs the sponsorship of **owners with stature and dedication.** Abigail Wexner brings these qualities to the sport.

MEDALS WIN OVER MONEY

Following the Olympics in Greece, offers were made to purchase the quirky Dutch gelding for millions of dollars. Abigail Wexner purchased Bud outright, ensuring that he would stay with Beezie and John and continue to compete for Team USA.

Bud won two cars, an Audi and a Mercedes, for his owners, along with impressive sums of prize money. However Authentic himself and the team that supports him are more impressive than the toys or the cash. As John Madden put it, "Luxury hood emblems are nice, but they can never compete with the feeling of an Olympic medal."

THE 2006 WORLD EQUESTRIAN GAMES

Beezie, Clark, John, and the cast of supporting characters headed to Aachen for the World Equestrian Games (WEG) to once again represent Team USA in quest of medals.

BOB LANGRISH MBE
EQUESTRIAN PHOTOGRAPHER

Beezie in action at Spruce Meadows on another of her famous mounts.

Much like the Olympics, the WEG takes place every four years. Its importance is second only to the Olympics. To say Bud rose to new levels of perfection during the WEG is an understatement. During the week of the team and individual competitions, Beezie and Authentic posted ten clear rounds. Their winning streak was absolute perfection in this sport where the technical difficulty is extreme. Their consistently flawless performance was beyond anyone's imagination.

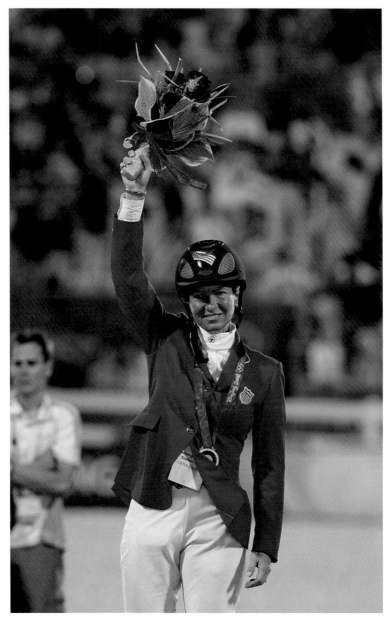

A Beezie Olympic moment.

There is a unique format at the WEG where the point standings during the week from the team competition are totaled and the top four riders are singled out for a process called the Final Four. The riders switch horses and ride someone else's horse over a single course. Bud was fabulous for each rider in the Final Four. The result was a Team Silver for the United States. If that were not enough to punctuate Bud's or Beezie's 2006 performance in Aachen, Beezie won the Individual Silver, faulting only at the last fence in the final jump-off—the only flaw on an otherwise perfect score card that cost the pair Individual Gold.

This team's winning percentage had become unbelievable. In addition to the Olympics, there were two wins at the American Invitational in Tampa and the Grand Prix of Aachen and two wins at famed Spruce Meadows in the renowned Queen Elizabeth Cup. In other words, the more important or momentous the occasion, or the harder the task, the more certain the desired result.

THE 2008 OLYMPICS IN BEIJING

Once again, McLain Ward's mount Sapphire and Bud share the plane ride to Beijing. This time, Team USA is made up of McLain, Will Simpson, Laura Kraut, and Beezie Madden.

In one of the first rounds, Bud was heading to the frightening triple combination, a vertical-oxer-oxer combination. Each element in a triple combination has a maximum of one or two strides between efforts. This makes such a test very difficult, without time for recovery. Suddenly Bud started shaking his head violently from side to side, causing Beezie to lose control and limiting their communication. The pair accumulated faults, the first of Bud's Olympic career. It was later determined that sweat under Bud's ear bonnet, which is worn to deaden the crowd noise, ran into his ear, making him uncomfortable and breaking his concentration. It just goes to show how incredibly sensitive these equine athletes are and how many details can affect the outcome of the sport at this level. There is an expression in football, "On any given Sunday..." that applies equally to show jumping.

Beezie and Bud soldiered on after the sweat-in-the-ear incident, putting in flawless rounds one after another; her teammates, Laura, McLain, and Will did the same. In the ultimate drama, Team USA's second consecutive gold medal is secured by Will Simpson in a final effort that put it in the record books for George Morris, the team's legendary coach, and Team USA.

> A lifetime of sacrifice, falls, broken bones, and shared dedication with the horse of a lifetime
> – Authentic.

This time, Beezie would enjoy the perfect Olympic moment, standing atop the podium on the world's biggest stage, listening to her country's national anthem with an Olympic gold medal around her neck. The story ends with a true fairytale moment. Beezie and Bud also went on to win an Individual Bronze in an exciting jump-off against six other people, including our own McLain and Sapphire.

BUD BECOMES COLLECTIBLE

Since that incredible Olympic moment in Beijing, Authentic has been cast as a Breyer horse. These are lifelike replicas of famous equines that children collect. Breyer is famous for capturing the detailed likeness of the horses they cast. Bud was unveiled in his toy-like Breyer horse form in 2007.

There was a funny moment associated with this process. Bud and his best human buddy and lifetime groom,

GRETCHEN ALMY

Bud with his best friend Clark Shipley.

Renowned Coach John Madden walks a course with Victoria Birdsall (2011).

Clark Shipley, spent an entire day posing for the Breyer photographers as part of the manufacturing process. Clark is a charming big bear of a guy with an ample sense of humor. Clark called John halfway through the photography session, aggravated and confused that he was not central to the photo shoot. He didn't understand how the Clark Shipley action figure was to be cast as part of the collectible set if he was not more obvious in the pictures. Can't you just see Clark brushing the hairs in Bud's mane while flashing his winning smile toward the camera? And maybe even his beloved Harley Davidson motorcycle would be included in the boxed set. Both Bud and Clark are total hams—cameras out, they are on.

I've known Clark for years. He's one of the first people I would ask questions regarding the care of a horse. Clark is also a constant source of positive vibes, just one of those happy people who love they are doing. I've never seen Clark have a bad day, though given the heartbreak that pervades this sport, he has lived with it all.

> One unknown aspect of Bud's animated personality is he gets hiccups. Horses cannot vomit, hence the danger with colic. **They are not supposed to be able to hiccup, but Bud does.** Sounds like a small thing to you or me, but it's comical if not mysterious that Bud is so unusual.

HONORING THE CAREGIVERS

There is an equestrian tradition which spans the Olympic Games, the World Equestrian Games, the World Cup Championships, and all the major venues in the sport. During

253

dal presentations when the riders are on the podium, the caregivers of the horses stand behind them, holding the reins and a bouquet of flowers. They are fully included in that special moment. The caregivers then assist their riders in remounting for the victory gallop following the playing of the champion's national anthem. This protocol is followed for a practical reason. During this drama, the horses are often at their most exuberant, and it takes experience and the presence of their best friends to calm them down. This aspect of the awards ceremony is done consistently with the world over to acknowledge the vital role in the success of the team played by people like Clark Shipley.

I asked Clark how he felt in Athens, in Aachen, and in Beijing. His instinctive and immediate response was, "Amongst the happiest minutes of my life. Emotional in a way I can't describe. Joyous and frozen in time." Clark can recall every second of those minutes, and he is the type of generous human being who would share it with anybody.

Beezie freely admits that while she has had the good fortune to have many incredible mounts, Authentic/Bud is her horse of a lifetime. As Beezie put it to me, "He's special because of his incredible generosity and talent, his courage, and his goofy personality."

Beezie rightly said, "They do the unnatural for us—tens of thousands of miles on airplanes, the work ethic, the crowds, and the quiet moments when Bud will lower his head allowing a young child to pat him while his adrenaline is in overdrive. That gentle touch is anything but the norm." Beezie, John, Team Madden, Bud, and Clark represent the pride of a country and demonstrate to all of us that the difference between ordinary and extraordinary is the level of sacrifice and effort made. It truly boils down to love and devotion. Dreams really do come true in Cazenovia, New York.

The first woman to earn over $1M in prize money

Won the $1M CN International Grand Prix on Judgment

A two-time winner of the Atco Power Queen Elizabeth Cup at Spruce Meadows

Beezie Madden & Authentic

2008: Individual Bronze and Team Gold medalist at the Beijing Olympics

2007: One of only three women to have won the Grand Prix of Aachen

2006: Team and Individual Silver medals at the World Equestrian Games

2004, 2007: Winner of the $200,000 American Invitational on Authentic, Tampa

2004: Team Gold medalist at the Athens Olympics

2003: Team Gold medalist at the Pan American Games

1989: American Grand Prix Association Rider of the Year

CH. 16

Kevin Babington & Carling King

Some people believe in destiny. Irish-born rider Kevin Babington will tell you he believes in destiny as long as you get up and do something to make it happen. The collective opinion of his peers is that he is one of the nicest and hardest-working riders on the East Coast. I've had a lot of fun with Kevin and gotten a fair amount of help from him in the many years that I have known him. Kevin is always in motion. You have to run to catch up. Work ethic and talent rolled into pure energy, with a dash of Irish charm and humility is the best way to describe this man. When I think of Kevin, I'm often reminded of the logo of the Notre Dame Fighting Irish, though Kevin is a bit taller than the little guy on the bumper sticker.

BOB LANGRISH MBE, EQUESTRIAN PHOTOGRAPHER
Kevin and Carling King; you can't build them too big for King.

This characteristic drive has helped Kevin fulfill his destiny with his famous partner Carling King. King was his equal, possessing the same drive, talent, and determination, though with a much-publicized grumpier disposition. In fact, I would describe King as a cross between a horse and a freight train rolling downhill.

My first encounter with Kevin was through a horse deal where I was the purchaser. The horse he sold me was everything he represented the exceptional animal to be and more, and he was poetically Irish as well. I have known Kevin and his wife Dianna for years now, and although I consider them good friends, I was surprised to learn so much about this great partnership and their untold history.

Kevin was born in 1968 in Tipperary, Ireland and grew up in the small river town of Carrick-on-Suir. His family kept horses at a farm in Kerry, but his formal riding career started at the age of nine when his mother signed him up for lessons to prevent him from getting into trouble. As a young lad, he would jump onto the backs of the local "Tinker horses" owned by traveling gypsies. These horses were left loose in the field near the castle on the edge of town until the guard would make the gypsies move on. Kevin saw this as an opportunity to ride. He would jump on the wild horses and ride bareback galloping them across the castle field, and clinging to their manes. With no way to stop them, he would simply jump off when he was ready for a change and get on another one. Dianna has assured me this is a true story.

SEEING A DISTANCE TO A FENCE

There was no Medal Final or American Hunter Pony Champions in his youth; just fox hunting, eventing, riding wild horses, and talent. Talent would carry him across the pond to America and to his destiny with King. His gift for riding initially landed him under the watchful eye of the late,

> Kevin has a
> # GOD-GIVEN ACCURACY
> when it comes to seeing a distance to a fence.

great Irish show jumper Iris Kellet and later with U.S. Olympians Frank and Mary Chapot. Kevin has a God-given accuracy when it comes to seeing a distance to a fence. This is horse language for where to place the horse in front of the jump so it has the best opportunity to deliver the horse and rider safely to the other side without knocking down rails or causing bodily injury. Seeing the distance to a meter 1.50 or 1.60 jump is like placing a basketball in the hoop for an NBA team. Not everyone can do it, and Kevin Babington is one of the best. Kevin has been patient enough to help me a time or two even though I'm sure it's hard for him to understand why the rest of us do not have the same inherent understanding that comes intuitively to him.

By the time King came into his life, Kevin had racked up miles on several national-level Grand Prix horses and even piloted his mount Tornado to National Grand Prix League Horse of the Year in 1994. Still, a superstar partner was missing until Carling King made his trip from Ireland to the U.S. in 1998. King was purchased by Kevin's student Saly Glassman to move up to the high amateur division. When Saly realized she had purchased more than a high amateur horse, she handed the reins to Kevin to see how far Carling King could go. What were the odds of this Irish athlete finding his horse of a lifetime in the form of an Irish Sport Horse?

KING BECOMES CARLING KING

King had humble if not precarious beginnings. He was bred by a physician and sold as a foal at the famous Ballinasloe Fair to a well-known horse dealer, Sean Kenneally. Ballinasloe is a true Irish horse fair. Sean recalled predicting that King, although not named at the time, would be a good jumper because he actually saw him jump over the back of another horse to get to feed. This is abnormal horse behavior, but typical for King.

He was sold as a two-year-old to a partnership that resold him as a three-year-old to a dealer named Sean Buckley. Michael, Buckley's son, rode and developed him until his sale to Saly Glassman. Michael recalled that he wasn't sure what to make of him as a three-year-old. King got a deep laceration on his stifle joint which could have been career-ending, and although he won a three-year-old loose jumping competition sponsored by Carling Beer, hence the name Carling King, he seemed useless as a four-year-old—his debut show resulted in over 20 faults in one class and over 30 in the next. Improvement was quick to show itself, however, when he started to learn to balance himself. He was as strong as a train with a temperament to match, and at the age of five he won the Royal Dublin Society Horse Show Five-Year-Old Championship. This class was later dubbed, and remains today, the Carling King Five-Year-Old Championship.

Not long after the Royal Dublin Show, Michael heard a horrific racket in the back of the trailer one day as he was transporting King to a nearby show. Pulling over, he saw a shipping boot sticking through the rear floor of the trailer. Envisioning the worst, Michael thought King had destroyed his leg by putting his foot through the floor of the moving trailer. As it turned out, the boot was through the floor but King had pulled his leg out and survived the ordeal with only a few scratches. It was a miracle he did not destroy his leg or suffer a serious injury. Soon after, he was jumping meter 1.50 classes, and was sold to Saly Glassman.

GRETCHEN ALMY

Kevin—A quiet moment with a young prospect.

RAW TALENT

The seven-year-old Irish-bred chestnut gelding was formidable and unmannerly, standing 16.3 with a flaxen mane and tail. He would snort like a dragon when he was pondering something. He was large, surly, somewhat green, but most of all, talented beyond anyone's expectations. "He was tough in the early days," Kevin recalls, "tough to flat and tough to hold in the ring to the point that I nearly took out the camera crew at Hickstead one year during a victory gallop. I just couldn't stop him. He was also tough to work around, but he was my partner in every sense of the word. We went through a few grooms—not everyone was able to handle him—but we had a mutual respect and a bond. He always knew we were in it together but he picked his people. You were either in or out with him. Luckily, I was in." I'm not sure how lucky it was to be picked or not; the horse was intimidating.

> King was usually so grouchy that it was a **rare friendly demeanor** that once clued Kevin into the **horse's silent agony.**

In 2004, King became extremely sick while in La Baule, France. He had an uncharacteristic number of faults in the team competition which left Kevin deeply worried and everyone scratching their heads. Once back at the stable, there was no doubt in anyone's mind that he wasn't well. He was leaning into the groom's arms with his head down and pressed against her stomach like a sick child. The following day, after being diagnosed and treated for ulcers, King won the Grand Prix of La Baule and returned to his former difficult personality to everyone's relief. Well, sort of to their relief; he returned to his usual fire-breathing self.

THE IRISH FEDERATION FINDS A NEW STAR

Kevin would have never gotten to France if he hadn't made it happen. His specialty of getting up and doing something would be his ticket to creating his own destiny. Once Kevin had the green light from Saly to take over the ride, in an unprecedented move, he flew King and a second horse to Europe in the summer of 2000. He then based himself in Germany at a friend's farm and called the Irish Federation to let them know he was available for a team spot and was in Europe if they happened to have an opening for him.

His approach was highly unconventional. Yet, soon after, Irish team veteran Eddie Macken was at CSIO Aachen (one of the most prestigious shows in the world) with a horse that became unsound, and they needed a final team member for the Nations Cup. They did not have an alternate available and were desperate to locate a qualified fourth horse and rider. Short on time and available horses, they called Kevin and gave him a chance to prove himself based on his success in America.

Standing 5'8, Kevin borrowed 6'0 Eddie's Irish team jacket and rolled the sleeves up, both literally and figuratively. Dianna pinned the jacket on the inside so it was not obvious that it was too big. When King cantered out into that German stadium that day, he was also cantering into one of the most famous careers in Irish show jumping history. He delivered a four-fault and then a clear round performance in that Nations Cup. That is analogous to playing your first pro football game as starting quarterback against the defending Super Bowl champions and winning. German arenas are packed with an educated equestrian audience and high performance pressure. Kevin's and King's cool performance catapulted them onto the international stage.

The following month, they were in the anchor-position for Team Ireland at the CSIO Hickstead Nations Cup in

Kevin and Carling King ride for the Irish.

England. They helped secure the Nations Cup victory, which had not been won by Team Ireland since 1937. An Irish victory on English soil after so long was a pretty big deal for Ireland. Before long, the Irish team secured ten Nations Cup victories with Kevin and King leading the way in seven of them. The following year, they returned to Hickstead, England, to contribute two clear rounds in that

Nations Cup and won the Hickstead Grand Prix the same week. They went on to help capture a Team Gold medal for Ireland in the 2001 European Championships and again captured back-to-back Nations Cups in the Washington International Horse Show and in the CSIO Royal Horse Show in Toronto, Canada, with Kevin and King anchoring the team efforts. It was a career shot out of a cannon.

It takes talent in both rider and horse to be ranked 8th in the world, and Kevin and King achieved this ranking at the height of their career. High-performing riders generally have two to four horses accruing points simultaneously. They rest one and bring out the fresh one on the following Sunday. Some riders have strings of horses and will fly into two separate shows in one weekend chasing points. It's not that Kevin pulled King out to compete in every available qualifier, but rather they consistently placed at the top of the order in the classes where they did compete. Kevin didn't have the luxury of lots of top horses at that time, so when he entered King, it was in the biggest classes, and King consistently responded in the most competitive manner.

IRELAND GOES TO ATHENS, 2004

It is hard to get a sense of what Kevin feels are his greatest moments, but his victories in England were some of the most meaningful. King gave him so many great moments across the spectrums of friendship and partnership. King also produced one of only two double clear rounds in Donaueschingen, Germany, which was the final qualifier for the 2004 Olympics. The course was a beast—large and technical. Those rounds secured Ireland's invitation to compete in the 2004 Olympic Games where Kevin and King finished 4th individually. For Kevin, enabling Ireland to get to the Olympics meant more to him than his own personal experience in Athens—yet more evidence of how selfless

Kevin is. I know him well; that's just the way Kevin is built.

Not all professionals are teachers, but Kevin very much is, and it follows his personality. I have seen Kevin beaming more when a student puts in a clear round than when he lays it down on the Grand Prix field himself.

KING BECOMES A COW

The personal relationship between Kevin and King is one Kevin feels will never be duplicated. They traveled the world together, and King was always a character. When laying over in Ireland during a European tour, Kevin turned him out in a field where cattle were grazing because that was how he had been raised. King was in his element—at home in Ireland, grazing among the herd, and eating nettles by the bush loads (sharp sticker bushes). "I was so happy I could give him that time to be an Irish horse in an Irish field one more time," Kevin told me. "You could almost see the stress run off him." He was home again and knew it. Eventually, King lied down with the herd and lazily munched on the grass that was in his reach. It was apparently a sight to see— one of the best horses in the world acting like a cow.

I bubble wrap my horses (meaning protective boots, front, hind) and do anything else I can to prevent them from hurting themselves when they are turned out. I add every manner of protective clothing and let my barn manager turn them out only when she is there to watch, much like a lifeguard at the pool. This is my quirk or insecurity, but apparently not Kevin's. Hearing someone of Kevin's stature in the sport recounting this story makes me feel a bit more foolish than usual. There is so much to be learned from highly accomplished riders like Kevin.

Jumping clear rounds across the globe vies for importance to Kevin with the times when he walked into the barn and King was so happy to see him. King would greet Kevin with a nicker and appear to say hello just for a moment before rushing back to his hay. No one else got a greeting. As for the grouchiness, it was very much an act in the later years. King had mellowed considerably but didn't want it getting around. He kept up appearances by pinning his ears and snapping his teeth in when his girth was being fastened.

CARLING KING'S GLORIOUS RETIREMENT

As with all athletes, there were injuries from time to time. A bout of pleurisy early in his career nearly killed King and damaged his lung capacity. The effects still plague him to this day. Maintaining his health demands nebulizers, pre-soaked hay, and anything Kevin can do to keep the dust down in the barn.

> There are many horses that can jump international tracks, as Kevin refers to them, but he told me **CARLING KING FELT LIKE MAGIC** on take off.

Late in his career, he started to show the telltale signs of unsoundness, but it was managed by superior medical professionals. In 2007, during the Florida circuit in Wellington, his veterinarian declared that a degenerative disease called ringbone could be managed for competition, but doing so could result in a life-ending injury. Kevin and Saly did not hesitate to retire him immediately. In fact, no other option was even discussed—the friendship and King's life came first.

The disease progressed, and it was time to act. Everyone left the barn that day in silence. Dianna recalls not knowing what to say to Kevin to comfort him. She said he was silent, which scared her. She was worried about the emotional fallout. It was heartbreaking to know there was nothing that could be done, looking at him so fit and strong, ready to win on Sunday, but it was over.

Kevin went to the barn alone that evening after hours, and, although what transpired is unknown, these final moments were surely among their most significant together. King's lifetime achievements were celebrated the following week with a retirement ceremony at the Palm Beach International Equestrian Center in the same arena he won back-to-back Grands Prix in 2004. There was not a dry eye among those who knew him. To see him retire looking so ready for the next competition was how Kevin wanted it to be. Carling King walked into the arena one last time, flanked by Kevin, Dianna, Saly, their families, Kay, his long time groom, Irish team members, former grooms, and lifelong friends. Kevin told me if he could find a horse with half of King's heart and scope, he would have a horse capable of competing at the next Olympic Games.

THE STAR SPANGLED BANNER RECOGNIZED

One day, a few years following his retirement, the U.S. national anthem echoed loudly through the woods behind Kevin's home. A fire truck exposition was underway at a local college. King recognized the anthem from the many times he had heard it played during Nations Cup award ceremonies. Dianna and Kevin were in tears as they watched King lift his head and pace the fence line, whinnying and characteristically snorting at the familiar music. As far as he was concerned, it signaled time to go back in the ring.

King now spends most of his days with the sun on his

BOB LANGRISH MBE
EQUESTRIAN PHOTOGRAPHER

Kevin and King on course going clear at the Olympics.

back peering over a garden wall by the Babington children's swing set. He has regular visitors from local pre-school classes and friends from Europe. His health is guarded because of his progressing lung disease, but he is content. He will remain at Kevin's farm for the rest of his well-earned retirement. As busy as Kevin is, he always makes time for his grumpy friend.

Saint Patrick's Day used to mean nothing special to me. I'm one of those run-of-the-mill American mongrels, as patriotic, in my own way, as all retired U.S. Marines. But from now on, when I think of Saint Patty's day, it will be with heartfelt affection for Kevin and Carling King.

2011: Winner of $100,000 Wells-Fargo Grand Prix of Devon on Mark Q

2004: 4th place individually at the Athens Olympics

2003: Winner of the King George Cup, Hickstead

Kevin Babington & Carling King

2003: 1st place Nations Cup Team on Carling King, St. Grallen, SUI

2003: 1st place at the Hickstead Grand Prix

2001: Gold Medal Team, European Championships on Carling King, Arnhem, NED

2001: 1st place at the Samsung Nations Cup CSIO Royal Horse Show on Carling King, Toronto

2001: Team Gold medal in the European Championships

2000: 1st place at the Rotterdam Grand Prix, Holland

1999, 2000 2001: Leading International Rider and Leading International Horse at the Madison Square Garden New York Horse Show

CH. 17

EricHasbrouck
&Miss Fio

LOVE AT FIRST SIGHT

Eric Hasbrouck had the love story of a lifetime with his favorite horse, Miss Fio.

In 1997, Eric was doing what a lot of top riders do—looking for his next Grand Prix partner. He had been fortunate enough to find a sponsor who would purchase a new horse capable of competing internationally, and he made it his mission to find one that could.

Eric ran across Miss Fio in Spain. He tried her once and fell in love with her. She was a smallish mare, just 16.1 hands. She was the type he had success with early in his career and performed very well in the trials over extremely

BOB LANGRISH MBE, EQUESTRIAN PHOTOGRAPHER
Eric in good form.

big jumps. Mares can be difficult, but the good ones try even harder than their male counterparts.

Like all of Eric's favorite mares, Miss Fio had **HEART** and **DESIRE**, and Eric had a good feeling about her.

Miss Fio, an Australian Thoroughbred, had been bred in Europe by Fernando and Enrique Serasola from Madrid. While they did very well with her, not everyone could get along with Miss Fio. Eric speculated that even though they knew she was a good horse, they did not like having to deal with her temperament.

THE PARTNERSHIP WORKED

She did not endear herself to everyone. "Most people thought, when they went in her stall, that she was going to try to kill them as often as not. I had a special relationship with her. She was all bluffing," Eric says. (My mare, Woodgate, has a similar personality. If anyone other than me enters the barn, Woodgate pins back her ears, snaps her jaws, and becomes a brute. This can be intimidating.)

Eric brought her home to the U.S., and from the start, she was everything he had hoped for. Their partnership was looking good in the Grand Prix ring, and by the time the season began in Florida, Eric and Miss Fio were placing consistently. In one of the bigger Grand Prix competitions, she was seventh, he recalls. Then, on one of the biggest Sundays, she placed third in the class.

"I was feeling really good," Eric recalls, but then he experienced every equestrian's nightmare. That Sunday night, after her great performance, Miss Fio was forced to undergo emergency colic surgery at the equine hospital in Palm Beach. The veterinary surgeon had to cut into her abdomen and untwist her intestine. The twist was caught early enough that it did not kill the portion of the affected intestines, so they were left intact. The operation was over quickly, but the bad news was this perfect little mare was now out of action and in need of a long stretch of recuperation. Fortunately, Miss Fio experienced a remarkably quick recovery and was able to rejoin the ranks within a few short months instead of six months, as doctors initially predicted. Everything was back on track for the pair.

1998 WORLD CHAMPIONSHIPS

Taking it slow, Eric got her ready for the next season. He knew Miss Fio had the ability to go far in competition, so they prepared during the winter in Florida for the upcoming trials that spring and summer. At that time, he had two horses doing very well: Freestyle and Miss Fio. Eric was in the top tier of the competitors throughout the trials. Miss Fio finished seventh out of eight rounds, but it was his other mare, Freestyle, who qualified for the world championships.

Eric was happy to have opportunities with either horse and was busy preparing both of them for competition. He was riding Freestyle in preparation for the world championship in Rome. This particular year, under the direction of the U.S. team coaches, the preparation was taking place at the Spruce Meadows Masters Tournament in Calgary, Canada.

It was September of 1998, and everything was going smoothly until Freestyle, on the first day, grabbed herself (which is horse slang for over-reaching with the hind hoof) and stepped on her front heel. She could not show the rest of the week. As fate would have it, Miss Fio was along as Eric's second horse. They did the bigger classes and were one of only two that went double clear in the Nations Cup. (Two clear rounds in a Nations Cup is perfection. It is rare and a big deal.) Team USA was second to the Germans that year.

The courses were difficult, but Eric was optimistic about the prospects for Miss Fio. She was phenomenal that day. Unfortunately, the system at that time did not allow Eric to take Miss Fio to the world championships, even though she was qualified in the top ten. The reality is that Miss Fio should have gone to the world championship, rather than Freestyle, but that was not the way the selection system worked. After recovering from her injury, Freestyle joined Eric for the world championships and turned in a solid performance scoring for the team.

> The amazing thing was that Miss Fio had come through for him with **zero preparation**, and **they won** one of the most important classes in the trials. Miss Fio had won a special place in Eric's heart as a **fighter**.

Eric was looking ahead to the next year and was intent on allowing Miss Fio to show everyone just how special she was. The Pan Am Games loomed on the horizon, and Eric was feeling good because he had two horses with a real chance to show. Eric was in a good position to help the U.S. team for the next couple of years, through the Pan Am Games and maybe even on to the Olympics.

BUMPS IN THE ROAD

That spring, Eric began to prepare for the trials for the Pan Am Games. When they started the trials, however, it was clear that something was very, very wrong—Miss Fio was not acting like herself. Before long, Eric and his terrorized barn staff figured out that Miss Fio had stomach ulcers. At this time, the equine industry was in the beginning stages of ulcer treatment for horses. Miss Fio became the poster child for the animal health company Merial, and Gastroguard, the industry standard drug for ulcer treatment. As a result of his hands-on experience, Eric even ended up working a bit for the manufacturer.

As would be expected, before she was treated for the ulcers, Miss Fio did not do well in the trials for the Pan Am Games. However, a mere four weeks after Miss Fio began treatment, she won a World Cup class. It was very dramatic! She never gave up and was always a fighter. Though many horses would have been unable to perform such a feat, Miss Fio once again demonstrated the heart and tenacity that Eric had fallen in love with.

The stamina Miss Fio demonstrated is something only a few special horses have shown in the past. Sometimes sensitive horses, especially the ones whose instincts are largely based on heart and desire, are too stubborn to give up when they are not feeling well. The only outward sign Eric's team picked up on was her severe cribbing habit (cribbing occurs when a horse holds onto a stall edge and sucks air into their system which can further aggravate their sensitive digestion), something that may have contributed to her stomach problems. It was not Miss Fio's nervousness but rather her fighting instinct that gave her this stamina. When she pranced into a large arena like Spruce Meadows with 55,000 screaming fans, she would grow in stature, not shrink. Eric could always count on her to give her best every time.

This is part of the reason why she was so **incredibly special** to him. It was not her results or athletic capability; it was her **personality**.

BOB LANGRISH MBE
EQUESTRIAN PHOTOGRAPHER

Eric on course at the Florida Grand Prix.

THE 2000 OLYMPIC TRIALS

With aspirations for taking her to the top, Eric had his eye on the Olympic trials in 2000. That winter in Florida, it was Eric's turn to have a setback. He sustained a fall from a young horse and broke his ankle, requiring two surgeries that kept him out of the saddle for several weeks, up until the trials began for the Olympics that year.

Miss Fio was doing well, and with her help Eric mustered the strength to perform at the trials and finish in the top ten. Even though Eric's riding ability was compromised, his friends continued to work Miss Fio. Michael Matz was particularly helpful to Eric during this difficult time. Michael Matz is a six-time U.S. national champion. He won Team Gold at the 1986 World Championships in Aachen. He is also most known for having trained Barbaro to win the Kentucky Derby in 2006. Eric was the last show jumper to have the opportunity to train with Michael before he left show jumping for the world of Thoroughbred racing.

Eric's special bond with Miss Fio gave him the confidence to ride with his injury. Riding with a broken ankle is worse than one might imagine—the joint in your ankle acts as a shock absorber when you land. Every jump you approach is going to hurt one hundred times more than it would normally. It is not a good mental state to be in while competing. Despite Eric's weakened condition, Miss Fio never wavered. Sadly, the duo came up short, and the dream of going to the Olympics was extinguished.

A Unique Spirit

Eric's love for Miss Fio never faltered. "My relationship with her was one of respect," he says. "We had that special trust; we knew each other. I understood her temperament and would never challenge her in the wrong way." Eric postulates that Miss Fio was difficult or cranky by nature, and it is quite possible that she may have been pushed around too much at some prior point in her life. As Eric explains, "She was fine with women, but with men she was terrible. There was a lack of trust on her part for whatever reason. She came to trust me, and I could pretty much do anything if I was careful and she knew it was me."

Miss Fio was a wonderful horse to ride, but she had her quirks. She could not stand still at the in-gate to the show ring; either the groom or Eric had to hold her. As long as she was held, she was fine. It wasn't that she did not want to go into the ring. She would anticipate what was going to happen, and she just could not stand still. She had to trot once she was in the ring and could never stand around and watch. Otherwise, she would rear up, spin around, and wheel, especially in a place like Spruce Meadows where there is a big crowd. As long as you respected her, she was perfect. Whatever the reason for her difficult behavior, Eric accepted it and considered it something his dear friend needed.

Miss Fio had her own style of jumping the fences. She had a tendency to jump with her belly down and her legs up; not exactly flat, but round in her own way; not too high or over-jumping; just enough to get over the jumps cleanly... most of the time.

Miss Fio was fast. Eric never took her in the speed classes, preferring to preserve her for speed when it really counted in the Grand Prix jump-off. Some horses start out great on Wednesday, perform well on a Friday, but run out of gas by Sunday. She was unlike most horses in this regard. Eric saved her for the bigger events, so she would get stronger and stronger. Eric discovered this fact at Spruce Meadows.

After showing four or five days in a row, with the extra demands of the $1 Million Grand Prix on the last day, he thought he would have to help her or override to finish the course. Miss Fio did not need any help. She was better than she had been on the first day of the competition. Eric never had to feel sorry for her going three days in a row or two rounds of the Nations Cup, as her history showed him she preferred the extra work.

DOES NOT LIKE MUD, WATER, OR FLYING

One thing Miss Fio did not like was mud. She never behaved badly on a muddy course, but, being small, she needed that extra big push off the ground to get over the jumps. Eric realized that deep and muddy footing was difficult for her, and he would not ride her in a show when there was mud on the course. Eric tells me, "One time in France, the footing was deep [meaning muddy]. When you are there representing your country and the owners are there, you just have to go on." Eric described this as an instance when he did not want to ride, yet Miss Fio jumped a clear round despite the conditions. That was when she first hurt her tendon, and that one day probably shortened her entire career by a year or two. Looking back, you could not know she was injured because she jumped a beautiful clear round and was not lame. But soon after, she had a series of related injuries, and eventually it caught up with her. I'm sure that day keeps Eric awake from time to time.

She was not the best water jumper in the world either, Eric admits. "Miss Fio did not like water. She jumped it a little flat, and once in a while, she would step on the tape. I didn't want to over-train. We would be jumping at home over a stupid plastic Liverpool, come out of the corner, and she would stop, spin around, and spook at it, hop over it three or

Eric did not know what to expect from her at a show, thinking she would refuse to jump over the water, **but she never did. It was as if she understood that would be hurtful to Eric.** It is funny how horses often cruise along in a competition when it really counts, but will refuse similar obstacles at home or during training sessions.

four times, and be a total jerk," he remembers.

One year at Spruce Meadows, Miss Fio had one of only two double clear rounds at the Nations Cup. There was a triple combination over the Liverpool right by the in-gate. It was one of the hardest jumps, and all the horses had trouble with it. I vividly remember watching them on Spruce Meadows Television. Miss Fio and Eric jumped it clear. She might have been difficult at home, but you could count on her 100 percent in the ring. At the famous Hickstead show, there were very spooky double Liverpools at the far end of the ring, yet again there were no problems.

"If you could give a horse a personality, which sometimes we do, yeah, she loved having an audience. The bigger the stage, the more she likes it," Eric says. We don't know what is going through the mind of a horse. It may be the buzz of the excitement, but whatever it is, they are able to focus and deliver what we ask of them.

Miss Fio did not like to fly. She tended to get nervous. Eric would fly with her, or he made sure the right caretaker was with her. She would lie down during the take-off. As soon as they would thrust up the engines, she would lean back, get ready, and sit down. She was fine after the take-off. Her travel mate would hold her, shaking her head a bit. Horses fly on chartered planes and are secured in stalls before they are loaded onto the plane. Often there are 15 horses flying together at a time. Horses are no different than humans—just like some people, some horses just do not like to fly.

SHE GOES OUT ON TOP

Eric continued to compete with her until she was 17. She did well and had many international wins. Eric says, "Because she tried so hard, I would not push her past her prime, go down the levels and become a junior jumper, or work for a

Eric feels the need for speed.

BOB LANGRISH MBE
EQUESTRIAN PHOTOGRAPHER

lesser rider." Fortunately, the owners agreed. The last class Miss Fio jumped in was in Palm Beach, and she jumped a clear round. Immediately after, she had a rerun of that old tendon injury and could not go in the jump-off. Her best friend, Eric, could not, in his heart, let her try. That was the day when Eric retired Miss Fio. She was 17, which is young for an equine superstar.

Horse owners will tell you that the horses who try the hardest tend to get hurt more often. All you can do is make sure they are fit and not over-show them. If you feel the conditions are unsafe, then you do not show. Even with care and maintenance, accidents happen. I respect Eric's decision to retire Miss Fio on the early side of her career and let her go out on top.

The relationship is similar to that of a parent and a child. The parent takes care of the children, educates them, and loves them. You would never do anything to hurt your child or put them in harm's way. In return, you know your child loves you. Receiving love and respect from your child is the greatest gift. It means you have given all you can give, and you did it right.

Miss Fio is now retired and happily resides in a New Jersey field. Eric checks on her regularly. One would think she might find a fellow equine to befriend or at least a dog or a goat, but she has not. Eric says that she prefers to be by herself and likes only a few people and no other animals. She was never a social horse. She was a persnickety thing! Eric was the only one she liked and her only rider for most of their time together. He was her special partner, and she was his.

Eric says, "There are better horses, but for me better is a relative term. I had a special bond with Miss Fio because of her personality, heart, and desire. Though her name sounds feminine, the little bay mare was anything but feminine. She would eat nails for breakfast!" He could trail ride her like she was a dog. "She was medium-boned; everything about her was medium except her heart. The other thing that was oversized was my love affair with her—I ache to this day thinking about how much I miss her."

A MAN WITHOUT A HORSE

Eric has had a long career in show jumping, though he is still a young man. He and his wife, Denise, manage Diane Walters's The Pavilion Farm in North Salem, New York. They train aspiring show jumping riders. Eric has also been a course designer for many years. He plays a major role in the Fidelity Investments Jumper Classic, where the exhibitors rave about him. He has served as Chef d'Equipe for the Samsung Super League team and has been on the Olympic Selection Committee for the Olympic Games. Eric is not currently showing any top horses, but his talents and his eye for that special horse are just waiting for the next opportunity.

> Grand Prix horses are freaks of nature. **One in 500,000** well-bred jumpers makes it to that level, having the athletic capacity, courage, and mind to handle a highly difficult job.

Listening to the memories relayed by the riders featured in this book, you realize that the equine part of the team is as special to the athlete as the horse's love for his or her rider. Individual horses mean much to the rider as a partner, as a friend, and as a special athlete. The horses all have a unique place in their riders' hearts that can never be replaced.

There are times when Grand Prix athletes are on a roll and have a string of Grand Prix horses or potential younger horses coming along. Eric is living through such a time presently. The search for the next Grand Prix partner takes time.

Eric's next great partner will come along when he least expects it. The journey is as important as the destinations along the way. Eric has prospered and sits at the pinnacle of the sport. His memories remain vivid as he waits to build his next partnership.

2009: Chef d'Equipe of the Dublin Super League

1999: National Champion

1999: Champion at the American Airlines Cup at Spruce Meadows

Eric Hasbrouck & Miss Fio

1998: Double clear at the Spruce Meadows Nations Cup

1998: World Championships, Rome

1992: Won the Gold Cup

CH. 18

Peter Wylde & Fein Cera

Since his early start as a child, Peter Wylde has had a remarkably successful career in show jumping. During his youth, he trained with Joe and Fran Dotoli in Milton, Massachusetts, where he started riding on his pony, Devil's River. Peter excelled on horses who did not need any leg, the ones everyone else feared to ride. Peter's equitation horse, Native Surf, was a Thoroughbred by the famous race horse Native Dancer. "The kids on the sideline were terrified that they might have to ride him," Joe Dotoli, who has remained Peter's friend and supporter, says, referring to the classes where the junior riders are required to switch horses. Native Surf had been ridden by George Morris in Green Confirmation

BOB LANGRISH MBE, EQUESTRIAN PHOTOGRAPHER
Peter and Fein Cera on course for Team USA.

classes. Native Surf was very difficult to ride and keep calm, but under Peter's guidance, the pair became the champions at the 1982 Maclay Finals at Madison Square Garden. Perhaps this laid the groundwork for Peter's ability to partner with the special mare Fein Cera.

Wylde maintains that meeting Fein Cera was a truly life-changing event. Fein Cera had a reputation within the industry as being a difficult horse to ride. She had come to him for sale in December of 2000 through Allison Firestone, another champion Grand Prix rider.

Allison had purchased Cera at age six and rode her until she was nine in a few fairly large Grand Prix competitions. In December of 2000, after a competition in Germany, Allison needed to return home to Florida and was unable to bring Fein Cera back with her. Peter, although born and raised in the United States, had moved to Europe as an adult and was living in Maastricht, Netherlands, where he had relocated his business. Allison and Peter had been friends for quite a while so Allison trusted him. She asked him to find Fein Cera a buyer and a new home.

THE 2001 WORLD CUP FINALS IN GOTHENBURG, SWEDEN

In 2001, Peter was at the top of his career. Riding Macanuto DeNiro, Peter had just won two silver medals at the Pan American Games and qualified for the World Cup Finals in Gothenburg, Sweden. In addition to bringing Macanuto DeNiro and Job, his speed horse, Peter made the bold decision to include Fein Cera in the lineup for Gothenburg. Though the two had just begun getting acquainted, Peter felt a connection with the horse.

Peter had long been friends with Olympian Conrad Homfeld, and he recalls a particularly touching moment: "When Peter and Job won the speed class by a full two seconds, they triumphantly galloped out of the arena to the blaring music of Bruce Springsteen singing 'Born in the USA'." Unfortunately, the following day was not quite as victorious for Peter. Joe and Fran Dotoli had made the trip to support their former student, and Joe comments, "DeNiro was a big chestnut suited to outdoor galloping courses more than a World Cup indoor arena. The horse was extremely nervous." DeNiro sustained an injury in the jump-off on the second day, and Peter dropped him from the remainder of the World Cup. Peter made the decision to change horses—DeNiro was out and Fein Cera was in, though Peter had not yet ridden Fein Cera in a major Grand Prix-level competition. The decision to use Fein Cera was made without the benefit of knowing how she would handle a championship-level event.

Peter's split-second decision propelled him from 20th to 6th place in the World Cup. "Fein Cera was one of two that jumped double clear," said Joe Dotoli, who described his first impression of the mare as "magnificent." Her breeding was impeccable, and the beautiful, 17.1-hand high-strung mare showed it in both her demeanor and her performance. For Peter, Cera's performance under pressure confirmed his suspicions about the horse. "I knew instinctively that she was a champion horse and the World Cup proved it," Peter says. "We had not done anything nearly that big up until then, and she went four and clear on the final Sunday of the World Cup. She had one rail down in the first class and was perfection in the second. She leapt into the international scene, and it was a big, impressive move. I think everybody saw she was a champion."

> It is **rare** for a rider to change horses mid-competition, but **Peter followed his instincts.**

THE 2002 WORLD EQUESTRIAN GAMES IN JEREZ, SPAIN

After their remarkable victory, Fein Cera's value skyrocketed, and Peter was quick to put together a syndicate to buy her. Cera continued to excel, and by the next year, she and Peter qualified for the 2002 World Equestrian Games in Jerez, Spain. Once in Jerez, the duo endured numerous challenges together (including a very large course), but finished with a clean first round. Cera's response to Peter was remarkable; though she was known for being very hot and sensitive, she responded beautifully to Peter's expert horsemanship and careful training program. Peter is known for being extremely hands-on with his horses (he even braids them himself, which is practically unheard of for a Grand Prix rider), and it is clear that Fein Cera flourished due to his attentiveness.

Representing the U.S. with his team, Peter won the Whitney Stone Cup for his selflessness and sportsmanship, and the Individual Bronze medal at the World Equestrian Games that year. Cera also performed like a champion at the World Equestrian Games; she produced two clears in the Nations Cup team rounds, and unique to the World Equestrian Games, Fein Cera went clear with each of the three riders when they changed horses during the Final Four. She was named "Best Horse at the Finals."

PREPARING FOR GREATER THINGS

Shortly thereafter, it became clear to Peter that with the right plan, he and Cera could continue on to the Olympics. As Peter puts it, "The intent was to keep her through the World Championships in 2002—that was my goal. I had put this group together to buy this expensive horse and planned to keep her for a year and half, get ready to do the trials, make the team, go to the WEG and do the best that I could, and then sell her. That was exactly what I did. During the WEG I had been talking to Missy Clark [a well-known trainer]. Many people had been

GRETCHEN ALMY

Peter in a quiet moment at the Fidelity Jumper Classic.

clamoring to buy Fein Cera at the WEG, but since Missy was my friend, she went to the front of the line. She had a number of people who were very interested in buying the horse." After the WEG, Missy's student, Sarah Willeman, and Turnabout Farm became the new owners of Fein Cera. A surprising turn of events made it possible for Peter to continue on to the Olympics with Fein Cera as his horse.

Around the same time that Sarah and Turnabout Farm acquired Fein Cera, Sarah sustained a serious back injury. Per her doctor's orders, Sarah was forced to take a year off from riding. Though the decision was devastating, Sarah agreed to the sabbatical and suggested that they leave the horse with Peter. Sarah knew that the pair had the potential to be Olympic contenders, and so in an enormously generous gesture, Sarah (with Turnabout Farm) urged Peter to continue with Fein Cera.

A SPECIAL CHEMISTRY

Though their reunion was certainly unexpected, no one was surprised at Peter and Cera's chemistry. As Joe Dotoli puts it, "Peter has always done well with hot horses. Those are the ones Peter always did the best with. He has a very calming effect on a horse. He's much better on a sensitive horse than one that requires pushing around." Fein Cera had a

"Fein Cera was actually a very complex horse. She had an incredible amount of blood. She was very, very hot, which most people don't really like in a horse. **I like horses that are hot and carry their own motor without you having to create the energy.** She's got incredible scope and can jump any course in the world."

reputation but she fit right into Peter's way of riding.

Peter was the only rider who could exercise her at his farm. If somebody tried to put too much pressure on her or ride in a frame or work her hard, she could be very difficult. She was a complex, complicated horse, but when you saw her in the show ring, she looked absolutely beautiful to ride. Peter always had a great feeling with her. This mare had beautiful technique, was a very good mover, and was very balanced with classic style when jumping. She had incredible range, and once she and Peter got comfortable with each other, the pair could pretty much do anything.

Peter concedes that riding Fein Cera was a challenge. "When most people saw her in the show ring they thought, 'That horse looks like anybody could ride her,' and in a way, it's true—when she was 'on' and when at a show, she was at her easiest, but getting her there was all about her mind. That was the tricky part with her." Despite Cera's finicky tendencies, Peter is quick to point out that she was a remarkable horse to ride. "She's the scopiest [most powerful] horse I've ever ridden in my life. I never once walked a course, whether it was at Aachen or the Olympics or the WEG or anywhere, when I thought to myself, 'Oh wow, this looks big,' because she always made me feel we could jump anything. That was definitely her strong point for me as a rider."

"She was not great going fast, however. If you went too fast with her, she would get too wild. I had to be cautious with her in the jump-offs because she would sort of lose her mind. Fein Cera was very nervous, and you wouldn't see it so much on the outside, but she was a worrier. She has a lot of this Holsteiner blood, so if she got too wound up or too excited, then she would rush too forward to the jump. Sometimes she was almost too aggressive. You had to take everything very quietly and very easily without her getting too excited. She was not for everybody."

Peter and Fein Cera—an Olympic moment.

"Most of the time, I rode her with no spurs. **I'd basically sit as quiet as I could and just steer.** She didn't take a lot of strength. She was incredibly ride-able and adjustable. You could do one less or one more stride with her, it didn't matter."

THE 2004 OLYMPICS IN ATHENS

For the next two years, Peter and Wendy Faust, his groom, focused nearly all of their attention on Fein Cera. In 2004, Peter was presented with an opportunity that most equestrians only dream of: the chance to go to the Olympics in Athens, Greece. Peter refers to his time in Athens as the highlight of his career, saying, "There are a lot of different sides to the Olympic experience. In a way, it's an ultimate goal if you're in this sport. It was a huge honor and a big deal for me to go and be able to compete there."

Though the experience was titillating, Peter is quick to point out the importance of staying focused. "Having said that, in the bigger picture, one event doesn't define a riding career, and I take pride in my horsemanship. I think it was Joe Fargis who said to me once when I was feeling down about a show that it's never any one show; it's your body of work over the years that you should be proud of, and that was about the best piece of advice anybody ever gave me."

While in Athens, Peter was acutely aware that he was in the middle of a once-in-a-lifetime opportunity, so he did everything in his power to live in the moment. His teammates chose to stay elsewhere in Europe until after the Opening Ceremonies, when they were summoned to Athens for the show jumping competition. Peter flew early to Athens, stayed in the Olympic Village for two days, and walked with the riders from the dressage and eventing teams in the Opening Ceremonies. He was the only member of the U.S. show jumping team who walked in the Opening Ceremonies.

His mother, members of his family, and Joe and Fran Dotoli and their daughter Annie (who is also a show jumper and captured third in the Maclay Finals as a

"Going to the Olympics was a dream, so I made a point of doing the Opening Ceremony which, being in Athens, it was spectacular to be there and walk with all the other athletes who are the best athletes in any given sport at the time. It gives you a different and interesting perspective on riding as a sport. It's easy to forget it is an Olympic sport."

junior some years behind Peter) were able to make the trip to cheer him on. They had not seen his special mare very often, as Peter kept her almost exclusively in Europe. Fein Cera had only been shown in the U.S. a few times—once during the trials for the World Equestrian Games, once during the finals for the World Cup in Las Vegas, and then for the Olympic trials leading up to the summer of the 2004 Olympics. She hated to fly, would drop weight, and had to have someone always standing at her head during the flight. She actually fell down on a plane once. By the time she flew into Athens, her team had the routine down and made it as comfortable and easy for her as possible.

The U.S. team performed remarkably well in Athens. Though the U.S. was initially awarded the silver medal, they ended up bringing home the gold because Germany was disqualified when the presence of illegal substances was discovered in one of their horses. Despite the team's tremendous victory, Peter and Cera were not at their best. When Peter reflects on his Olympic performance, he says, "In reality, I actually didn't have a very good performance myself. Fein Cera was clear the first day, and that was very exciting because we were tied with the Swedes in the Nations Cup, and we had a clear round in the jump-off which helped us win the silver medal. We had a mixed performance though, with two good rounds and two average rounds. It wasn't what I had hoped. It was towards the end of a long summer for Cera. I think the selection trials took a lot out of her. I must say, I left some of my best rounds behind us prior to the Olympics. She was not in her best form when we arrived at the Olympics, and this was very difficult and frustrating for me, but horses are horses, and she tried the best she could at the time. We gave it our best effort."

The 13-year-old beautiful big bay mare with the impeccable German breeding had shone in the Olympic ring nonetheless, alongside Sapphire with McLain Ward, Royal Kaliber with Chris Kappler, and Authentic with Beezie Madden. Joe Dotoli would later say, "In my opinion, if you put a list of the top 20 horse-and-rider combinations in the United States, this group would have to be on that list." Though Peter had moved to Europe and gone on to do great things, he had always maintained a connection with the Dotolis and they were extremely proud of him. During the Olympics, Joe decided he wanted to write a book about his experiences with Peter. The Dotolis were running the Ox Ridge Hunt Club and had run a horse business for many years. They decided to make some life changes. Joe and Fran retired to an island in Lake Champlain, Vermont, and Joe wrote his book *Wylde Ride* (there are very few books like this available for young riders, and I highly recommend Joe's).

GRETCHEN ALM

Peter in his always eloquent form at the 2010 Winter Equestrian Festival.

CERA'S LEGACY

After the Olympics, Peter continued to perform with Fein Cera in Europe for a while longer. Peter retains only the fondest memories of Cera. "She was never in a bad mood," he says. "She was always quite cheery, and [except when around] Wendy and I, she was quite shy. She was not a horse that comes looking for treats and we give all our horses treats. I think it just goes with her internal personality. She is a very sweet, very kind horse who never puts her ears back ever, not even around other horses." Even though Peter's farm has incredible grass paddocks, Wendy would always take Cera for grass by hand. The stable is on the Dutch border and the property abuts a national forest, where Peter loved to ride Fein Cera and trot on the sand trails.

Today, the beautiful Fein Cera has been bred a couple of times, and due to her high value, the birth was by a surrogate mother through embryo transfer. "We took her out of the sport to collect the first embryo, then put her back to work and rode in three more Grands Prix in the fall of 2007. She placed in all three. Then we had to decide: do we take her to Florida to compete or concentrate on producing offspring? I didn't want to fly her to Florida and compete in the end of her 16th year, coming up on 17 years old. There wasn't anything she hadn't done in show jumping through nine seasons of Grand Prix all over the world. She didn't have anything left to prove."

Cera herself has retained her fine figure and currently resides at her birthplace, the famous Harm Thormahlen Holsteiner farm. Peter, who is arguably in the prime of his career, frequently visits his old friend. Though he currently resides in Europe, as he has for many years now, he is known for his intense work ethic, his patience, and his talents as a rider in all parts of the world.

2004: Team Gold medal at the Athens Olympics on Fein Cera

2002: Individual Bronze medal at the World Equestrian Games, Jarez

2002: Fein Cera won Best Horse in the finals of the World Equestrian Games

Peter Wylde
&Fein Cera

2001: 6th place final standing at the World Cup finals, Gothenburg

2001: Winner of the CSI Grand Prix, Dortmond

2001: Style of Riding Award at CHIO, Aachen

1999: Team and Individual Silver medals at the Pan American Games, Winnipeg

1999: USOC Male Equestrian of the Year Award

1996: Winner of the Presidents Cup Grand Prix, Washington, D.C.

1982: National Maclay Medal Champion at Madison Square Garden

Ch. 19

Peter Leone &
Legato

Between an Olympic horse and rider, there is an extraordinary and very unique partnership. A special union is forged during all the months and years that bring them along the sometimes bumpy road to the Grand Prix arena, centered in an Olympic stadium. It is a pattern we have seen repeated with several of the horse-and-rider combinations we have examined. To have a "Sunday" horse is something very special, with so many aspirations and efforts going into this level of the sport. (For the less-initiated to the sport's slang, a Sunday horse is a Grand Prix horse prepared to compete in the biggest 1.60m classes at the international level. Think of it like your Sunday best.) The horse must be up to the sport physically and mentally, and must have that magical ability to perform flawlessly time and time again when it counts. The rider must be physically fit, dedicated to the sport, very talented, and totally trusting of the horse. When these bonds are formed, the partnership takes horse and rider through the various trials and obstacles put in their way, and a lucky few make it to the top.

No one understands or appreciates this more than Peter Leone. A true gentleman and an athlete, he is both gracious and passionate when discussing his partnership with Legato that eventually led to their selection for the 1996 Olympic Games. It is a special story of determination, talent, and a never-say-never approach to reaching a goal, no matter how many obstacles are put in the way. I have been fortunate to know Peter for years. He is completely dedicated and a real pleasure to interact with, except for his preference for the New York Yankees and New York Giants. Peter and I make regular bets on the New York versus Boston major league teams. I am sorry to report that I have sent Peter more New England lobster and chowder than I have received New York cuisine in return.

THE FIRST ENCOUNTER

It has been 15 years since the 1996 Olympics, and even longer since Legato first came into Peter's life. He realized almost immediately that he had a special horse.

Peter's trip to the 1996 Games began in the early 90s, when all of Peter's hopes and dreams were suddenly centered on the four-year-old horse he found in a small indoor arena on a rainy day in Belgium. He didn't know for sure if this might be the one—the horse who had what it took to go all the way. He recognized the horse's raw talent and allowed himself to hope that possibly, just maybe, this horse would be the one who would allow him to realize his lifelong dream.

Peter knew Legato came from excellent lines, and though most of his sire's (Jasper) offspring tended to be small, Legato was an ample 17-hand bay gelding. Peter said the horse looked like an unusually large version of Jasper. Legato's dam was a French mare. He was a very classy-looking horse. On that rainy day, Peter remembers, "I was looking at horses with a very renowned legendary horseman from Belgium, Francois Mathy. My family and I have done business with Francois for over 30 years—since 1978—and many of our top horses and U.S. team horses have been found through him. From my world championship mount, Ardennes, to my world cup final horse, Oxo, then to my brother Mark's horses, Tim and Artos, and my brother Armand's horses, Walenstein and Lasandro, we have found a lot of good horses through Francois."

Peter and his two brothers were known as Team Leone when they were all competing at the same time, and they were very competitive. This family dedication would serve them well, but especially when Peter needed it most. Without them, Peter would have lost his foothold on the path to the Olympics, and the horse would never have had the chance to shine.

That rainy day in Belgium, with his trusted dealer accompanying him, Peter was excited to ride Legato for the first time. The arena was very tiny, but riding outdoors was not an option. Peter made do.

GREAT ATHLETES RIDE RAIN OR SHINE, HOT OR COLD, AND PETER IS NO EXCEPTION.

Peter knew after just one jump, one fence—which he jumped approximately 15 times over 20 minutes—Legato was all talent. According to Peter, Legato came off the ground very lightly, like a bird. For a large horse at this age, Peter could tell Legato knew exactly where his legs were. Peter could feel how intelligent and aware the horse was of the obstacle in front of him. Like the opposite poles of magnets which refuse to come together, Legato would not touch the jump. He soared over it! Whatever height Peter set, Legato jumped with power, attentiveness, and confidence. It is a quality you dream about when you ride a show jumper. Peter told me he looked at Legato in the stall after he rode him and, even though Legato was bandaged up and ready for bed, Peter saw that look in his eye—Legato had the look of a winner. Peter could see Legato had an inner confidence, and he moved with a sense of quality.

GETTING ACCLIMATED

Peter brought Legato home to his family's Ri-Arm Farm in New Jersey. "I didn't jump him for four months after I got him home," Peter says. "Now with most people, that's the first thing they do. I saw no point in jumping him as that was the easy part for Legato. I brought him along slowly and put all the pieces in place on the flat and then spent a lot of time introducing him to gymnastics."

Peter, who is known for his patience and kindness as a trainer, let Legato tell him

> Riders do listen to their horses, and **THE HORSES DO LET THEM KNOW JUST HOW THEY ARE FEELING.** Often it is that cue that determines what classes they enter and how much the rider is comfortable asking a horse to do.

Peter with his best buddy.

when he was ready. By the time the horse was six, Legato was Peter's number two horse on the U.S. team in Italy. He was riding Oxo first, as his Nations Cup horse, but Legato continued to impress Peter day after day. Peter and Legato earned ribbons in every class they entered. This horse's ability was incredible for one so young. Peter had the feeling Legato could do it.

Legato was turning out to be everything Peter had hoped, and he was not the only one who thought Legato was something special. In 1992, when Legato was a six-year-old, Peter rode him on the Grand Prix field at Gladstone, New Jersey, during the Festival of Champions in a George Morris clinic for up-and-coming riders or older riders with up-and-coming horses. George Morris was impressed when he saw what Legato could do. Peter beams when he remembers George saying, "Peter, this is an Olympic horse!" George has been central to so many careers and his keen eye often determines which horses and riders get to wear the U.S. colors in international competition. This comment lit Peter up like a lamp. Four years later, George's prediction was proven right. Peter had believed it all along, but having the confirmation of one of our country's greatest horsemen does not hurt your confidence.

In 1992, the Saturday Grand Prix in South Hampton was not what it is today. It was barely 1.50m, and Peter was still riding as an amateur at that point. Today this venue builds a test closer to 1.60m. As a result, Peter and Legato entered the Grand Prix and were third after a fall. Peter gave Legato some mileage in Florida that winter, then went home to New Jersey and did the Garden State Grand Prix. The horse was becoming predictably consistent class after class. Peter went on to the Grand Prix at Old Salem in New York and had yet another indication of how well they were doing. Robert Ridland designed the course, which was very different. The course was on grass with both water and ditches, which is not always the case. The duo was again double clear! Legato jumped around the Grand Prix like it was a schooling jumper course. Legato rode very smoothly, handling the course as if it were an easy training exercise.

> "He was everything I ever thought he was going to be. Robert Ridland even said to me, 'Peter, my God, that's a horse!'"

A BUMP IN THE ROAD

Flying high, Peter had to get up the next morning and go to work. He had a full-time job at the time as a national sales director of Liberty Travel—a position that had nothing to do with horses. (This element of Peter's story is hard for me to grasp. I can only think of him as the ultimate professional he is today.) Bright and early Monday morning, he was representing his company during a seminar at sea on a cruise ship that departed out of New York with 400 travel agents on board. While he was on the ship, he got an emergency call. Legato had been seriously injured during the night in his stall.

"He had gotten cast in his nice big stallion stall at our farm. He had been banging against the side of the stall, trying to get up, and a piece of wood splintered and went right into the stifle joint. It chipped off two pieces of stifle bone and severed most of the center patella ligament, which is basically the knee, and ruptured the joint capsule. This was just 24 hours after our incredible Old Salem Grand Prix, where he had just been so amazing." Peter explained that Legato went into surgery and was then stuck in his stall for the next 90 days playing with a rubber ball. Discussing this incident with Peter today, you can see the anguish on his face, even all these years later.

Peter in perfect form.

All Peter could do was visit the horse and count the days until he could start a careful program of rehabilitation. There are masterful veterinary surgeons and excellent care for these high performance animals and, fortunately, horses often come back from injuries. But this injury was extreme, and the odds were not the best.

AGAINST ALL ODDS

The effort that Peter put into bringing back his potential Olympic mount was the same effort Peter would have put into any of his client's horses today—that is the way Peter is built. His Olympic goal was still on the horizon and he was manic. Once Legato had healed enough to start working lightly under saddle, it was a carefully regimented schedule, beginning with 60 days of riding at the walk. It was similar to the Rocky comeback story. Peter regularly walked the hills and worked with him, slowly and carefully. The dedication it takes to bring a horse back from injury can be frustrating for a rider, who is anxious to get out and ride and do what they do best. It is a testament to Peter's great horsemanship that he stuck with Legato from the beginning, determined to get him back in shape. It paid off. Like Rocky, Legato and Peter overcame the setback and were ready once again to meet the challenges in the ring.

By the time the Winter Equestrian Festival began in Wellington, Florida, Legato was eight and not yet in his prime. As Peter recalls, "I went in my first Grand Prix, which is a World Cup down here, and he jumped it freakishly well. He was double clear! So bringing him back from a career-ending injury took an extraordinary effort on the part of the vet, Dr. Furlong, and a gifted surgeon, Dr. Greg Staller. I had to deal with the whole range of emotions from 'We can overcome' to 'Your career is not over; we can get back in the game.' It was a real journey."

Later that year, Peter began to realize that he and Legato had a shot at the 1996 Olympics. He was thrilled and carefully planned his competition schedule so that the horse had a taste of competing in Europe. Peter rode him on the U.S. show jumping team at the Dublin Horse Show and then continued with his building block approach to get Legato ready for the Olympic trials. Along the way, they captured second place at the Nations Cup in Aachen and won both the World Cup Grand Prix at South Hampton and the World Cup Grand Prix in the famed Devon Oval. They skipped the indoor classes that fall because Peter's trainer, Michael Matz, did not use the indoor competitions a decade before as a prerequisite to the outdoor summer championships. Peter adopted Michael's approach. They went into winter break in late 1995 after a year of excellence showing in the big classes. "All systems go!" Peter said. At the beginning of 1996, they geared up again for the next round of competitions designed to prepare Legato for the Olympic trials.

SETBACKS – MINOR THEN MAJOR

As is often the case in show jumping, it was Peter's turn to have a physical setback. It was not a huge injury, but Peter broke the fifth metacarpal in his hand, which was enough to interfere with riding. Joe Fargis, a fellow rider and 1984 Olympic gold medalist, introduced Peter to his surgeon, who worked with the Miami Dolphins football team. The surgeon, Dr. Virgin, told Peter he was not going to simply fix him so that he could ride again, but his job was to get Peter back in the saddle so that he would not even be thinking about his injured hand.

This is the ideal mindset of a sports physician—thinking "How can I get you back in the ring?" and not "How long do I hold you back?" I have a similar relationship with my surgeon, Dr. Peter Asnis, who is the team surgeon for the Boston Bruins, and who Charlie Jacobs put to work on my busted knee. (My thanks to Charlie Jacobs, owner of the Boston Bruins and a fellow equestrian, and Dr. Asnis. Dr. Asnis's comments to me before my surgery were much the same as those received by Peter from Dr. Virgin.)

Peter and Legato completed the first two trials successfully. The trials were completely objective, with eight rounds that included two discard opportunities where the rider could throw out those scores. By the end of the first two trials, he was in third place. Once again, he was on his way and could say, "All systems go!"

When it came time to ship Legato to compete in the third trial in Pennsylvania, Peter did what all riders do who are showing several different horses simultaneously. He was not just riding his best horses, but he was working concurrently to bring along several young and inexperienced horses. Accidents frequently happen on young horses. Peter was in the jump-off of what was then called a preliminary jumper class at the Garden State Horse Show. His horse hung a leg and flipped over a vertical. Peter got pile driven into the ground.

Peter had never broken a bone in his life until 1996, and now it was an Olympic year! He shattered his collarbone 48 hours before the third Olympic trial. Following on the broken hand, the injuries were adding up for Peter. In the ambulance, Peter told his wife, Marcella, "Get me to Dr. Virgin!" The scene was similar to the accident scene in the Kevin Costner film *For the Love of the Game*. Peter knew that Dr. Virgin was the most important person he needed to see at that moment.

Once back in competent medical hands, Peter learned more about the collarbone than he ever wanted to know: It's like a chicken bone—it's hollow. Peter's collarbone was totally shattered. He missed the third trial, but Dr. Virgin managed to put five screws into the remaining bone fragments to hold it all together so that Peter could compete in the remaining Olympic trials.

Helping his country earn an **Olympic Team Silver medal** represented the **pinnacle of achievement** for Peter and his family.

UNDER PRESSURE

Timing was tight, and Peter was under a great deal of pressure. The next two trials (Trials #4 and #5) were only two weeks away at the Old Salem Horse Show. There were to be two different and important rounds on the same day.

Peter admitted to me that

winning a medal for the United States in the Olympic Games was a family dream and his own personal dream as well. Peter and his brothers grew up with George Morris as a mentor. It was the team medal, more than the individual medal, that meant so much to Peter because it represented the strength of the country, as opposed to one individual's strength.

Teamwork was what saved Peter and Legato, as Team Leone sprang into action. Peter's brother, Armand, who is both a doctor and a lawyer, helped him with a myriad of details. His other brother, Mark, also an international Grand Prix rider, kept Legato active so the horse would stay fit and ready to compete. Peter was working with a personal trainer, but realized, with hard work, he would just barely be able to make it to Trials #4 and #5 at Old Salem—if he could stand the pain. Armand, who had become involved with the U.S. Equestrian Team and FEI, was very familiar with the rules and knew competitors could not take any painkillers.

The fortitude of many of us, both horses and riders, has been tested at horse shows at Peter's level. I have experienced it personally. These prohibitions are how the FEI keeps the sport drug-free.

Show me another sport with this type of dedication. Riders ride hurt all the time and, more often than not, they are paying for the privilege to do so, not the other way around.

PLAYING BY THE RULES

What was permissible, under the FEI rules, was to locally infiltrate the fracture site, meaning Peter could get injections of lidocaine and longer-lasting numbing agents which were injected directly into his collarbone. The rules did not allow other injections or medications. The Leone family and medical staff came up with a plan that was sanctioned. They got permission from the jury to allow Peter to ride without a jacket because it would be very painful to pull a jacket over his hand and shoulder.

Peter and his brothers walked the course, and then Armand drove Peter to the Mount Kisco hospital, where Armand had made arrangements with an anesthesiologist. They met with the anesthesiologist, who gave Peter the approved injections. Mark had warmed up Legato in their absence. Peter entered the ring and put in a four-fault round.

Riding at that level and achieving the score he did, just two weeks after shattering a bone, is indeed inspiring. Two hours later, Peter had to ride again, and by then the injection had worn off. The pain interfered with Peter's ride, resulting in an unusual 12-fault score. This was his second discard; he had no room for any more errors.

Two weeks later, the next two Olympic trials would be held at Devon over a course designed by Linda Allen (she would actually design the Olympic course in 1996). I have worked directly with Linda, who is a brilliant course designer, for three years in conjunction with the Fidelity Investments Classic. She is a great lady and really fun to work with.

Peter's challenges were not over. In each of these trials, he learned how to handle the injury better. He continued with his rehab, but every time he jumped a large jump he would re-break the collarbone. For this pair of trials, Team Leone made arrangements to have the local anesthesiologist come to the show. Peter walked the course, and then went to the little medical room under the Devon grandstands, where his shoulder was numbed so he could ignore the injury during the competition. Amazingly, he went clear with half a time fault. He was still in the game!

GRETCHEN ALMY

A quiet moment in Florida (2011).

For the two trial exercise at Old Salem Farm, Peter and Armand came up with a better plan. On this occasion, they injected and numbed the injury a second time, immediately before the second trial of the day. This revised approach worked and Peter and Legato went clear again with only three-fourths of a time fault. The dynamic pair was one clear round away from making the Olympic team. The last trial was three weeks later at the historic USET headquarters in Gladstone New Jersey.

Thanks to the extra time between trials, Peter was able to warm up his own horse. He had an anesthesiologist administer the injections into the collarbone at ringside. Peter and Legato had a magnificent clear round and won the final trial, earning themselves a berth on the Olympic team.

ATLANTA, PART OF TEAM USA

The Olympics were held in Atlanta just six weeks later, and he was able to ride without any medical help. Legato was with him the whole time, boosting his confidence and helping him move past the pain every step of the way. "I took care of Legato when he was badly hurt and, in turn, Legato did much the same for me when I was in need." Peter felt he owed it to Legato to work through a few broken bones. "I couldn't have made it without my brothers and my mom and dad. When I was first riding with my collarbone broken my dad said, 'I think you have to stop.'" Peter's parents are both radiologists, and they were there at that final trial along with Armand and Mark. Peter found out afterward that his Dad and Armand were too nervous to watch and waited out in the parking lot, listening to the announcer. This can be a tough sport for parents and siblings, but nothing builds character like doing whatever it takes to win.

It was magical how Legato sensed Peter's compromised condition and made up for his weakened state, carrying him to clear rounds and an Olympic dream. Legato was in Peter's eyes the true hero in their amazing journey. Peter told me it was his duty and honor to his horse and country to ride through the discomfort.

This team mentality worked both for him and

against him at the Olympics, however. He made team representation his priority. "Of course, it's every rider's dream to take a shot at an individual medal. But I have to say I didn't take it upon myself to know exactly how the individual riders were selected for our team for the individual medals. I knew the qualifying format for the individual finals used three rounds (the first competition was the first individual qualifier and the two rounds of the team competition were qualifying rounds two and three). The top few would be eligible to compete in the individual final. Prioritizing the team competition, I did not jump in the friendly warm-up and planned to use the first individual qualifying competition as my prep. My plan was to have Legato peaking for the team competition and then have enough horse left to take my best shot in the individual finals. Instead of jumping in the friendly warm-up round, I cantered around the arena, introducing Legato to the Olympic venue. So, as planned, I went in the first individual competition and allowed Legato to have his warm-up performance. We had the first jump down, which is a bit unlucky, one front rail and one back rail—not a great individual score. But most importantly, my horse and I were now ready for the two round competition to be held two days later. All along I thought how we did in the Nations Cup would determine which of our riders would represent the U.S. in the individual finals."

The U.S. won the silver medal in the team competition, and Peter put in a four-fault round and a clear round in that effort. Overall, he had the best scores for the U.S. team. The German powerhouses, as had become the norm, took the gold. Michael Matz had four faults in both rounds, Anne Kursinski went clear and eight, and Leslie Howard went 14 and clear, leaving Peter's record the best for the members of the U.S. team.

Our Olympic medalist on course with Legato—an Olympic moment.

THE INDIVIDUAL FINAL

Though Peter had the best scores in the team competition, he was shocked to learn he was not on the U.S. squad for the individual final. He had a horse that was peaking and ready for more. While Peter and Legato qualified for the individual final along with all three teammates, the U.S. could only enter three riders into the individual. Because of his score in the first individual ride, the Chef d'Equipe

Peter at the Fidelity Jumper Classic, an annual sure thing.

TONY DE COS

left Peter off the team for the individual final. It was an incredibly disappointing reality. But his lifelong dream had come true, and he made a significant contribution to his country's Olympic medal performance. Peter had done what he came to the Olympics to do and put in the rides of his life for his country.

Peter had been passed over before when he felt he had the scores, and this was to be a common theme that would plague him more than once in his career. Much of the result was due to the selection criteria. The U.S. Olympic Committee had a very subjective means of determining who went to the Olympics, not just based on scores, but on a number of other criteria. Then they shifted to strictly objective means of selection that was not ideal either, because the top scoring horses might be eliminated if they slipped or threw a shoe. Some combination of the two approaches would ultimately prove to be the best formula for putting together a U.S. Olympic team. It has evolved to a combined approach today, and the results have been two consecutive gold medal Olympic teams.

> "I was rewarded by something bigger and greater than myself. It was a precious spiritual moment in my life."

Nonetheless, Peter had his Olympic medal and his horse of a lifetime. Not long afterward, he was asked by a writer of a book on faith about how he felt during the medal presentation ceremony—did he experience an encounter with faith or something bigger than himself in the Olympic moment? Peter responded, "I have to say, when I was on the podium, yes, I felt like God rewarded me and my family for doing the right things over the years. Something in the way I lived my life, something in my principles."

A Second Sunday Horse

Legato was for Peter that special, wonderful, perhaps once-in-a-lifetime horse. Peter then went almost ten years without an extraordinary partner for the biggest rings and venues. I know, talking to Peter today, he is all the more grateful to be at that place in his career again, with his chestnut horse, Select. He is blessed again with a real Sunday horse. He started riding Select in 2010, and they went all the way to the Pfizer $1 Million Grand Prix in 2010 and a clear round in the $500,000 Winter Equestrian Festival final class in 2011. To qualify for either of these two competitions, you have to have a top-tier horse and have proved it that season. He is unabashedly delighted to allow himself to say that, with Select, "I'm finally in the hunt again!" The heartbreaking truth is, even for people as talented as Peter, those top horses sometimes come after years of searching, and years of droughts in between.

As I talked to Peter, I could not help but notice the horse's groom, Santiago, fussing over the horse. While Peter talked fondly of his spiritual relationship with the wonderful mounts he has had, it was obvious that he adores Select, too. Still, Peter says, "I'm not a kisser. I give him just a manly pat, and he knows who I am." As he said this, I could see the affection in Peter's eyes and realized that, like all of us, he lives for his horses. Through all the challenges, injuries, and disappointments, Peter's dedication has never wavered. And it won't; excellence is a lifelong quest for Peter.

Peter, like many of the extraordinary people in this book, is as much an example of world-class character and kindness as he is of world-class talent. It is people like Peter that cause me to say show jumping is indeed the world's most beautiful sport.

Six World Cup Finals, placed in all six; best finishes include 5th place on Ardennes 1982, Gothenburg and 5th place on Threes and Sevens 1989, Tampa

Three-time winner of Grand Prix of New York—1978 on Semi-Pro, 1992 on Oxo, 1998 on Legato

2010: Won the Devon Grand Prix on Select, Devon, Pennsylvania

Peter Leone & Legato

1998: Won the Presidents Cup and double clear in the Nations Cup for the win on Crown Royal Legato, Washington, D.C.

1998: Won both the Saturday Night and Sunday Afternoon Grands Prix to win the "Golden Whip" on Legato, Nörten-Hardenberg

1997: North American Champion at Spruce Meadows, Calgary

1996: Team Silver medalist at the Centennial Olympic Games on Legato, Atlanta

1988: Won the American Gold Cup on Threes and Sevens, Devon, Pennsylvania

1982: 4th place at World Championship Team Competition; Double Clear in Third Leg of Individual Final on Ardennes, Dublin

1982: First all-brother Nations Cup Team in show jumping history (Peter on Semi-Pro, Mark on Tim, Armand on Loecky), Lucerne

Ch. 20

Jeffery Welles
&Armani

When Jeffery Welles is in the saddle, it is immediately clear to spectators that this man means business. However, for Jeffery, show jumping is not just his business—it's his life. Jeffery's career spans over four decades and began when he was just six years old. He has competed in over a hundred World Cup Qualifiers and has been on four FEI World Cup teams. Jeffery is a remarkably talented horseman in his own right, but like so many others in the sport, he contends that his excellence is due at least partially to those who have supported him unconditionally in his career. When asked to reflect on his cherished support system, he was quick to single out one horse in particular: Armani.

Tony De Costa
Jeffery in good form.

327

OKAY ARMANI!

In 2002, when Armani was seven years old, Jeffery met the horse for the first time in Belgium. Jeffery and his companions, Emile Spidone and Paul Hendricks, watched Armani's owner Christine Tallieu-huot ride the horse and take him over a few small jumps. Christine, an amateur Canadian rider, married a Belgian and worked as an exceedingly talented horse trainer in her adopted country. Christine was searching for a rider to purchase Armani and take him to the top of the sport. At first, the men were not impressed by what they saw. Their attitude quickly changed, however. Jeffery recalls, "He looked nice going over the little jumps but we weren't overly excited. Then she put the jump up to a 1.30m (that's about 4ft. 5in.) or a little bit bigger, and he really opened behind and just jumped it explosively. We all looked at each other and said, 'Okay!'"

When the men voiced their interest in Armani, Christine was hesitant to allow Jeffery to ride him. She was extremely protective of Armani, and she was unaware of Jeffery's riding prowess. However, after a quick conversation with Emile and Paul, Christine relented and permitted Jeffery to ride Armani. He recalls, "I got on and jumped five or six jumps, and from then on, Christine was very happy and totally on board." Though it broke Christine's heart to think of parting with Armani, she recognized the way that Jeffery brought out the best in Armani and knew it was time for the rest of the show jumping world to see it.

Jeffery, Emile, and Paul remained nearby for the next two days and went to see Armani in a show. As he remembers, "A couple of days later, we went to see him at a horse show, and he was jumping almost two feet higher than the jumps were set. It was something like a 1.20m class because Christine hadn't shown him in very big classes—she'd brought him along very slowly, and he was soaring over the jumps, so we were saying, 'Okay, now we've got to try to find the money for this horse, whatever it takes.'"

Jeffery and his Triton Ventures partner, Gareth Gair, ended up buying half of him with Bill Kimmel, a man they had met in Old Salem, near their Brewster, New York, farm. They brought Armani to the U.S. and put a lot of heart and soul into moving the horse up to the higher classes for which he was truly destined. His first U.S. horse show was in Lake Placid, New York, in July. Jeffery notes, "He never looked askance at anything, even during that fragile transitional period when moving from a familiar situation to a new environment. When he stepped into the ring at Lake Placid onto the grass field, he was just amazing." Armani's new trainers kept Christine's pace with him and took it slowly for the remainder of the year. Eventually, they began to introduce him into the more challenging classes. When Armani was eight years old, he won his first Grand Prix class in Old Salem, New York.

> "I must say that from the very first time in the ring, he was a gentleman. **He was all business**; very careful and brave."

TROUBLE IN PARADISE

Things were going extremely well for Jeffery and Armani until they encountered their first stroke of bad luck. Armani, for all his gentlemanly behavior in the ring, had a strong tendency to misbehave in the stalls. When the horse became bored or agitated, he often kicked the walls of his stall. While at the HITS show in Saugerties, New York, in 2003, Armani

A quiet moment—mutual admiration.

kicked a hole in the wall of his stall. His leg became stuck, and in an effort to free himself, the horse frantically yanked his leg out of the wall. In doing so, Armani pulled a ligament in the stifle and hock area of his leg. This injury meant show season was over for Armani; he was ordered to four months of stall rest. For a restless horse like Armani, stall rest could be torturous. He was permitted to move only ten steps out of his stall a few times a day to be cold-hosed, which aided the healing process. Apart from that, Armani was forced to remain in his stall while the season continued without him.

Armani's recovery process was particularly difficult for Jeffery. "It was devastating for me," he says. "It was the time of his life when he needed to get mileage. The Olympic trials in 2004 would have been my goal, but he was still young. He was nine years old and so brave and so straightforward. He has a championship mentality and ability. Unfortunately, the 2004 trials were no longer possible. Even though he came back from the injury well, we couldn't get ready for the trials realistically. We brought him back very slowly. The ligament totally healed, and it never came up again." Armani's recovery was based largely on the horse being walked around the trails. Jeffery, Ed Copeland, and Gareth Gair alternated walking Armani for multiple hours each day.

THE MEDIA FINDS A STORY

By 2004, Armani was back on the show jumping scene with a vengeance. He performed astonishingly well in a series of large Grands Prix in 2005—it was tough to believe he had ever been injured. He was second in the American Invitational, chasing right behind Beezie Madden and Authentic, Armani's half-brother. That year, Jeffery and Armani had the great honor of representing the U.S. in Europe on the Super League tour, where the best of the best compete in the quintessential proving ground for world-class show jumpers. They blew away the competition. The pair won the King George V Cup in Hickstead. In addition, they were on the winning Nations Cup team in Aachen and in Barcelona, the final Grand Prix competition in the Super League, where they jumped two clear rounds for the team.

Jeffery is extremely modest about their astonishing comeback, saying simply, "It was really nice that summer to finish with Barcelona and the U.S. winning Super League 2005." The press, however, recognized that Armani and Jeffery had done something truly amazing and latched on to the story tightly, which rarely happens in the show jumping world.

> Jeffery was recognized in *USA Today* for his outstanding rides in the Super League and named **Athlete of the Week**.

Shortly thereafter, *Chronicle of the Horse* reported to its equestrian readers: "Two completely faultless rounds have earned Jeffery Welles, the show jumper from Ridgefield, Connecticut, recognition from *USA Today*. The national newspaper named Welles, 43, its athlete of the week for the performance that propelled the U.S. team to a tie for second in last weekend's Samsung Nations Cup Final, a finish that put the U.S. team atop the year-long series standings. Welles rode Armani, a 10-year-old SelleFrancais gelding owned by Bill Kimmel, Sandy Yeager, Kimmel-Yeager Equine LLC, and Triton Ventures. In July, Welles and Armani then went on and won the King George V Cup at Hickstead (England)."

UPS AND DOWNS

2006 was another extremely successful year for Jeffery and Armani. The pair was named as an alternate on the U.S. World Equestrian Games (WEG) team in Aachen, Germany. Since they were not going to ride in the WEG, Jeffery shipped Armani to Spruce Meadows and had double clear rounds in the Nations Cup and placed in the CN Grand Prix. Armani performed especially well on grass footing, as evidenced by his success at two separate Grands Prix at Spruce Meadows on his 2004 summer tour. After the last show of 2006, Armani's career went on hold again, but this time it was for a planned surgery on his stifle. The wear and tear of competing regularly at the highest level had taken its toll on Armani's meniscus. It would be nearly a year before he came back to reclaim his earlier level of fitness and ability. Ever resilient, Armani came out of his recovery period just as tough as he had been before. In late 2007 and early 2008, he came back "super strong," Jeffery says. "We did some classes earlier in the circuit and he was jumping fantastically—the best he'd ever jumped." Despite his extremely successful recovery, tragedy struck the pair once again. The opportunity to ride at the Olympic trials was sadly lost due to the strain of a tiny ligament in Armani's hoof, which was the result of an injury the horse had sustained earlier in his life.

BACK ON TOP

You can't keep a good horse down, though, and so once again, after a period of rest and healing, Armani was ready to start jumping again in 2009. He came back strong yet again, and in 2010, he had two double clear rounds to win the $200,000 Gene Misch American Invitational in April. You may recall from earlier chapters that the American Invitational is the Super Bowl of U.S. show jumping. "I know him so well at this point, it is just so great to still have him and have him jumping like this," Jeffery said at the time. Armani's ability to recover from an injury and win the class he'd placed second in five years earlier was confirmation that he still had what it takes to be a world-class competitor. His new half-owner, Abigail Wexner, who came on board to replace Bill Kimmel, is also the owner of his half-brother Authentic and helped to make it possible for Armani to continue his interrupted career. Now 15 years old, Armani had such a good summer season that he qualified for the fantastic Pfizer $1 Million Grand Prix at what is referred to as HITS on the Hudson in September 2010. At HITS, Armani did not fail to impress; he captured 5th place in the first million-dollar class in America.

"People ask me what would have happened if he hadn't had these injuries. Our lives would have been extremely different. Even with his injuries, he certainly did very well," Jeffery says. Unfortunately, after the Pfizer Million, the ligament in Armani's foot was sore once again, and it was recommended that he take some time off. Armani soon grew bored, and since he was constantly straining to reach the grass outside his fence, his caretakers allowed him to wander around the 23-acre farm unsupervised. After some time like this, Jeffery observed Armani bothering the other horses in their paddocks. Shortly thereafter, when he saw Armani jumping a ditch on his own, he knew it was the right time to start him back to work. He bemusedly recalls how Armani seemed a little displeased by having to be clipped and groomed and made to look like a show horse again.

"He's fast in the ring, and he's so brave. He keeps his head together when he's galloping and doesn't get frazzled. **He puts his eye on the jump;** that's where all his attention is. Most of the great horses you see are totally focused on the fences."

Jeffery fondly remembers traveling the world with Armani during peak times in his career. "He has always been such a dependable horse. It didn't matter what show or what venue—if he was sound and going well, I knew we had a chance to do well. He attacks the fences and never backs off," Jeffery says.

Armani has his own style of jumping up with a huge round jump, which is where he can lose time—those precious fractions of a second of extra hang time. The more relaxed he is, the rounder he jumps. "He's very elastic and puts in a powerful final two strides before jumping, coiling up a little bit, then with a thrust that seems to come from nowhere—not a big explosion but a 'snap' up off the ground. It's a feeling you rarely get from a horse," Jeffery says. "It didn't matter what kind of combination they built for a class—not that he didn't make mistakes, but there was no particular worry when we went to shows, except keeping him relaxed. He gets wound up in certain settings, but he is more relaxed in a big open ring like those at Aachen or Spruce Meadows or The Fidelity Jumper Classic."

THE SUPPORT NETWORK

Today, Jeffery is adamant about the fact that he simply could not have achieved success with Armani without the help of his support system. He remains eternally grateful to all those who helped him buy horses throughout his career. He also holds a special place in his heart for Oliver O'Toole, a well-known groom whose name is now etched on a Perpetual Trophy at the Winter Equestrian Festival. Oliver accompanied Armani to Barcelona, but unfortunately cancer claimed the promising young groom's life at a mere 30 years old. A Swedish groom, Emma Nielsen, cared for Armani while he was on another European tour. Without these wonderful people to care for and befriend Armani, showing a horse at this level would not

GRETCHEN ALMY

Loving partners, taking time to remember when.

be possible. Everyone who encountered Armani was drawn in by his charisma, including the vets who cared for him at Fairfield Equine in Connecticut: Drs. Mitchell, Weinburg, and Edward, and Dr. Nixon at Cornell Equine Hospital.

Today, though Armani's career is a bit more relaxed, he is still ridden regularly and enjoys spending time outdoors. Jeffery remains cautiously optimistic about Armani's return to an intensely competitive lifestyle. After the horse won a class at Abigail Wexner's farm (where the Albany Classic is held on grass), George Morris approached Jeffery. "He always loved the horse. We spoke after the show, and George asked me if I think he has a championship left in him for the WEG. I had to say I'm not really sure. He doesn't owe us anything. If he can comfortably get back into the show ring, he will." Jeffery tells me he will pick his next classes on the grass fields—the footing Armani prefers—but if he finds him to be unhappy or sore, Armani's welfare will always come first and foremost. Regardless of what Armani's competitive future holds, it is certain that the horse will be admired and cared for. As a rider myself, I have tremendous respect for Jeffery's love and passion for his horse of a lifetime. Jeffery Welles is a superstar by all standards and no doubt we will yet see him in an Olympic stadium.

2nd place at the $200,000 American Invitational on Armani, Tampa

2010: Winner at the $200,000 Gene Misch American Invitational, Tampa

2009: New Albany Classic Grand Prix, Hampton Classic on Armani

Jeffery Welles &Armani

2007: Winner at the King George V Cup on Armani, Hickstead

2007: Winner Team USA at the Nations Cup Super League on Armani, Aachen

2005: Winner Team USA at the Nations Cup Super League on Armani, Barcelona

2005: 1st place at the Winter Equestrian Festival Challenge $25,000 Cup CSI3

2005: *USA Today*'s Athlete of the Week

Ch. 21

Chris Kappler & Royal Kaliber

As a child, Chris Kappler lived with his family in Wayne, Illinois, a town with a large horse community. Chris had a very ordinary early childhood and participated in the usual sports and activities. When he was eight years old, he was introduced to riding by his mother, Kay. She began taking riding lessons at the country club where the family belonged. Kay's newfound hobby piqued the interest of Chris and his sister, Katie, who also began to take riding lessons.

Initially, Katie and Chris rode only once or twice a week, but their interest increased and they began to ride more frequently. Within a few years, Katie and Chris purchased their first horses, and the family became immersed in riding.

BOB LANGRISH MBE, EQUESTRIAN PHOTOGRAPHER
Chris and Roy in an Olympic moment in Athens (2004).

> What began as a hobby blossomed into a **FULL-BLOWN PASSION**, and Chris and Katie began showing at the local hunt club.

When Chris was about 12, he and Katie started training at a barn named Our Day Farm in the Chicago area. These training sessions marked the beginning of their riding careers.

Chris qualified for the Indoor Medal Finals at 13, which was considered extremely early by all standards. He was regularly riding an equitation horse, Count to Ten. While this horse undeniably put Chris on the map, in many ways, Count to Ten put Our Day Farm on the map as well.

WORKING WITH GEORGE MORRIS

Chris met U.S. Olympic coach and trainer George Morris at an indoor event held at the Pennsylvania National Horse Show where Chris was competing and George was one of the judges. George called Chris back on top (a show jumping or equitation expression for the cream of the crop in a given class who are asked back in ranked order for further testing). To compete in any event at the prestigious Garden is a tremendous accomplishment for trainers and riders. Chris placed third in the Medals Finals that year.

George Morris and other top professionals were at the finals scouting for talent, both young riders and their horses. On the day of the finals, Chris's mother impulsively approached George Morris and asked him, "What should I do with my son?" George told Kay that Chris reminded him of the extremely talented Conrad Homfeld and that he would very much like to have Chris train with him at

Hunterdon, his world-renowned farm. They were invited for two weeks during the Christmas season at the end of 1984.

After their stay at George's farm, Chris and Katie were invited to Florida to compete at the Wellington show grounds. At that time, Wellington was only a three-week event (unlike the 12-week event it is today) and took place at the Polo Club, which to this day remains part of the Winter Equestrian Festival. One of George's collaborators, Frank Madden, helped Chris with equitation, and George mentored Chris in the jumper classes. Chris and his family worked out their schedules so that Chris could attend school in Chicago and commute for training back and forth to Florida.

The Kappler family acquired a farm where they were now running a business. Chris and Katie worked wonderfully together and trained one another's horses at the ten-stall barn. Chris was increasingly involved in the small business at the Kappler barn. For the most part, he concentrated on his own riding, though he did have a few clients he was training.

With Frank Madden's assistance, Chris found Kandi, an equitation horse. Chris had a great last junior year with Kandi at the Maclay finals in 1985 where Chris and Kandi placed second. After the Maclay finals in 1985, Chris declared himself a professional. The decision is irreversible—once you do it, there is no going back to amateur status. While he did not know at that point if he would be internationally competitive, he loved every part of riding. "If I could make a living at it, this is what I wanted to do. I was never so certain of anything in my life," Chris tells me. "The riding, the people, working with

Deciding to become a **professional** at the **age of 14** was a tremendously unusual decision.

young horses—I just could not get enough of it. There were not enough hours in my days to give me my fill."

Though his parents were extremely supportive of Chris's career choice, they also stressed the importance of a college education. Katie was attending college, and Chris was being pressured by his parents to continue his education. In an effort to appease them, Chris enrolled in Aurora College. After one day of classes, Chris knew that college was not for him. "I just couldn't do it. I couldn't leave my horses for any length of time, so I left Aurora and immersed myself full-time in the horse business," he explains.

THE NEXT BIG BREAK – CONCORDE

Later in 1985, Chris's family received a call from George Morris. While in Canada, George encountered a horse named Concorde. While Concorde had a difficult reputation, he was an all-star jumper. Industry insiders would call Concorde "scopey," meaning that he was very powerful and able to jump extremely large jumps, but Concorde had ridability problems. George was able to make a deal to ship Concorde to Florida so that Chris could have some time to try him out.

George advised the family, "If you like the horse, buy him." George's advice proved to be extremely valuable. Chris maintains that Concorde was the horse that transformed him into a rider. The horse had a lot of trouble at the in-gate and the water jump, but Chris and George worked tirelessly on Concorde's issues, and soon Chris and Concorde developed a close bond.

Chris began to divide his time between working with George and Concorde in Florida and rushing home to Illinois to work with his clients on the farm. Though Chris began to win competitions with Concorde almost immediately, the horse was still so difficult that George reluctantly suggested Chris send Concorde back to his prior owners.

GRETCHEN ALMY

The horse in the photo with Chris is Royal Reflection, owned by Kathy Kamine. The mare is an offspring to Royal Kaliber; she is currently seven and was born the year he died.

While Chris usually listened to George, this time he would hear none of it. He had **fallen in love with Concorde**, and bought him.

Chris was 18 years old at this point and had already developed a reputation for being able to deal with difficult horses. His talent and his competitive streak prevented him from giving up on Concorde.

Chris enrolled in large Grand Prix classes, and with Concorde as his partner, he started to win. In the Grand Prix classes, the general rule is the bigger the prize money, the more difficult the course designers make the course. If you are riding in a $150,000 class, you can expect bigger jumps, more technical distances, and a bigger challenge than the jumps in a $25,000 class.

In 1988, Chris had the privilege of riding Concorde on his first winning Nations Cup Team at the Royal Winter Fair in Toronto, Canada. A Nations Cup is a country-versus-country competition in which four riders represent each nation and complete two rounds, with the worst score from each round dropped from consideration. It is a pressure-cooker situation; the equestrians are riding for their entire country and desperately want to contribute to the keeper score (or overall score that is counted) for their team.

Chris's Nations Cup success opened the door to the United States Equestrian Team. Chris felt that his hard work had finally paid off, saying, "The work and time you put into your horses developing that relationship just begins to feed to that next level." When he next qualified for World Cup finals, he was the highest-ranked American, placing tenth with the temperamental Concorde. Chris and Concorde continued to compete together with success through 1993. In the period between 1986 and 1993, Concorde and Chris earned over $500,000 in prize money. Concorde enjoyed an extremely long career, which many experts would argue is characteristic of horses with difficult personalities.

CHRIS MOVES TO HUNTERDON

In 1993, George and Ray Texil (a talented equestrian and George Morris's former title rider) parted ways. Shortly thereafter, George asked Chris to work for him full-time. This was not an easy decision for Chris to make. He was leaving behind his family and his rapidly expanding horse business. However, his mother told him, "There is absolutely no question—you have to go." In many ways, it was Kay's unwavering devotion to the sport that propelled Chris to leave home and go work for George. Though the Kappler family recognized that this was a tremendous opportunity, Chris's departure from his support system and from the family business that he essentially started was full of emotion and difficulty.

Chris was able to bring some of his older horses with him to George's farm, which helped him with the transition. George's vast knowledge of the sport and Chris's passion made the two a perfect match. George's interest in the sport remains with him to this day. George is over 70, but still rides multiple horses each day. To this day, George is magical to watch. Chris recalls how, even at the end of a cold, grueling, and exhausting day of training, George refuses to give up. He will continue working with any student wanting his help.

Chris continued to work directly for George through 2005. A few years later, George sold Hunterdon, his famous farm, to Chris's clients, Steve and Lori Racioppo. Chris remains Hunterdon's resident pro.

By 1995, Chris had acquired a string of successful

Chris in action in Florida, always in the hunt for the winner's circle.

horses: Zanzibar, AbraCadabra, and Seven Wonder, which enabled him to achieve a milestone in his career: he won his first American Invitational. The Invitational, founded by the recently deceased Gene Mische, is a famous evening Grand Prix held every April, under the gleaming stadium lights, in Tampa, Florida's Buccaneer football stadium. The Invitational course is huge and built like an Olympic course, thanks largely to the work of its designer, Steve Stephens.

Chris has the unique distinction of winning the American Invitational three times and placing second twice. His achievement is especially notable for the fact that he is the only competitor to have ever placed first on three separate occasions. Chris was ranked first on the United States Ranking list in 1995, which made him eligible to embark on his first European tour for the USET.

CHRIS MEETS ROYAL KALIBER

Following Chris's tremendous success in early 2000, things slowed down considerably. Though he was still competing, it was clear Chris needed to find more superstar horses. In 2002, Chris was traveling through Europe on a horse-hunting trip. Europe remains the preferred venue for horse-hunting because of the high volume of show jumpers born and raised there and because the sport is held in such high esteem. A high-ranking champion jumper rider like Chris is considered a celebrity in Europe, comparable to an all-star major league baseball player in America.

On one such trip, Henk Nooren, Chris's European agent, brought a horse named Royal Kaliber to a farm for Chris to try out. Though Chris was initially hesitant, he liked the young stallion and expressed interest. However, Chris returned to Florida without purchasing Roy (as he would come to be known). As the weeks passed by, Chris was unable to keep Roy off his mind. He flew back to Europe, and to his delight,

Roy was still available. Chris's trials with Roy lasted about three or four days, with each day better than the last. Chris, with Kathy and Hal Kamine, made the decision to purchase Royal Kaliber.

That spring, Roy had his first big show in Lake Placid, New York. Roy was a huge horse, powerful and exuberant. He was able to jump both high and wide with ease, but Chris did not want to rush Roy. He took it slowly, placing Roy first in intermediate classes to build the horse's confidence. By this time, Chris recognized that Roy was special and the two were developing a deep and trusting bond.

In 2002, Royal Kaliber and Chris competed at the Cincinnati Horse Show, known for its large and difficult courses. Chris felt ready for this class; he had no other horse suitable for the challenge—Roy was his only option. Chris had a lot of confidence in Roy's abilities, and he delivered. The horse jumped magnificently, and the pair went double clear, meaning they did not lower a single fence in the first round or the jump-off.

> Chris proudly remembers, "When Royal Kaliber trotted into a stadium, as big as he was, **he grew another ten inches, and lesser horses around him would shrivel.**"

The following year, when Roy was ten years old, the pair competed with great success throughout the Winter Equestrian Festival. Though the course was exceedingly difficult, Roy and Chris placed consistently, class after class. They were second again at the American Invitational in April at the end of that winter season. Roy handled the big courses with ease—in fact, big seemed to suit him best.

CHRIS ON THE ROAD TO THE OLYMPICS

Their success at the 2004 Invitational marked the start of a winning streak. After the Invitational, they won in Palm Beach and in Devon. A year earlier, Chris became the first rider in ten years to be subjectively selected to the U.S. team for the Pan Am Games in the Dominican Republic.

Being subjectively selected means that based on Chris's and Roy's history of performance together, the coaches allowed them to skip the selection trials and appointed them members of the team. Subjective selection is unpopular and adds tremendous pressure to the team. Despite the controversy, subjective selection also has its fair share of benefits. The selection process is physically grueling and often exhausts the horse before they even have a chance to make it to the main event. However, being a subjective selection pair did not ensure Chris a free ride to the Pan Am Games. He had to compete first in Aachen, Germany, and he had to place well there to maintain his spot. Chris traveled to Aachen with the rest of the team, comprised of Beezie Madden, Margie Engle, and Lauren Hough. Chris took Royal Kaliber and another horse named Premiere.

"Royal Kaliber and Premiere were like having **Michael Jordan** and **Larry Bird** on your team, and the rest of the line-up was like having a string of **Dennis Rodmans**."

In Aachen, the team experienced great success. They were double clear in the important Nations Cup rounds and fourth in the Grand Prix. Chris won the Style Award that year at Aachen, which is a tremendous honor for an American to receive in Germany, where the sport is tremendously important. Chris left Europe brimming with confidence. He went on to the West Coast that year and competed in a big $250,000 class in California with Roy. This competition, where Roy and Chris placed third, was the final prep for the Pan Am Games. The Pan Am Games were very important because they were the qualifying games for the Olympics—if the U.S. team did not medal, then they did not qualify for the Olympics. At the competition, Chris had only one rail down in the first round. He ended up winning Individual Silver and the team collectively won gold, thus qualifying for the Athens Olympics.

Chris ended his season that year with a competition at Spruce Meadows. Royal had done a lot of flying, and Chris felt the best thing was to give him a break for the remainder of the year. The two would have a fresh start in Florida, and Chris used the break to help him recover and peak for the Olympics.

THE EUROPEAN TOUR

At the time of the Olympic trials, Chris had been riding Roy for four years and was extremely emotionally attached to the horse. His trip to the Olympics with Roy was a tremendous achievement, and his lifelong dreams were unfolding before his very eyes. Much of Chris's show jumping career had been based on risk-taking and with the Olympics looming it was clear that all the risks were well worth it. While qualifying for the Olympics was gratifying in itself, it was not enough for Chris. He is quick to point out, "It wasn't about just going. I really, really wanted the results. I just didn't want to go and have the team jacket and the Olympic clothes. I wanted to bring home the glory for my country, my family, and my staff, and failing was something I couldn't, wouldn't bear."

GRETCHEN ALMY

Chris and Luis Fernandez, who is a critical part of Chris's operations success.

The European Tour began in Hackenburg, Germany; Hackenburg was the prelude to the Olympics. Royal Kaliber and Chris were competing in a Grand Prix in the jump-off round. The jump-off is the second timed round against the clock and has a reputation for being risky in relative terms; with added speed comes challenges. When Chris and Roy were turning to the last fence, the horse slipped from behind. It was a minor mistake, and Chris thought nothing of it until the following day, when he noticed some swelling in Roy's hind ankle.

Chris began to panic. Aachen, the last stop on the European Tour, was merely two weeks away, and Roy was lame and sore. With no chance of making a speedy recovery, Aachen was out of the question for Royal Kaliber. Tim Ober, the USET team veterinarian, examined Roy. Tim and his team were unsure what they could do, but they started aggressively working on him using lasers, cold therapy, wraps, ultrasound, and every kind of local therapy imaginable. Though the team was working feverishly to nurse Roy back to health and Chris was riding him lightly, there was still no way that he would be able to compete in Aachen. As a result, Chris went on to Aachen without Roy and took Premiere instead.

Chris and Premiere placed fourth at the Grand Prix in Aachen. Though Chris was steadily upping his workload with Roy, the two made little progress. About three weeks later, Frank Chapot, the U.S. team coach, came to Chris to inform him that he was under a lot of pressure. Chris and Frank both recognized that real improvements needed to be made before the Olympics. Roy was finally looking and feeling better, and Chris managed to jump a few jumps with him, which was a tremendous accomplishment based on the circumstances. Frank Chapot and George finally declared Chris, Roy, and the rest of the final U.S. team ready for the Olympics.

THE 2004 OLYMPIC GAMES

Royal was doing well as the team prepared for their jog for the FEI officials. A jog is a preface to every major international competition: horses are presented to a panel of officials, and the horses are jogged in-hand, not ridden. The purpose of a jog is to determine the horses' physical readiness for the competition. Beezie Madden's horse, Authentic (also known as Bud), nearly caused the team to miss their first Olympic triumph due to his colic distress. Adding to the mounting tension preceding the jog was the fact that McLain's mare, Sapphire, developed a horrific leg infection from a tiny cut a couple weeks earlier. Since medications are not allowed, the team worked tirelessly to treat the infection without antibiotics.

Between **Sapphire's infection, Bud's colic, and Roy's ankle injury**, the fact that the U.S. team made it through the jog at all was an **absolute miracle**.

In the Olympic warm-ups, Roy rose to the challenge. Though Chris would later admit the horse was a bit rusty, he performed splendidly, with one rail down in the first round. The pair worked well together for the rest of the warm-up sessions or early rounds, prior to the Nations Cup. On the morning of the Nations Cup, or the team rounds, Chris began his day by riding Roy at 6:00 AM to calm his nerves and loosen him up. The team performed well in the first round, and by the second round, scheduled to begin at 10:00 PM that evening, the U.S. team was tied for second place. At this point Team USA was sitting on eight faults (or two rails) between the four U.S. riders, meaning two team members had clear rounds. The second round went off in much the same fashion as the previous rounds; Roy was fantastic and consistent.

Originally, Team USA was awarded the silver medal, but shortly thereafter it was exchanged for the gold medal.

Chris studies the next obstacle.

Germany was stripped of the gold medal after one of their horses tested positive for banned substances. Upon receiving the gold, the team moved on to the rounds that would determine the individual Olympic medals.

The first round course was huge with very few clears in sight. There was to be a timed jump-off for silver and bronze medal placements. After the earlier rounds, the horses were cooled out and attended to for hours. Drug tests that included blood and urine samples were administered, and by the time all of the tests were completed, it was nearly 3:00 AM. Chris, Beezie, and McLain all said later, that this 24 hour experience was both emotionally and physically as challenging as the riding. Imagine all of the highs and lows in a single day—first the competitors were unsure if they had placed at all, and suddenly they were awarded the silver medal (later to be the gold).

THE INDIVIDUAL MEDAL COMPETITION

Chris maintained his focus, and he was scheduled to ride fourth in the individual medal competition. In the first round, there was only one clear, and Roy jumped spectacularly. The second round, however, was much larger and more difficult. With one rail down, a discouraged Chris feared he had lost his chance to win an individual medal.

Due to the difficulty of the course and the fact that no one jumped clear, there was to be a jump-off for the silver and bronze medal placements. Rodrigo Pessoa of Brazil and Chris were jumping-off for the silver medal. The winner would take silver, and the slower of the two would take bronze. The early part of the jump-off went well for Chris, and Rodrigo had the last fence down. Chris strategized that he could either go fast with the chance of one rail down, or he could go clean and win it outright.

Chris decided that it was not the time to be

conservative—he chose to go fast. As the pair jumped over an extremely wide oxer, Chris sensed that Royal did not land correctly, but with no other choice, he had to continue. In retrospect, Chris says that Royal felt strange to him for the remainder of the round, though he concedes that it was not obvious the moment it happened. The combination of double verticals came up, and Roy's discomfort nearly caused the horse to falter in the in-and-out, but Roy, ever resilient, somehow managed to jump both elements clean. Roy and Chris jumped one more fence before things quickly turned from bad to worse.

When they were two obstacles away from winning the silver medal, Chris felt Roy stumble. Without any hesitation, Chris pulled up and jumped off Roy. In this moment, you could have heard a pin drop in the stadium. Some 60,000 spectators were struck silent as they looked on, collectively dumbfounded. Chris instinctively knew something was wrong with Roy, and he summoned the horse ambulance. The ambulance came in the ring and took Roy to the clinic immediately. Chris's forfeit put him in third place and earned him a bronze medal rather than the silver that was two jumps away from his grasp. In a particularly touching display of good sportsmanship, Rodrigo marched back onto the field and gave Chris a much-needed hug.

Chris knew that Royal Kaliber was extraordinarily determined and that if he had not stopped, Roy would have finished the course on three legs if necessary. But Roy was so important to Chris; he simply could not put the horse at risk. This intense sense of camaraderie is something that you will not find in any other sport—the respect and admiration that Chris felt for Royal Kaliber was immeasurable.

TRAGEDY STRIKES THE MIGHTY STALLION

A few days later, Royal Kaliber was diagnosed with colon enteritis. In essence, the injury to his leg, coupled with the stress of being in an unfamiliar place and the stress of the competition, greatly affected Roy's weak digestive tract. Since Roy was unable to fly with colon enteritis, he was forced to stay in Athens when the other horses left. Horses are naturally social animals, and the fact that Roy was left alone undoubtedly affected his already-fragile psyche. Tim, the team's vet, stayed with Royal, hoping to get him well enough to fly from Athens to the Sommern Clinic, one of the best veterinary clinics in Europe. But Roy was unable to eat, and he began to rapidly lose weight.

> **Chris willingly gave up the silver medal,** as his partner's well-being was far more important to him than the fulfillment of his personal goals.

Forty days passed, and Roy grew weaker by the minute. After consulting numerous specialists, it was decided that surgery was the most viable option to remove the bad intestine. They flew in Dr. Jack Snyder, one of the best equine surgeons in America, to perform the amazing four-hour surgery. In an effort to heal Royal, they removed a portion of his intestines.

After the surgery, Roy's condition seemed to improve dramatically. He resumed eating normally and regained some of his strength. They moved Roy to a familiar local farm, thinking that familiar surroundings would aid his recovery. Three or four days after he was moved, Roy became sick again, and all the adhesions were reforming in the intestine. Not willing to lose hope, the team decided on additional surgery. However, in the operating room, it became devastatingly clear that there was nothing else the doctors could do for Roy—they had to let him go. Roy was humanely put to sleep. The mighty stallion closed his eyes for the final time in the operating room.

Roy was a bona fide athlete, a warrior who left everything on the field at the Olympics. He was extremely unusual in that he was equal parts strong-willed, hardheaded stallion, and sweet, loving companion. Moreover, Roy was Chris's very best friend. The horse loved the shows, even though it sometimes took four people to get him in the ring because of his excitement.

When the team made the decision to let Roy go, he died the warrior he was for most of his life. He is remembered not as a sick horse at the clinic but as the Olympic champion he was to the bitter end. Today, Chris stores Royal Kaliber's ashes in a Team USA trunk with Roy's bridles and equipment, which are also kept in this precious place. Chris keeps the trunk with him at all times. Wherever he travels, Roy's ashes follow.

Chris and Roy were deeply connected. Though the loss of Roy was devastating for Chris, he is the type of individual who always looks for the positive in any situation. Chris says, "Roy was here to give me what I wanted more than anything, and he did." Chris finds comfort in the fact that Roy spent his final days on the biggest stage, doing his best in front of the entire world.

Chris has employed the same groom, Luis Fernandez, since 1992. Luis was Roy's groom and still grooms for Chris to this day. Chris told me when Luis retires, so will he. He concedes, "I couldn't do it without him." Throughout Royal Kaliber's entire ordeal, Luis and Chris's wife, Jenny, remained faithfully by his side. The bill for Royal's care was astronomically high. The USET stepped in and took responsibility for most of it. While it was not necessarily their obligation to take on, Chris remains extremely

Chris fondly remembers Royal Kaliber, saying,

"He just made life fun.

I couldn't wait to ride him in the morning and would ride him again in the afternoon. I rode him on Mondays, even if it was just a walk, because we couldn't bear not to be with one another in that way every day."

grateful to them, as well as to the owners, teammates, and friends who had Roy's best interests at heart.

The ultimate form of human devotion in life is arguably to give everything you have and make sacrifices for the sake of achieving your goals. Perseverance in the face of pain and hardship signifies true devotion to one's cause, and Chris and Royal Kaliber undoubtedly exemplify all of these qualities. The pair truly gave all they had, and together they made Olympic history. Roy in the end gave his life for Chris. As the saying goes, what doesn't kill you makes you stronger, and what Chris lived through makes his strength of character hard for the rest of us to imagine. Never was a horse loved more than Roy; never was an Olympic story so inspirational and at the same time heartbreaking. Roy will never be forgotten. Honoring his horse's memory is now Chris's life quest, and honor it he has.

2004: Team Gold medalist at the Athens Olympics on Royal Kaliber

2004: Individual Bronze medalist at the Athens Olympics on Royal Kaliber

2004: Team Bronze medalist at the Nations Cup on Royal Kaliber, Aachen

Chris Kappler
&Royal Kaliber

2003: Individual Silver medalist at the Pan American Games on Royal Kaliber, Santo Domingo

2003: Won the $150,000 American Grand Prix Association Championship on Royal Kaliber, Wellington

2003: Won the $75,000 Devon Grand Prix on Royal Kaliber

2003: Sweep of the first Triple Crown of Show Jumping on Royal Kaliber; First rider to ever win classes with the most prize money in the U.S.: the American Invitational and the AGA Show Jumping Championship, on consecutive weekends. Won the third leg, the American Gold Cup, Devon, PA

2003: Team Gold medalist at the Pan American Games on Royal Kaliber, Santo Domingo

1995, 2003, 2009: American Invitational career wins

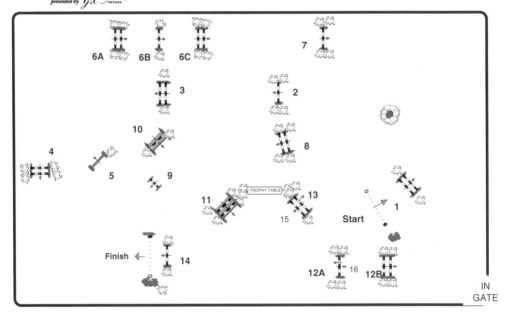

Steve Stephens's American Invitational course diagram (2011).

STEVE STEPHENS

364

CH. 22

Show Jumping Fundamentals

This chapter is for those uninitiated to the sport of show jumping. If you are a fan of the sport or a rider yourself, you can skip this chapter. For all the parents, aunts, uncles, and friends of participants in this sport, this chapter is for you. We will go over some of the basics of show jumping so you can enjoy *Unbridled Passion* without getting lost in jargon.

CLASS FORMATS

There are two types of formats that you need to understand. There are **speed classes** that are comprised of a single round, meaning a single jumping course where the rider with the fastest time and least number of **faults**, or fences lowered, wins. In some cases, faults are converted to added seconds; other times, faults mean you move to the back of the class standings behind all clear rounds. If it is the former rule, a very fast horse and rider could still win.

Traditional rounds mean you jump the first track or course and, as long as you do not go over the time allowed, your time does not matter. If you **clear**, meaning you finish with no faults and under the time allowed, you go on a shortened course against the clock. In this format, the fastest rider in the second round with the fewest faults wins, with other participants getting second, third, and so on.

OBSTACLES AND JUMPS

There are several different jumps and obstacles. The first is a **vertical**, meaning a straight up-and-down fence with no width or spread. You jump to clear the top of the obstacle.

Author standing next to a typical vertical obstacle.   TONY DE COSTA

366

Oxer front view. TONY DE COSTA

The second kind of jump is called an **oxer**. This jump has both a vertical and horizontal component, where the horse and rider will need to go both up and over the jump. This jump is considered much more challenging because of the width.

Oxer side view—5 ft. 9 in. wide. TONY DE COSTA

Swedish oxer.   TONY DE COSTA

There is a second variation of the oxer called a **Swedish oxer**, named after the country where it was first employed. In the photograph above, you can see that the rails form a cross. It is very important to jump through the middle.

The other type of spread fence is called the **triple bar**, which is built like an ascending staircase. The spread element can be as much as nine feet. This can make the horse need to stretch to cover the rails. A common mistake here is that the horse will stretch for the triple bar, then fail to compress his or her stride length to go over the next set of rails at the following fence, which is often a tall vertical.

Finally, at the Grand Prix level and in smaller courses, you will often see water added. For smaller classes, the water is referred to as a **liverpool**, and comes in the form of a tray full of water placed underneath a vertical or oxer. This can sometimes spook a horse. If the horse stops or knocks a rail down, four faults are added. In Grand Prix classes, the big water comes in the form of a tray of water as wide as 16 feet. Stepping in the water or on the plastic strip on the landing side will also be scored as four faults.

A triple bar may be as wide as nine feet.   <small>Gretchen Almy</small>

WALLS

Walls are funny things. Much like a vertical fence, a wall is a straight up-and-down, clear-the-top, element equation. The horse senses that they are more solid than some airy vertical fences and offer a more inviting approach. That said, to the rider they offer the additional challenge of playing with the mind because they look more solid and imposing. Walls also offer jump builders and course designers a real canvas to paint on. The one pictured on the following page is from the jump inventory at the Fidelity Jumper Classic, and we have fondly dubbed it the "sea world" wall for its blue color and background of fish and turtles painted on its surface. At times, a block on a wall can also be dislodged with less force than it takes to rub a rail out of its cups, making it a more delicate fence to jump cleanly. I always say to myself, "Oh God, if I hit this, there will be more things for my horse to step in or on and hurt himself." It is a mental game I've invented to terrify myself. Nonetheless, if you jump it cleanly, it does not detract from your score. Knock a

A somewhat colorful but representative wall jump.

block off, or send the whole thing flying, and it's four faults just like a single dislodged rail.

DISOBEDIENCES

Disobedience in show jumping jargon is a stop or a refusal on the part of the horse to obey a rider's command to maintain forward motion. If a horse rears up or stops at a liverpool, (the equine equivalent of saying, "Oh, hell no!") the rider is given four faults. More than two disobediences on the course in any class results in the dreaded double buzzer, signifying elimination.

FALLS

No matter how fast a horse runs or how high the horse can jump, gravity is a constant. And if gravity wins, you lose. Falls happen to everyone at one point or another, and whether the rider falls from the horse or the horse falls himself, the result is instant elimination. If a horse drops to a knee but regains her balance, and the rider remains seated, the pair may continue.

A rider may also fall victim to confusion—one can leave the course or forget the sequence of jumps and jump over the wrong fence. Either example is cause for immediate elimination. All jumper riders dread this kind of memory lapse, but it happens.

SUMMING UP

There are no style points awarded in show jumping. This makes the sport relatively simple and non-subjective. You either incur faults or are fault-free. The fences are either left standing or they are not. You stay on the horse or you fall off. The art of show jumping is easy to understand and incredibly difficult to master. Now that you are better acquainted with the fundamentals of the sport, please enjoy the rest of the book.

Jeff and Roxett power through the B element of a triple combination.

CLOSING THOUGHTS

John Madden, Beezie Madden's husband and a world-renowned coach and horseman, told me once, "If you're not blindly in love with horses, get out of the sport before you begin. Proceed at your own risk because you are going to experience failure, heartbreak, and injury. Persevere and you will end up with a wall full of memories, gratification like none other on earth, and all your days will be filled with admiration for the generosity of the horses you're blessed with." I remember John's words verbatim. I am confident I have quoted him with complete accuracy, and John was right. I am living proof of the truth of his words. At the core of show jumping is the love affair between the horse and the rider that is evident in every chapter of this book. I shared my own love affair with my horses, and one in particular, in the first chapter of this book.

I have left show rings with my soul mate Roxett (Rocket), knowing I succeeded not because I performed flawlessly, but because he covered up my mistakes and stretched his mighty physical limits to get done what I should have made easier for him. I don't care what anybody tells you; I've felt him grow in stature in the more important moments when we were in a crowded stadium, the music was blaring, and the atmospherics meant more to him than they did to me. I know in my heart Rocket thrived in these moments and emphatically understood his role in the sport. I know of no other partnership in sport with this kind of mystical connection. I hope, in this book, I have given you a glimpse of what this relationship looks like.

It is hard to understand how horses find it within themselves to bond with their human partners in the way that they do. We experience it with other animals, of course, like our dogs, for instance; I have several. Tess and Lola run when they hear me come home each night and there is an unconditional love and affection at the core of my relationship with them. My dogs are always happy to see me even if other people in my life are less enthused (sometimes with good reason). What is different about horses, and show jumpers in particular, is the incredible effort, courage, and concentration extracted for our benefit from a seemingly endless reservoir of generosity. What we ask of the horses in this sport is extreme. How they respond is magical.

In this book, I frequently referred to show jumping as "the world's most beautiful sport." There are many reasons I feel justified making that statement. The venues the sport frequents are often picturesque or outright stunning. The colorful and meticulously decorated obstacles that grace the courses our sport is constructed around are a visual delight. The flags that wave, indicating our national affiliations, are colorful, and the gloriously elegant accessories that enhance the ceremony and pageantry of the sport are all there if you're paying attention. The horses themselves are amongst the most graceful, powerful, and visually stunning life forms on the planet. All of these truths validate my assertion that show jumping is the world's most beautiful sport. I have reiterated this statement not for these reasons alone, but also because the nobility, character, generosity, and courage of the horses, who are the central miracle explored in this book, warrant such distinction. The dedication, sacrifice, and moral fortitude of the human half of these partnerships is also a thing of beauty.

I expect you can now understand why I have placed Authentic, Big Ben, Glasgow, Fein Cera, and the other equine stars featured in these pages on the pedestal I have. In a like manner, there is something inherently courageous about the human halves of the teams I have showcased—Margie Engle riding in the Olympic trials with a broken hip; Kevin Babington completing in a Nations Cup round in Aachen with a broken hand; Peter Leone in the Atlanta Olympiad with a broken collarbone; McLain Ward riding in the same condition in Germany; Chris Kappler jumping off his mount Royal Kaliber in the midst of a jump-off at the first sign his horse might be at risk; Debbie Stephens returning to the ring she had been airlifted out of paralyzed 93 days before. These heroic acts provide role models of dedication and distinction for the next generation of riders to emulate, admire, and learn from.

Roxett and Jeff jump clean at the Master Classic Syracuse Sport Horse Invitational.
RANDI MUSTER PHOTOGRAPHY

JEFF PAPOWS
TA: 73
Jump Faults 8   Time
                  49
Time Faults
Total Faults 8   Rank

GRETCHEN ALMY

The author and his horse, Tenacious, finish a Masters round at the 2010
Fidelity Jumper Classic.

For those of you immersed in the sport of show jumping, I hope this book has given you a deeper, more personal connection with the stars of the sport who are making news every week around the world. If you have gained an understanding of the personal insights, unique relationships, and sacrifices these athletes have made, then I have succeeded as an author. If you are connected to a young person or novice just starting out in the sport and you have gained a better understanding of what he or she aspires to be, then, again, I feel I have accomplished what I set out to do.

Below is a catalogue of my favorite observations of my experience writing this book, just as I have catalogued the career highlights of each athlete profiled in this book:

Confirming my friends in the sport are as special as they always seemed

Realizing that every athlete's love affair with his or her horse is like my own

Experiencing the intimacy and the honesty with which these riders have shared the depths of their feelings for their equine partners

The Author's Most Compelling Moments Writing this Book

Reliving Olympic moments with these exceptional athletes and understanding how extraordinary and different the experiences are for each of them

Witnessing the outpouring of support from photographers, caregivers, coaches, and every person connected to the sport and the enthusiasm with which they rushed to help me get these stories published

Observing the diversity of ethnic backgrounds, cultures, and economic circumstances from which each of these stories began

Witnessing a culture where the extraordinary is an everyday, ordinary expectation

Experiencing kindness and generosity shown by the people and horses alike

I have some specific advice for my younger readers starting out in the sport who have taken the time to read this book. Each of the men and women profiled here started just as you are. All of these incredible athletes dreamed, just as you do, of that day when they would first wear the scarlet jacket, ride for their country, and stand on an Olympic podium. All really important visions of future accomplishment start with just that—a dream. There are many incredible riders featured in this book, but they are not incredible only because of who they are. They are also incredible because of what they have sacrificed to get where they are. You, young readers, can be the stuff of future chapters in this sport. Dream the seemingly impossible, and go out and make it your reality.

Olympic dreams begin here.

TONY DE COSTA

TONY DE COSTA

Emma and Effie dream big.

UNBRIDLED PASSION